Made in the Shade: A Zentangle® Workbook

Cris Letourneau, CZT

Made In The Shade, a Zentangle Workbook

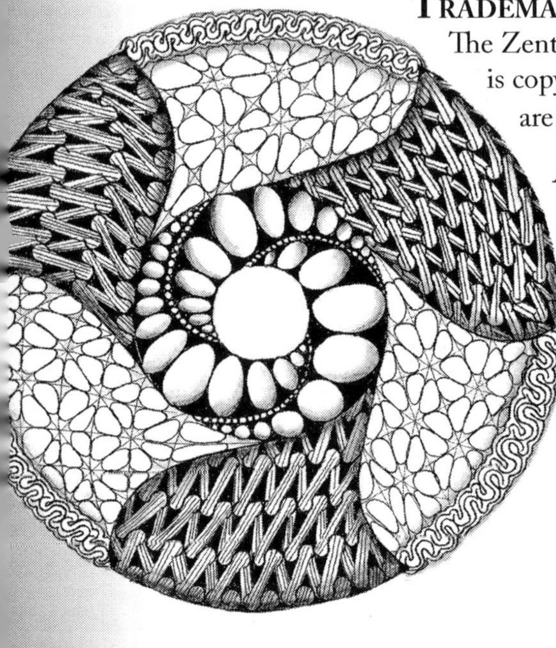

Acknowledgments

All art in this book has been reproduced with permission of the respective artists, and every effort has been made to ensure credits are accurate. Art on Contents page is by Brinn McFetridge. Images on page ii are from January 11, 2010 Zentangle Newsletter and are used with permission. The photo on page ii is by Geneviève Crabe. Artwork on the back cover is by Alexa Letourneau. (She gets her talent from me.) Unless otherwise specified, all artwork is done by the author.

Published by Cris Letourneau, CZT, Pickerington, Ohio
ISBN-13: 978-0615753225
ISBN-10: 0615753221
www.TangledUpInArt.com

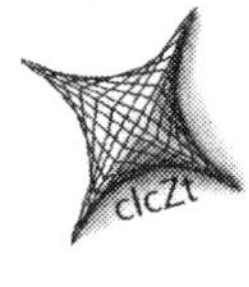

Thanks to the following artists for their generous contributions to this book:

Michelle Beauchamp, CZT
Launceston, Tasmania
shellybeauch.blogspot.com

Margaret Bremner, CZT
Saskatoon, SK, Canada
enthusiasticartist.blogspot.com

Amy Broady, CZT
Nashville, TN
tanglefish.blogspot.com

Emily Classon, CZT
Lowell, MA
momzenartist.blogspot.com

Paula Dickerhoff, CZT
Huntsville, AL
wannatangle.com

Ellen Gozeling, CZT
Sassenheim, Netherlands
www.kunstkamer.info

Alice Hendon, CZT
Keystone Heights, FL
thecreatorsleaf.blogspot.com

Diana Hirsch, CZT
Canton, MI
wolfhowlings.wordpress.com

Kelley Kelly, CZT
Newington, CT
thepathuntangled.com

Mimi Lempart, CZT
Florence, MA
tangledplanet.blogspot.com

Alexa Letourneau
Pickerington, OH
artzyalexa.blogspot.com

Jane MacKugler, CZT
Londonderry, VT
dicksallyjane.blogspot.com

Jane Menard, CZT
Clarksburg, ON Canada
tanglejam.blogspot.com

Brinn McFetridge, CZT
Poquoson, VA
brinnmar.com

Caren Mlot, CZT
Mt. Pleasant, SC
tanglemania.com

Sue Sharp
Toronto, ON, Canada
inquisitive-sue.blogspot.ca

Maria Vennekens, CZT
Leiden, Netherlands
vennekensmaria@hetnet.nl

Sonya Yencer
Pickerington, OH

Special thanks to Emily Classon, Paula Dickerhoff, Diana Hirsch, and Alexa Letourneau for their editorial comments, suggestions, and encouragement during this process. I couldn't have done it without you.

For Birdie, Never stop dreaming.

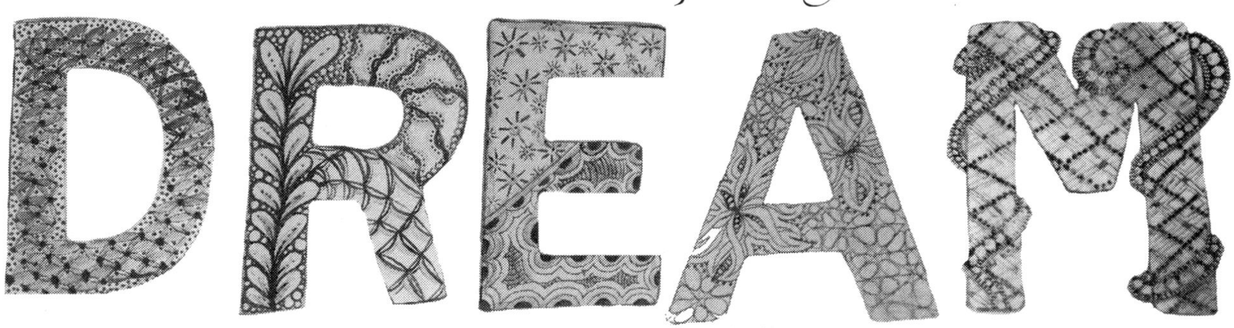

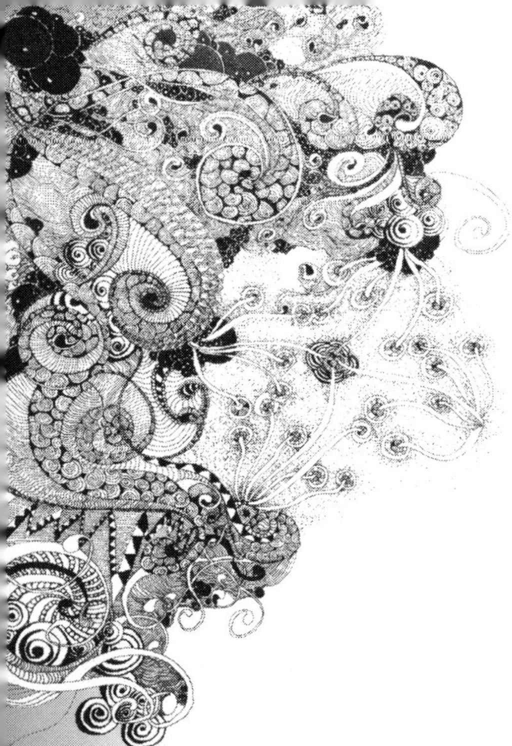

CONTENTS

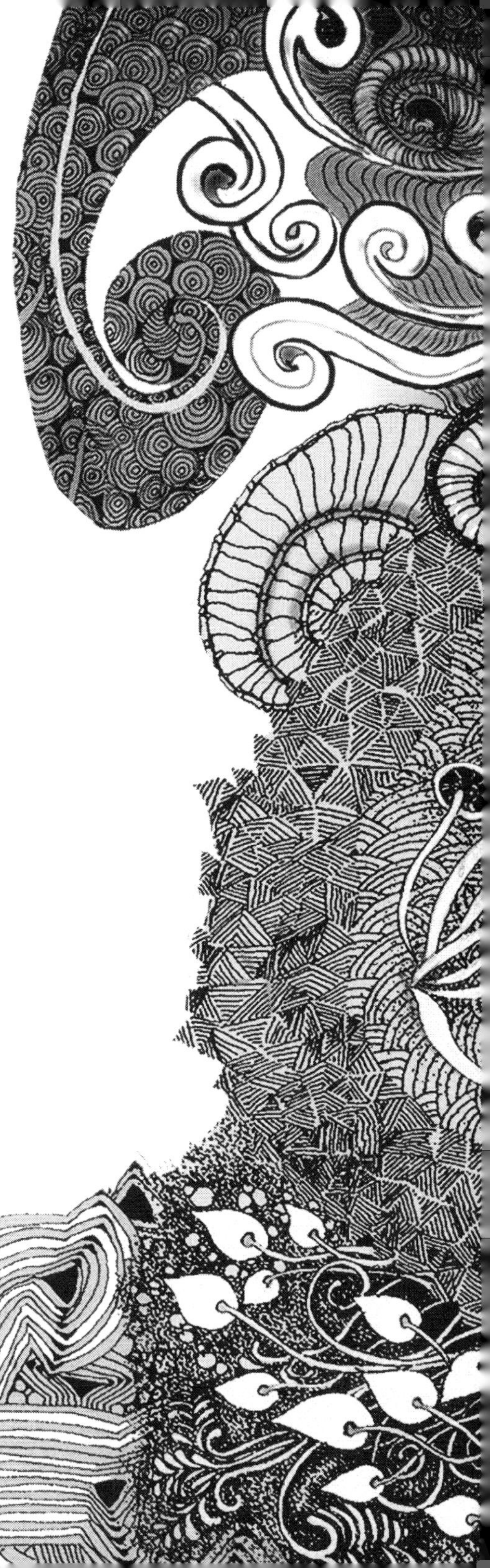

Food For Thought: One Tangle Shaded Four Ways

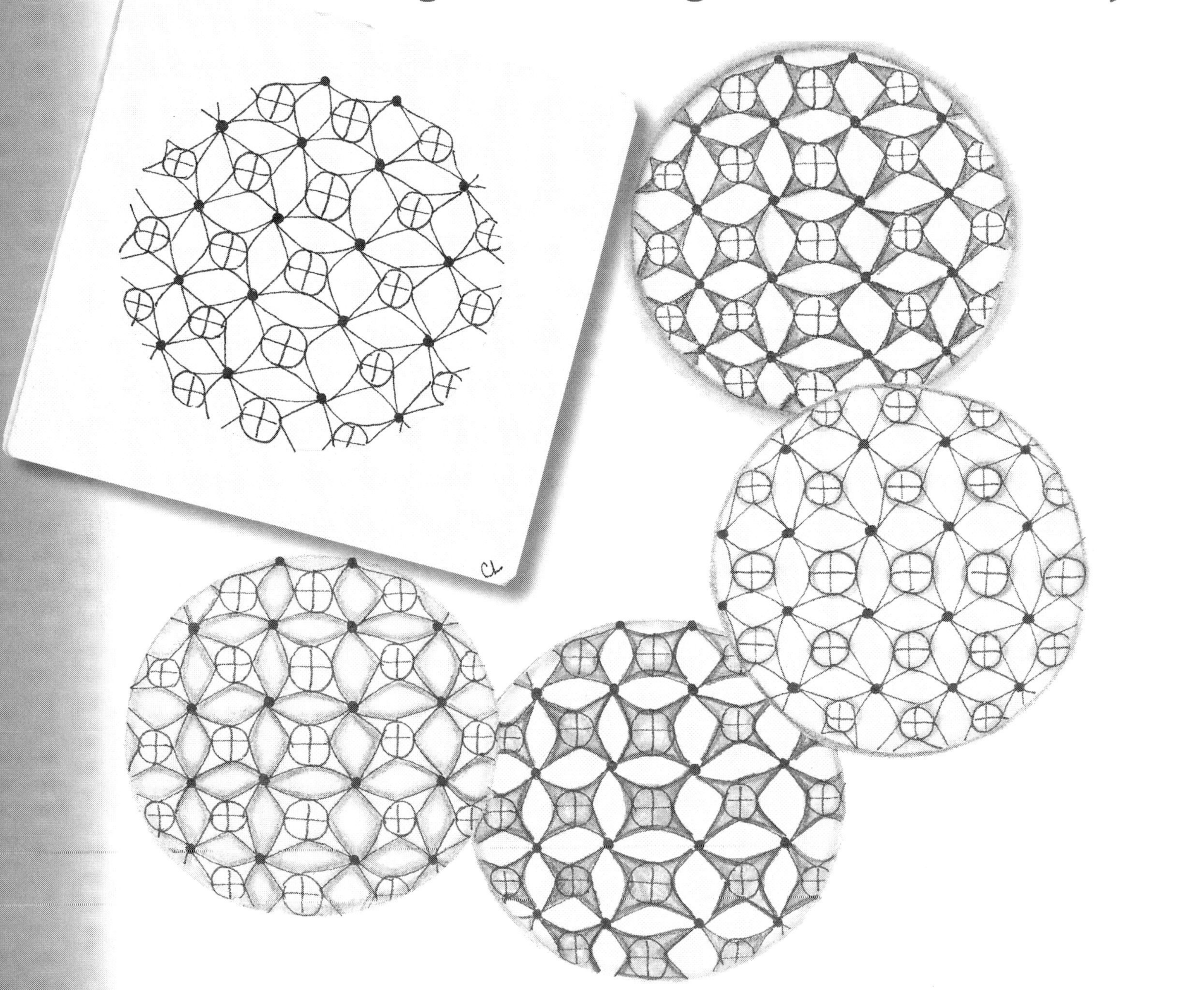

INTRODUCTION

I love to shade my Zentangle tiles. To me, they don't look finished unless I have gone in with my pencil and added touches of gray to the black and white. However, despite my enthusiasm, when I teach Zentangle 101 classes, I am constantly surprised at how many of my students are reluctant to shade their creations. I have found that there are usually one of two reasons for this. First, many lack confidence in their pencil work and are afraid to "ruin" their beautiful artwork by shading it. Others simply don't know where to begin.

I wrote this book for my students as well as others who want guidance and practice with their shading. It provides plenty of tips and techniques, but more importantly, it has plenty of room to practice shading in a non-intimidating way. By working through the exercises, beginning shaders may gain confidence and skills to shade their Zentangle art beautifully.

Chapter 1 defines some art terminology and gives introductory information on pencil use. It also has instructions and exercises to learn both pencil and pen shading. Chapters 2-5 contain tips and techniques for shading simple shapes, individual tangles, and completed tangled artwork. Finally, Chapter 6 has over 40 images of tangled tiles, Zendalas, and Zentangle-Inspired Art to practice shading in a variety of styles and inspire you to take risks so you can learn and develop your own personal style.

One final note: this is not a beginning Zentangle book. There are many wonderful books available to help you learn to tangle (see Resources), but the best way to begin is to go to Zentangle.com, find a Certified Zentangle Teacher (CZT), and take a beginner class. The guidance you will get by working with a CZT is invaluable. Once you understand the Zentangle method, this book will help you enhance your work by learning artistic shading.

So, grab your pencil, and let's begin.

Tangling by Sonya Yencer
Shading by the author

WHY SHADE?

Have you ever completed your art only to find that it looks a bit "flat?"

Sometimes you may look at it and feel vaguely dissatisfied even though there is nothing clearly wrong with it. Sometimes it might need a little pizazz or maybe it seems too busy. Sometimes it is hard to tell what it needs, but you know it needs "something." Well, that something may be shading.

By adding a little gray pencil to your black and white art, amazing things are possible. If you want some practical reasons to shade, you can:

- Make your art pop.
- Add a 3-dimensional look to your work.
- Make busy tiles look less busy.
- Cover up an accidental streak, smear, or misplaced mark.
- Call attention to your favorite area.
- Hide or draw attention away from your least favorite area.
- "Jazz up" mundane tangles.

NOTE: *Since* ***Zentangle*** *is a trademark, it isn't used as a noun or a verb. Therefore when referring to the art created using the Zentangle method, I will use the term "tile" or "art" instead of calling it "a Zentangle."*

If you want a more philosophical reason, one of the many Zentangle metaphors, how about this? According to, Rick Roberts, co-founder of Zentangle, Inc.,

> "*Not everything in life is black and white, but all shades in between.*"

If you want a more visual reason, look at Figure 1 to see the dramatic impact Rick created by shading his tile. The original tile is beautiful, but see how much more exciting it became after Rick shaded it?

By learning to shade, you too can take your tangles from flat to fabulous.

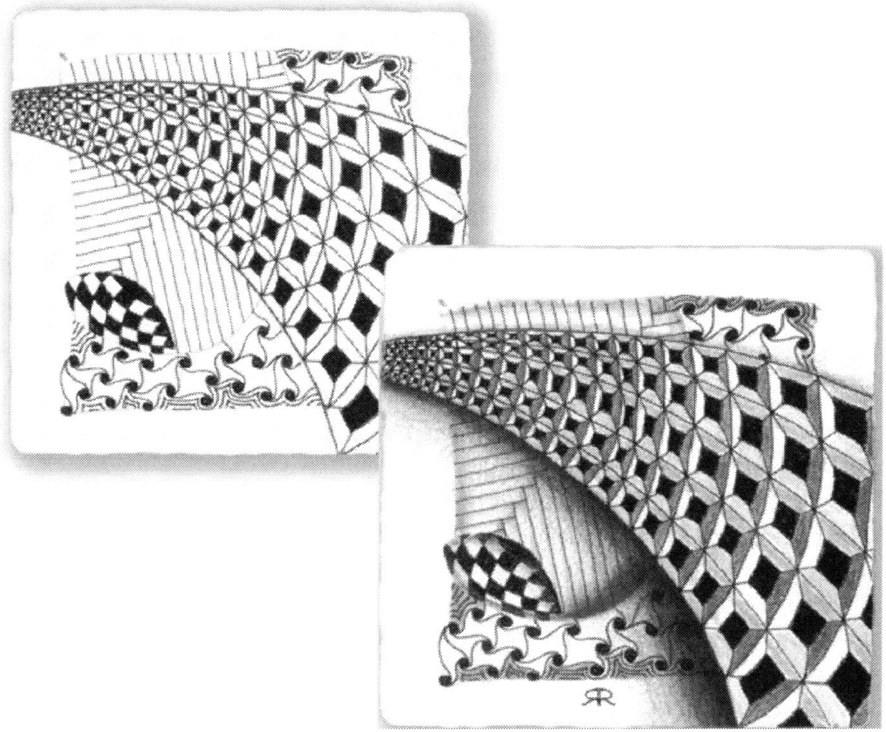

Figure 1. *Look at the difference shading makes in this Zentangle tile by Rick Roberts.*

SHADING AND SHADOWS

Before describing any techniques for shading, I want to define the terms shading and shadow as I use them in this book.

- **Shading** is a verb that means adding different shades of gray and black to your tangle to define or enhance it.
- **Shadow**, a noun, is a darker area representing a lack of light.

Did you know there are several different kinds of shadows? If you hold your hand over your book, a hand-shaped dark area will appear. This is

NOTE: *Colors are used to shade colorful art, but in black and white art , the shadows are gray and black.*

what most people think of as a shadow. In art jargon, this is called a **cast shadow**. There is another type of shadow that is important to understand when shading. It is called a **form shadow**. A form shadow is simply the part of an object that the light is not hitting, so it is darker than the rest.

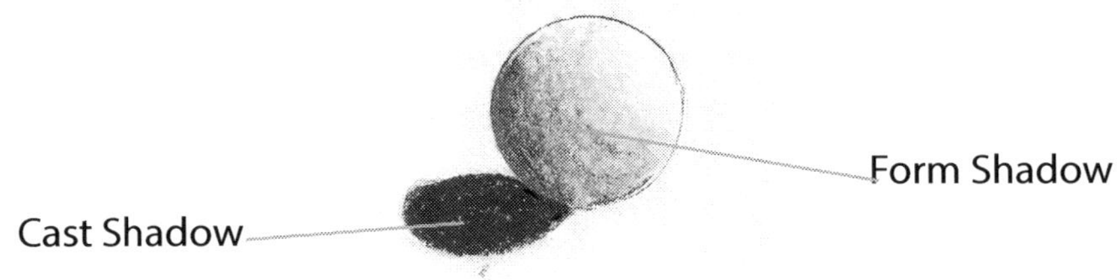

Figure 2. *Cast shadow vs. form shadow illustrated.*

When shading tangles, I use cast shadows to show that one element is on top of another. Any time I'm shading inside an element, that is a form shadow.

TIP: *Hard shadows evoke full sun, harsh, strong heat. Soft shadows bring to mind shade, diffused light, cool, calm, relaxed.. You can use either to bring out whichever feeling you want in your art.*

Shadows can either be **hard** or **soft**. A hard shadow has a clear, sharp line separating the dark area from the light. There is a high contrast. A soft shadow has no clear line of demarcation, and there is a large area with many shades of gray.

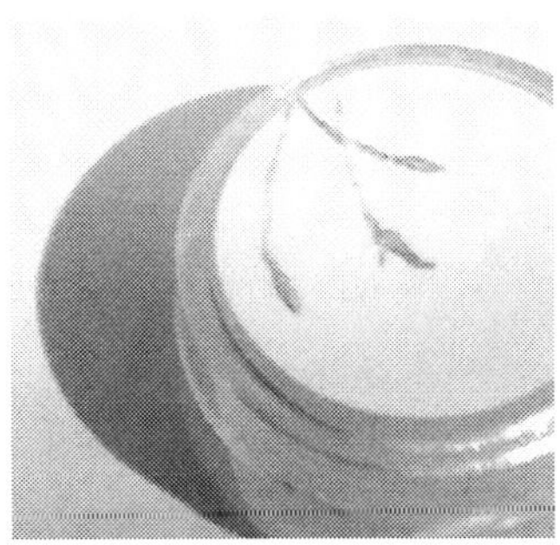

Figure 3. *The edge of a hard cast shadow is clearly defined.*

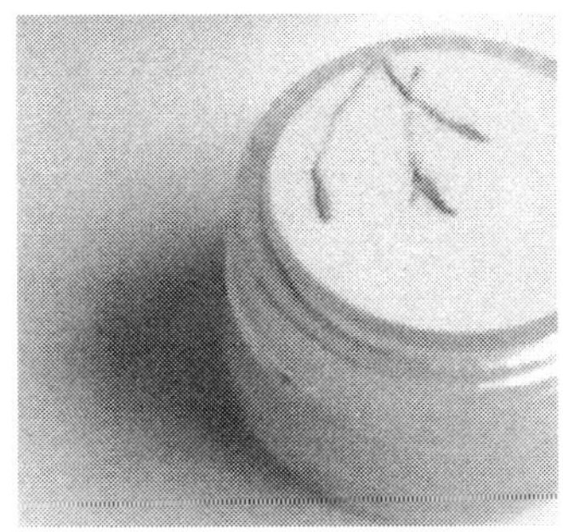

Figure 4. *The edge of a soft cast shadow gradually blends.*

Cast shadows can either be soft or hard while form shadows are soft.

In Figure 3, the cast shadow has a clear, sharp edge, but look carefully at the shadow itself. Do you see how the area within the shadow isn't a single shade of gray? Compare the gray at the top with the gray at the bottom. You will see that the shadow at the top is lighter than the shadow at the bottom, but the change is so subtle and smooth that you may not have even noticed it the first time you looked.

NOTE: *According to Sandra K. Strait, "If you've studied drawing at all, you've seen advice about locating your light source. Don't worry about that for tangling. That's all you need to know on this subject." I agree with her.*

In your shading, you have the choice of making your cast shadows either hard or soft. As you can see in the photos, either hard or soft cast shadows can be realistic. Form shadows, on the other hand, are naturally soft and have many shades of gray that blend seamlessly from one to the next. In order to draw them that way, you must be able to recreate this soft look where there are no sharp edges and no clear distinction between one shade of gray and the next. If you do not render them softly, they will not look like a shadow. Look what happens to our lovely sphere when all I did was give the shadow a hard edge.

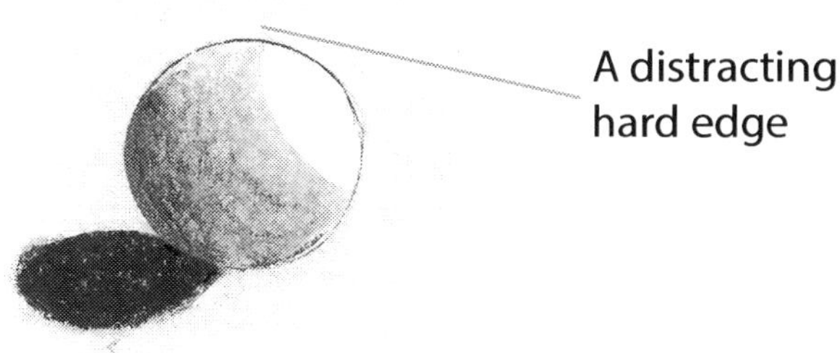

FIGURE 5. *Look at the difference between this ball and the one in Figure 2. When the edge of the shadow is made hard, the whole shading effect is thrown off and it looks as if part of the ball is painted gray, like a billiard ball.*

As a tangler, I'm sure you already see patterns everywhere you look. If you carefully observe light and shadows as well, you will notice a big improvement in your shading.

Prestrung Zendala #13

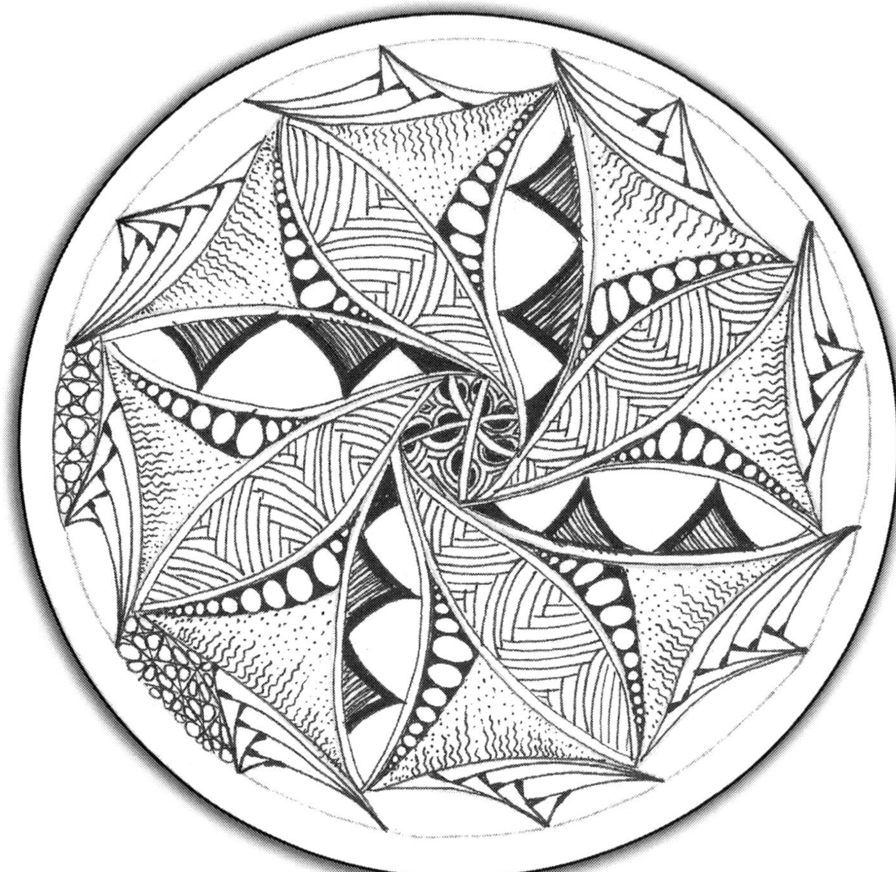

Tangles used: MSST, 'NZEPPEL, BETWEED, HIBRED, IXORUS

CHAPTER 1 GETTING TO KNOW YOUR TOOLS

One of the most wonderful things about the Zentangle method is that anyone can do it; you don't have to have formal art training and years of practice to create a beautiful piece of art. People who never dreamed they were an artist take a beginning Zentangle class and suddenly realize that they are! I have seen this excitement change to frustration as these people want to take their art to the next level, but they don't have the skills to achieve the results they want.

This chapter helps fill the gap by teaching some art skills as they apply to shading tangles. It guides the reader through a series of steps designed to help them learn to use and to get the most out of the most basic shading tools: a pencil and blending tool. Then information about additional tools and techniques is provided to allow a greater range of expression.

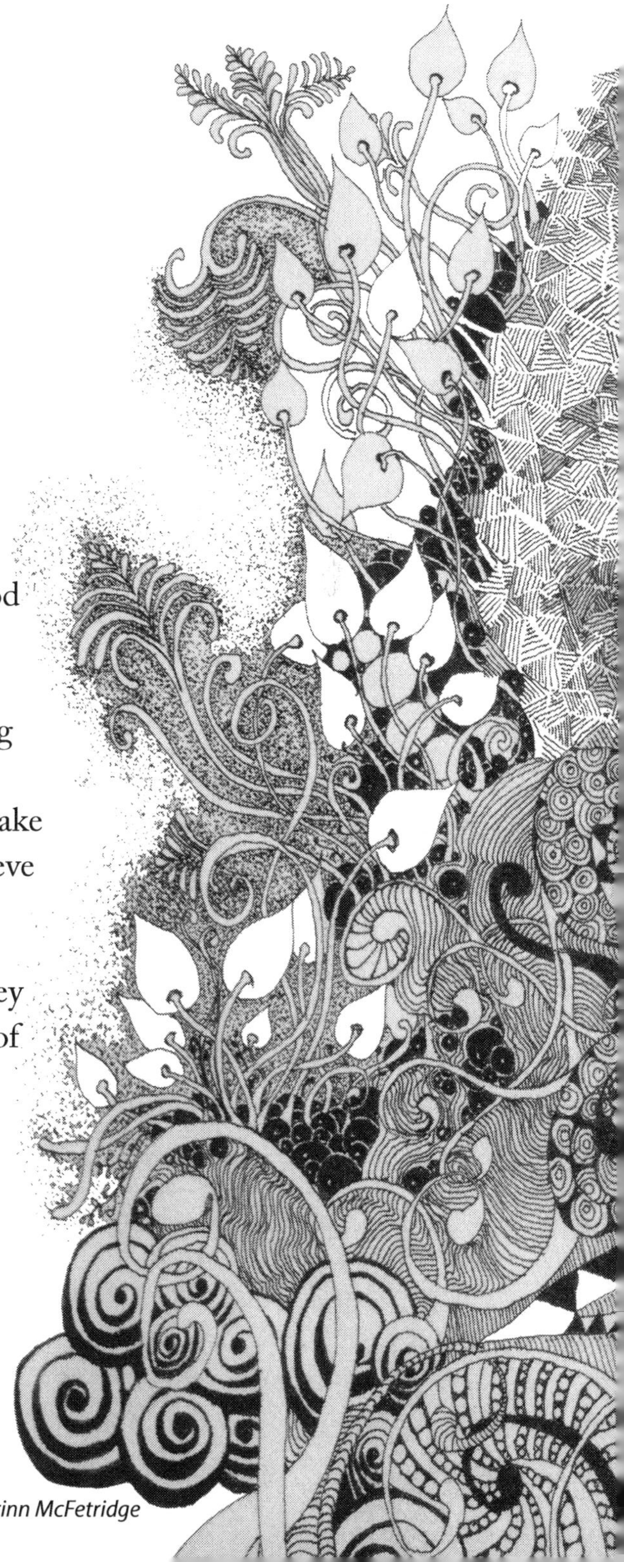

Original art ©Brinn McFetridge

SIMPLE PENCIL SHADING

NOTE: *In this section, we'll focus on shading with just a single pencil, preferably your Zentangle pencil. Information about other types of pencils can be found in "About Pencils" on page 22.*

Shading tangles can be done beautifully using the simplest of tools, a pencil. While you probably have been writing with a pencil since you were a young child, it is unlikely that you have spent much time just using your pencil to see what marks it is capable of producing. If you want to improve your shading skills, I recommend that you do just that. Experimentation and practice are the best ways to learn what you can do with your pencil.

Pencil Grip

But before you begin to shade with your pencil, you must hold it correctly.

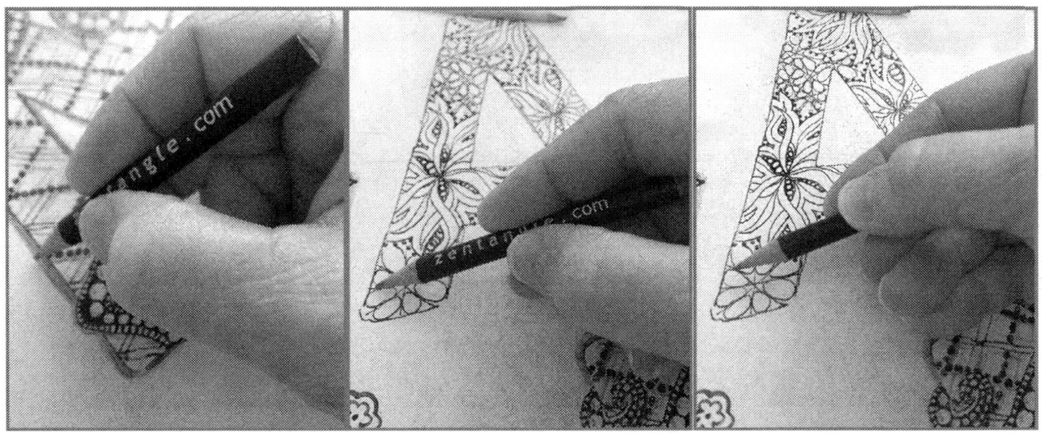

FIGURE 6. *My pencil grips: traditional tripod grip (left), extended tripod grip (center), and relaxed grip (right).*

Most people were taught the tripod grip and use it when they are writing. With this time-tested grip, you can write or draw quickly and easily, have good control, and little hand fatigue. But, there are other grips that are popular when drawing and sketching. Most of the time when I am shading tangles, I need the precise control of traditional tripod grip because the areas I shade tend to be tiny. I hold the pencil further from the tip, the extended tripod grip, when I want to shade something bigger. My relaxed grip is for filling a large area very lightly. The overhand grip is also popular for shading. If you hold the pencil almost parallel to your paper and shade with the side, you are using your version of the overhand grip.

As you work through the exercises in this section, try out some different grips to see what works best for you. It is likely that you will switch grips depending on the size of the area you want to cover and the style you want.

No matter which grip you prefer, take care to hold the pencil lightly but securely. If you tense your hand and hold the pencil very tightly, your hand will tire easily, and your fine motor skills will be weakened, causing your art to suffer. If you hold it too lightly, you will lose control, and again, your art will suffer.

TIP: *The proper grip is one that lets you work for a long time without fatigue and gives you enough control to create the shading effect that you want.*

Getting to Know Your Pencil

The purpose of this exercise is twofold. First, it is a warm-up for the other exercises and second, it is for you to become familiar with the variety of strokes and styles you can produce. Take a few minutes and play with your Zentangle pencil to see how many shades of gray you can produce. As you do this exercise, pay attention to your pencil and how it hits the page.

- Explore the difference between a sharp pencil and a dull one.

  Before starting, intentionally dull the point by scribbling hard on some scrap paper and experiment with a dull pencil. Then, sharpen it to a fine point to see what a difference that makes.

- Try different motions.

  Try moving your pencil with just your hand and wrist, and then see how it feels keeping your hand and wrist still and moving your elbow. What happens if you move your whole arm from the shoulder? Which gives you more control? More freedom?

TIP: *As you work through this exercise, take notes in the margins about what works and doesn't work for various techniques.*

- Vary your grip.

  Experiment with your grip to see if you feel more comfortable using your regular writing grip or with one of the other grips described. Try moving your hand closer to the tip and then further away to see what a difference this makes.

- Try different pressures.

  Do you prefer making dark marks by pressing hard or keeping light pressure and layering your marks?

TIP: *Need more practice? Experiment on the back of a Zentangle tile, so you can see how your pencil will perform on an actual tile without having to "waste" it.*

Exercise 1: ***Experiment to see how many different kinds of marks you can make using just one pencil.***

Did you discover anything during your experiments? In the following pages, I give you advice based on my experience. As they say, "your mileage may vary." Use this workbook to try out different techniques so you can decide which work best for your style and comfort.

Shading Technique

Should you shade with a dull pencil or a sharp one? With the point or with the side?

I remember being taught to *never* shade with a sharp point because it can scratch the surface of the paper, making a mark that is impossible to blend away. I was taught that using the side of the pencil is the only way to get a smooth fill. While working up the examples for this book, I was amazed to discover the opposite to be true! I was able to get smoother results using the point rather than the side of my pencil. Take a look at my results.

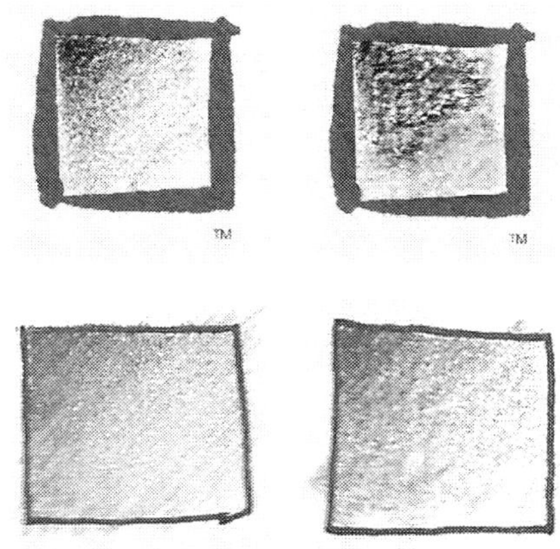

Figure 7. *The difference between shading with a sharp point (left) and a dull one (right) on both a Zentangle tile (top) and copy paper (bottom)*

The reason for this is the way a pencil interacts with the paper's surface texture, called its **tooth**. Paper is manufactured with tooth to give the graphite something to stick to. You can see the subtle "hills" and "valleys" in the magnified tooth detail photo and feel them when you rub your finger across the surface of the paper. When I used the side of the pencil, the lead just skipped over the valleys and the mark only stayed on the hills. Using a sharp point let me get the pencil down into the valleys.

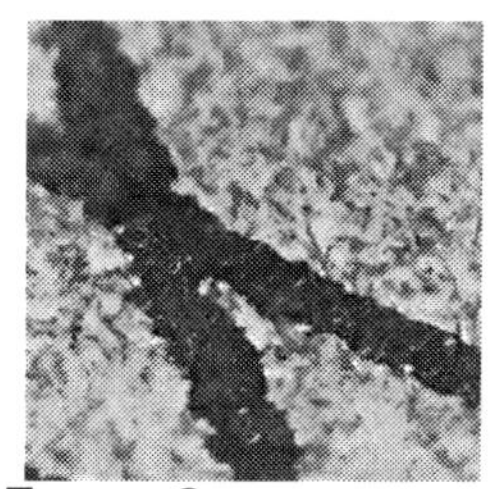

Figure 8. *Tooth detail, magnified.*

The more tooth in your paper, the more you will be able to see the difference between using techniques that allow you to get your graphite down into the low parts and techniques that let you keep your marks only on the high parts. You may want to try some of the shading exercises in this workbook on some Zentangle tiles or textured drawing paper to see for yourself the influence paper has on your results.

TIP: *Using a sharp point lets you get your graphite down into the tooth while using the side or a dull pencil lets it skip over the low parts and stay only on the top.*

Shading with a sharp pencil point makes it is easier to get into tight places. Since Zentangle tiles are small, this can be helpful when shading details.

Making a Smooth Fill

Shadows, whether hard or soft, are smooth. The eye can see details more clearly in bright light, so the lack of light in a shadowed area causes even rough textures to even out. Learning to make a smooth fill will help you make beautiful, realistic shadows.

Fill the boxes below smoothly. Use both the tip and the side of your pencil to see which enables you to get the smoothest results.

Tips for getting a smooth fill.

- Use light or medium pressure.
- Keep your motion steady
- Keep your pressure even.
- Keep your lines very close to one another.
- Turn your paper to work in the way that feels most natural.

TIP: *Everyone has a way of drawing lines that feels most natural to them. I prefer diagonally. Take a few minutes working on a piece of scrap paper to see what is easiest for you. Then when you are working, turn your paper so you can work in that direction. It can be awkward to do this when working in a book, but it should come naturally when you are working on a tile.*

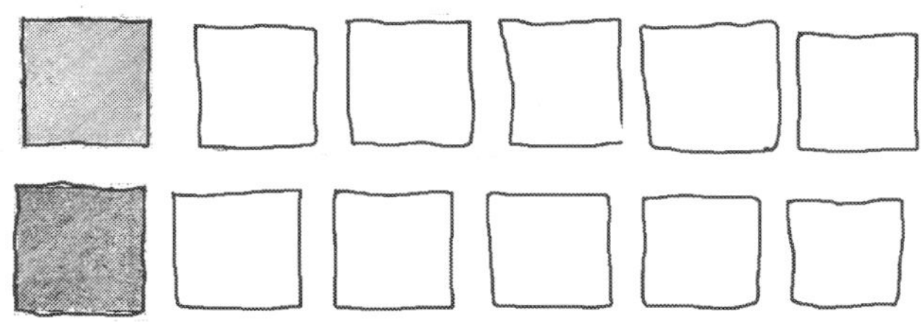

Exercise 2. ***Fill the boxes smoothly, trying both the tip and side of your pencil.***

There are a lot of boxes so you can keep going until you get one you like.

Make a Value Scale

In art, **value** is defined as the lightness or darkness of a color. A related term is **contrast**. High contrast is created when very dark values are next to very light values. This adds interest. You can see this in the value scale for Exercise3. Do you see how your eyes are naturally drawn to the bottom where the contrast is greater between the dark box and the white paper?

I only used a single pencil to draw this value scale, a standard Zentangle pencil. I filled the top box with the lightest mark I could make, barely brushing the tip of my pencil against the paper. I made the middle values by layering and also by gradually increasing the pressure of my pencil. The bottom box took several layers of medium pressure. If it takes less than 5-6 passes to get your darkest value, you might be pressing too hard.

Practice making a value scale in Exercise 2. Barely brush the lead over the paper to get a very light gray; press harder or draw over the same area repeatedly to get darker shades. You can use my scale as a guide, but don't worry about copying them exactly. Don't feel bad if it takes you a few tries to be able to get all five values; it did me, too.

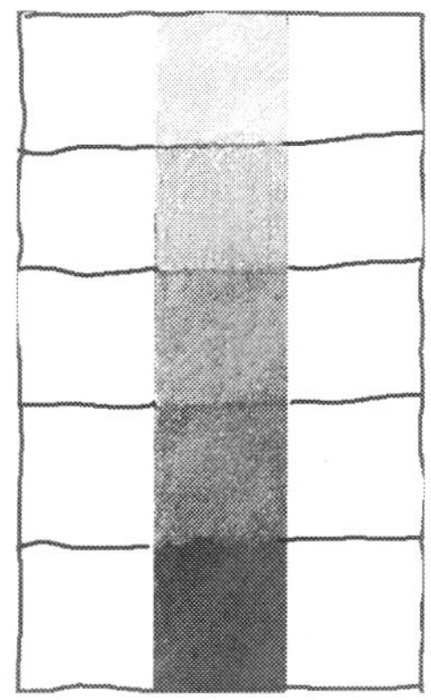

Exercise 3. ***Make a value scale.***

TIP: *Placing light values adjacent to dark values draws the viewer's eye and makes your art more interesting.*

Which values did you find easiest to create? For most people, creating the darker values is easier than the lightest values. It takes considerable practice to balance the precise amount of control and pressure needed to consistently produce the light values.

Making a Gradation

A **gradation** is a gradual blending of values from one to the next. Done perfectly, it is impossible to tell where one value stops and another starts, just like in the soft light photo shown in Figure 4 on page 4. Being able to render a flawless gradation is a skill that is essential for realistic pencil drawings and can take many hours of practice.

Luckily, it is possible to shade tangles beautifully without spending hours learning to perfect your gradations. There are several reasons for this.

1. First, Zentangle itself is abstract l, so "imperfect" gradations will likely be seen as an artistic choice rather than a jarring mistake they would if they were in the middle of a portrait or landscape.

2. Secondly, the areas you will shade on a tangle are usually quite small, and it is not necessary to have the same level of expertise to make a short gradation as it is to make a longer one. For example, the long gradation on the right is more difficult to make than the shorter one on the left.

FIGURE 9. *Two gradations. More skill is needed to draw the longer one.*

3. Lastly, there are tools that can help you smooth out your gradations. These are covered in the next section.

The slow change from one shade to the next is done by changing the pressure of the pencil against the paper. By learning to control that pressure, you will be able to do amazing pencil work.

Try for a seamless transition, but be patient with yourself. You are training your eye as well as your fingers. It can take a lot of practice to learn to make a smooth gradation. If it is difficult starting with a light touch and increasing pressure, try reversing the process. Start with heavy pressure and gradually lighten the force.

Think of learning to make a gradation like learning to play scales on a musical instrument. You may be able to play beautifully without ever learning a G-flat minor scale, but the dexterity you gain from practicing that difficult scale makes it worth the effort.

As you do this exercise, pay attention to your grip and the muscles in your hand, arm, and shoulder. If you find yourself tensing up, change your grip or move your paper higher or lower or at a different angle, or just take a break. There are no boxes here because learning to make a smooth gradation is difficult enough without needing to stay inside the lines.

Tips for Smooth Gradations

- Start by using the lightest pressure you are able to. You can correct values that are too light by going over the area with heavier pressure. If you press too hard to begin with, you might be able to erase, but adding more is always easier than taking away. (See "To erase or not to erase, that is the question" on page 37.)
- Make your lines parallel. Lines going in different directions will not look smooth.
- Avoid overlapping or leaving space between your lines. Overlapping will cause the area to be darker than you want, and leaving space will cause the area be lighter than you want.
- Take your time. It takes longer to make the lines close and consistent.

EXERCISE 4. ***Use this space to practice making gradations.***

TIP: *Instead of relying solely on changing the pressure of your pencil on the paper, you can also use layers of pencil to make your darker values as in Exercise on page 13.*

ADDING TO YOUR TOOLKIT: USING A BLENDING TOOL

Now that you've had a chance to do gradations the hard way, are you ready to use a tool to make things easier? It is possible to do amazing blending using only pencils, but it is easier and faster to get smooth pencil marks if you use a tool to speed the process along.

TIP: *Blending tools can help make your fills smoother, but they are not a panacea. Extremely uneven lines can sometimes be impossible to correct using a blending tool.*

You have probably discovered that sometimes your pencil marks are uneven, despite your best efforts. If this happens, you can use a blending tool to smooth things out. The most readily available tools are called phalanges, more commonly known as fingers. They are always "on hand", are free, don't wear out, and are easily cleaned, so it makes sense to explore finger smudging before trying other tools.

Practicing Finger Smudging

Use the boxes below to practice finger smudging. First, fill part of the box with pencil. Then rub your finger over the mark with the goal of filling the box. See what happens if you vary the direction of your smudging, up and down versus side to side. You may have to press fairly hard to spread it around. The amount of pressure needed will vary depending on the tooth of the paper, the softness of your pencil lead, and the amount of pressure you used when applying your pencil marks.

TIP: *If you don't like getting your fingers dirty or if you have oily skin, place a tissue over your finger before you do this exercise. The oils in your hand can leave fingerprints or make spots on your paper that are darker than the rest.*

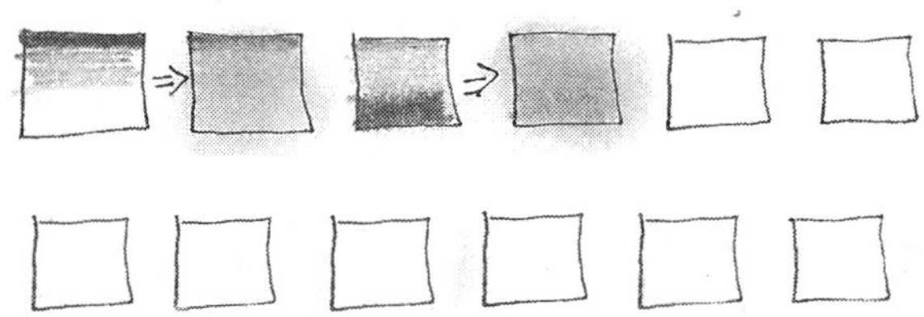

EXERCISE 5. ***Fill the box part way and then use your fingers to blend your pencil and fill the box.***

Did you have trouble keeping your pencil inside the lines? You can see that I did. Keep this in mind if you decide to smudge your tangles with your finger. If you want a piece that is organic or loose, or if you are blending a large area, then your finger might be the right tool for you. If, however, you are trying to shade tiny tangles or want you want something more control, you will want to use a different tool.

Types of Blending Tools

Some people, Maria Thomas, co-founder of Zentangle, comes to mind, can shade brilliantly by smudging with just their fingers. I am not one of them. I don't get enough precision with my fingertip. When I try to smudge with my fingers, I make a mess. If you, like me, do not enjoy finger smudging, you might want to try a different blending tool.

The most popular blending tools are tortillions and blending stumps. These terms tend to be used interchangeably, but there is a difference. Both are made of soft paper and are used to push the pencil marks around.

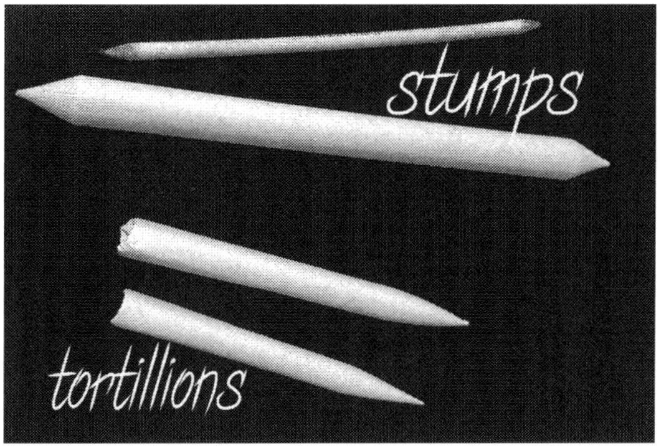

FIGURE 10. *Tortillions and stumps - different tools for the same job.*

Tortillions are tightly rolled, hollow cored and pointed only on one end. Blending stumps have points on both ends and are solid in the middle. They are made of paper pulp or paper felt that has been molded or pressed into shape. Since they are not hollow, they tend to be sturdier.

I use both blending stumps and tortillions, keeping several sizes of each in my tangling kit. I just choose the one that is the best size for the area I am blending. If you don't have a tortillion or stump, there are several items you probably do have that you can use to blend with. Why not try one or more of the following potential tools?

TIP: *A blending tool can be anything that will blend cleanly without damaging your paper. Avoid anything with dirt, chemicals, or oils.*

Everyday "Blending Tools"

- **Cotton swabs**. They work well, but tend to wear out quickly, so grab a handful. Interrupting your work to go fetch more is not very zen.
- **Art brushes**, especially stiff bristled ones.
- **Make-up brushes** or applicators.
- **Paper towels**.
- **Fabric**.
- **Tissues**. Be careful, sometimes they will pick up graphite rather than spreading it around.
- **Chamois**.
- A piece or corner of a **sponge**.

This exercise is a repeat of Exercise 5, but instead of using your finger to smudge, try using one or more different tools. Make some dark marks and some light marks to see which is easier to blend. Vary how hard you press with your blender to see what a difference that makes. Take some time and see what you can do with your blender. Experiment and have fun. See what tool you like best. It might turn out to be your finger!

TIP: *Practice blending on some paper with tooth to see what happens.*

TIP: *You might want to go back to and try your tool on one of your gradations to see how easy it is to smooth things out.*

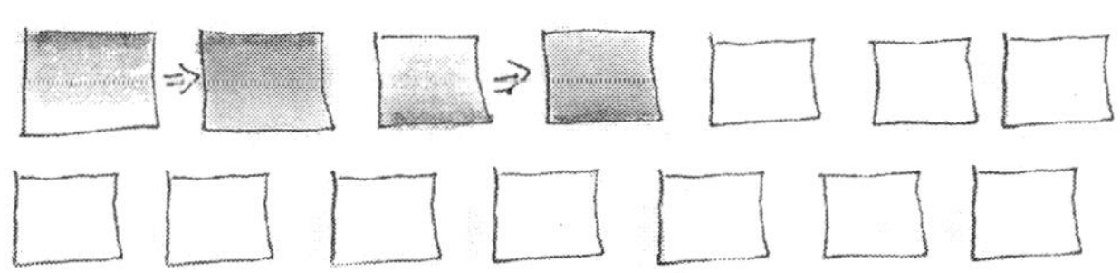

Exercise 6. ***Use a tool to blend and fill these boxes.***

Was it easier this time to stay in the lines? It certainly was for me. If you want to improve your shading results quickly, really get to know your blending tool(s).

Tool Tips

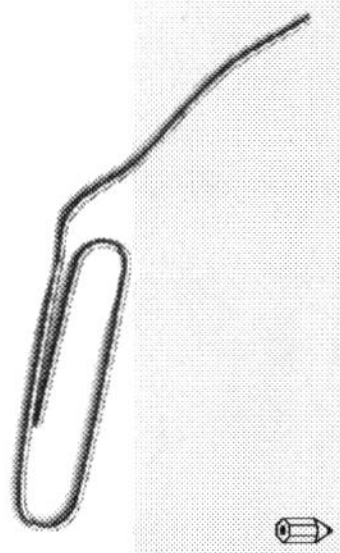

- If you use a tortillion, be careful that you don't push straight down on the tip because you could cause the end to cave in. It this happens, unwind a paper clip, then push it up through the bottom of your tortillion to poke the point back out.

- If your blending stump becomes bent or worn, you can sharpen it with a hand-held pencil sharpener. If it is too thick for a pencil sharpener, use fine sand paper or a nail file.
- Use a kneaded eraser to clean your tool. Or you can clean it by rubbing it on scrap paper until it stops leaving marks.

NOTE: For the remainder of this book, I will just use the generic term "blender," and you can use your favorite tool: blending stump, tortillion, cotton swab, or even your finger.

Pencil-less Pencil Shading

Instead of cleaning a dirty blender, you can use it to shade and skip the pencil fill altogether. This is a great way to produce a delicate shadow.

If you like using this technique, you don't have to wait for your blender to get dirty. You can intentionally dirty it. One way to do this is to rub your pencil over sandpaper or a nail file and collect the graphite powder in a small container. Then you can dip your blender in the powder. Another method is to scribble darkly on a piece of scrap paper and the rub your blender over that to pick up graphite.

TIP: *Do a quick test on some scrap paper to see how dark the mark will be. If it is too dark, simply rub it over your scrap until it is light enough.*

Unintended Smudging

I've had people ask how to avoid accidentally smudging their work after it has been shaded. I personally have never had a problem with this, even with the tiles that get passed around in my beginner classes. If you do, though, you can purchase a can of spray fixative that is used for charcoal and pastel drawings.

To avoid accidentally smudging your art while you are working on to, do not rest your hand on the pencil marks you have already put down. Zentangle tiles are small enough that it is possible to get your pencil all the way to the center without ever needing to put your hand on your tile. If there is a spot that is hard to reach, just turn your tile until it is easier to reach.

If, however, you are working on a larger piece and cannot avoid resting your hand on your artwork, here are a few tips to help reduce these accidental smudges.

Tips to Reduce Accidental Smudging

- If you are right handed, work from left to right and top to bottom, or from the middle to the edges. If you are left handed, work from left to right and top to bottom, or from the middle to the edges. If you shade this way, you won't have to rest your hand on your already completed shading.
- Place a clean sheet of paper under your hand. This will keep the oils on your hand away from the pencil on your art. The oils that keep your skin soft and supple are what pick up pencil marks and smear them.
- Wash your hands frequently to avoid transferring any marks from your hand to the paper. If you don't want to get up and take breaks to wash, keep some baby wipes on hand to clean up. Just make sure to dry your hands thoroughly before you touch your art.

Before moving on to other tools, I wanted to share how I use my blenders.

Method 1

I shade about half the object with medium pressure then blend, moving from dark to light, lifting your blender up at the end of the stroke, and starting back again in the dark area. I use long strokes, pressing hard at the start, and fading off at the end.

When it looks similar to the third box, switch to tiny strokes, moving back and forth within a tiny section. Start in the darkest section, 1. When that is smooth, move on to section 2, then continue section by section until section 5. Section 6 should stay white. If section 1 doesn't seem dark enough, I go back over it to darken and blend it again into section 2.

I use this method when I want to make sure I don't shade too darkly or when I'm shading a small space.

Method 2

I start by shading just a small section darkly; then I blend little by little using tiny sections as above until I get a nice smooth transition.

I use this method when I'm shading outside an object, and I have no boundaries to fill.

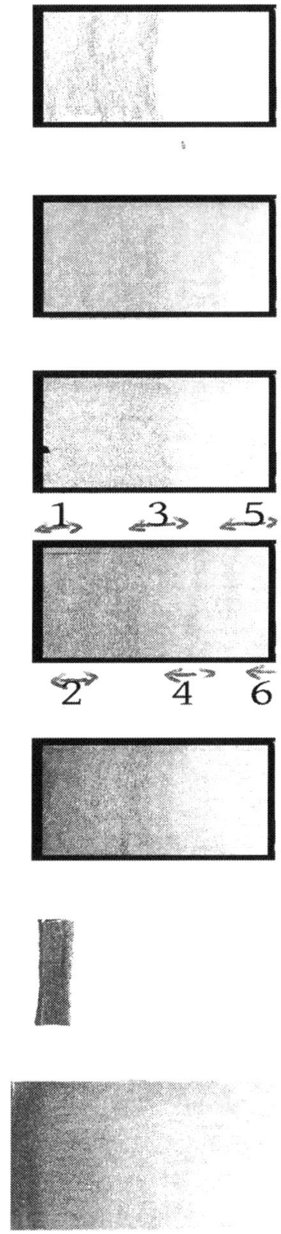

Figure 11. *Here are a couple different blending techniques that work for me. Try these, but experiment to see which technique(s) you prefer. The most important thing is understanding how to use your tools to create the effect you want.*

EXPANDING YOUR TOOLKIT: USING A VARIETY OF PENCILS

NOTE: *The official Zentangle pencil is similar to an HB.*

TIP: *Artist pencils are not essential, but they are an inexpensive way to help you create a range of values without needing to vary the amount of pressure you use when drawing.*

While you can get great results with the standard Zentangle pencil, having a set of drawing and sketching pencils can make it easier to get the results you want. If you only have one pencil, it is tempting to press really hard to get your darkest value. That is not a good idea. Besides causing your hand to tire quickly, pushing too hard can flatten your paper, destroying the tooth. Also, if your pencil lead is soft, it could break. If the pencil lead is hard, you could tear a hole in your paper. It is better to switch to a softer lead if you need a darker mark. Likewise, if it is hard for you to produce the lightest values, it can be easier by switching to a harder lead. Using a range of pencils allows the pencil to do some of the work for you.

About Pencils

NOTE: *Another system uses just the numbers 1-4. In that system: 1 is equivalent to a 2B, 2 is an HB, 3 is an H, and 4 is a 2H.*

NOTE: *Sometimes you may find a pencil labeled F which is halfway between an HB and an H.*

Artists pencils are graded using a series of numbers and letters. The most common scale uses a letter (H or B) and a number (2-9). Pencils are labeled B, which stands for black, or H, which stands for hard. In H pencils, bigger the number, the harder the lead is, so a 4H pencil is harder than a 3H. Similarly for B pencils, the larger the number, the softer the lead, so a 6B is softer than a 5B. The most common pencil, the one you used in school to take tests is equivalent to an HB, hard and black. It is in between the H pencils and the B pencils and is a great all-around pencil

Although commonly called "lead", the center of your pencil is actually a mixture of powdered graphite and clay. Soft lead contains more graphite than hard pencils. The higher graphite content enables you to get a darker mark, but these marks smudge easily. If you use a very soft lead you need to be more careful not to smudge your work accidentally. It can be difficult to obtain and maintain a sharp point with a very soft pencil so detail work can be tricky. The softer the lead, the more often you will need to sharpen your pencil. Harder leads have less graphite, so the marks produced will be lighter, but the pencil will hold a sharp point longer, so it is used more often for detail work.

If you don't like sharpening your pencils, you can get a set of mechanical pencils. They come in a variety of widths, from .13 mm to 5.5mm, and softnesses, from 4B to 4H. Not all softness are available in all lead sizes. Besides never needing sharpening, mechanical pencils have the advantage of consistent line width.

I have a set of pencils ranging from 4H (very hard) to 8B (very soft), but I rarely use anything other than a 4H, HB, 2B, or 4B for shading my tangles.

Learning about Your Pencils

You can easily find charts that show how dark a mark each pencil will make, but just because a value is on the chart does not mean it is one you will be able to make easily. If you make your own chart you will be able to see the results *you* can get with the pencils you have.

NOTE: *There is no standard across manufacturers, so just because two pencils have the same grade, if they are by different manufacturers, they may not perform equally.*

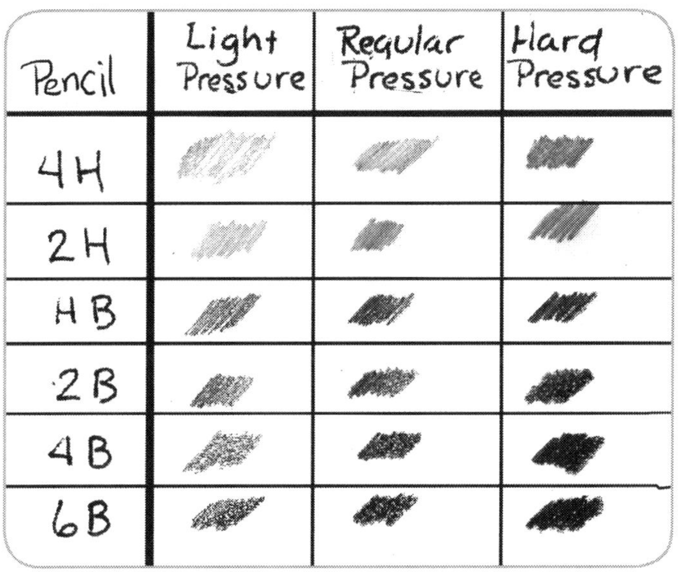

FIGURE 12. *Chart showing the values I can make using various pencils.*

NOTE: *What feels like regular pressure to you may change as you work. If you do a brief warm-up and take breaks before your hand tires, you will have a more consistent "regular" pressure.*

TIP: *You might want to make another similar chart keep with your tangling supplies for quick reference.*

One thing to note is the term "Regular Pressure." Everyone is different in what feels "regular" to them. I naturally use a lighter pressure than my daughter. Using the same pencil, her marks will be darker than mine unless I am pushing harder than normal or she is making a concerted effort to write lightly. This is why it is important for you to do these exercises. You want to know how the pencils work for you, not how they work for me.

Pencil	Light Pressure	Regular Pressure	Hard Pressure

Exercise 7. ***See What Values You Can Make Each of Your Pencils.***

Just as you did using a single pencil, use the values in this chart as a reference and take a few minutes to practice making a gradation with each of your pencils. Like Exercise 7, this is just so you can see the difference in your pencils. It will help you decide which pencil to use to create the result you are looking for. (Do not compare your gradations with mine. I used Photoshop to crop mine into neat boxes.)

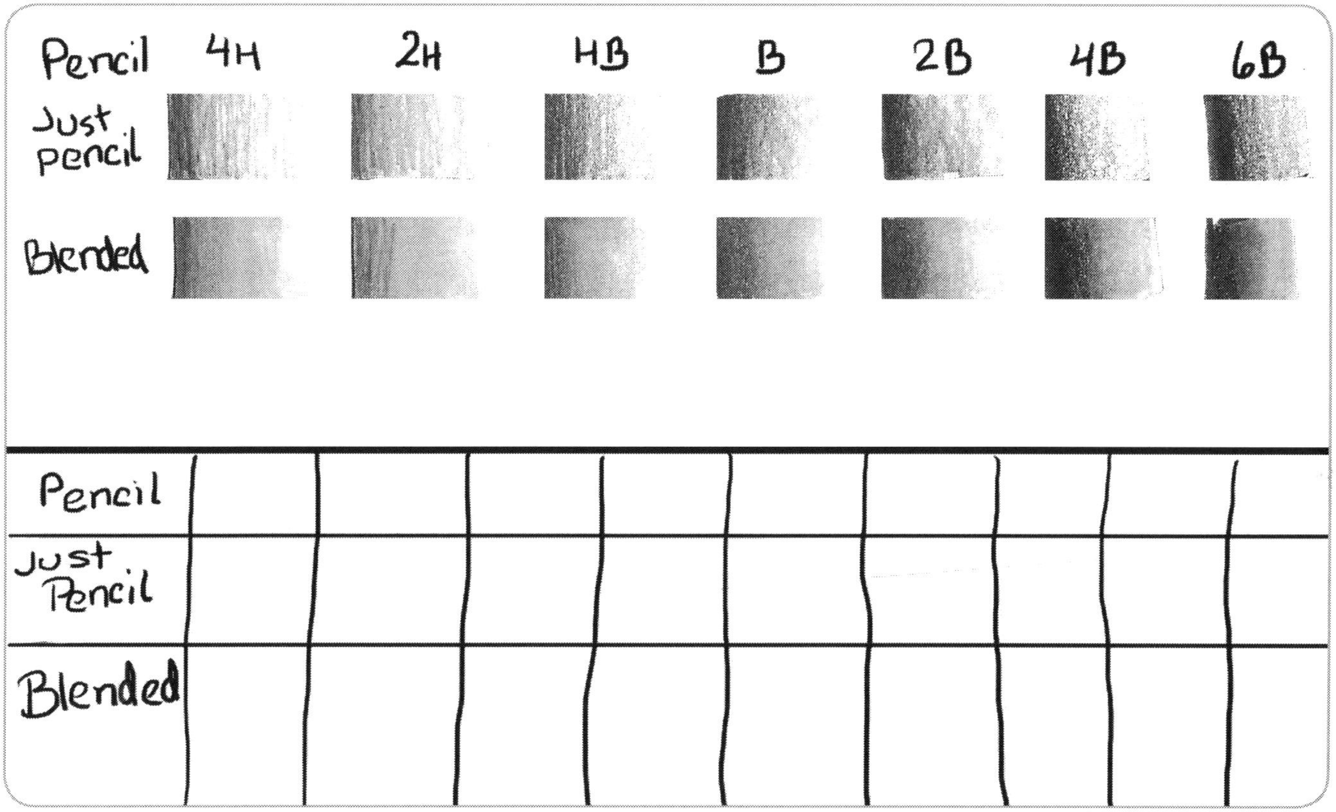

Exercise 8. ***Make a Gradation with Each of Your Pencils.***

Combining Multiple Pencils to Make a Gradation

Sometimes the result you are looking for is easier to create using more than one pencil. Using your chart from Exercise 7, make a long gradation from very light to almost black.

If your gradation is a bit rough at first, here is a trick you can use to smooth it out. Take your hardest pencil and gently go over your gradation again. Start using medium pressure at the darkest side of your gradation and work towards the lightest pressure on the light side. The hard pencil will fill in any white space, and it also acts as a blender, pushing the softer graphite layer down into the paper, both darkening and smoothing.

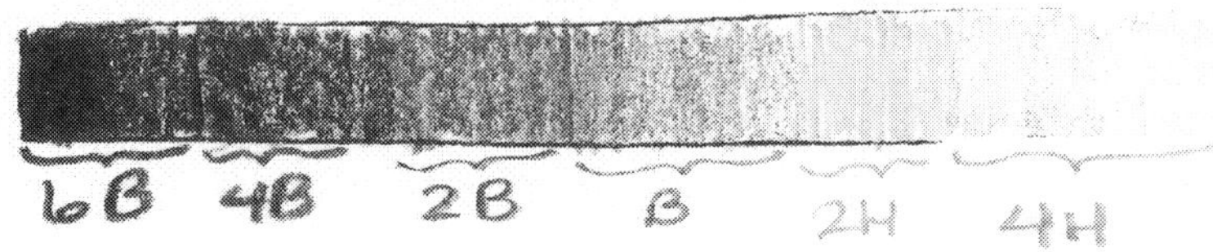

EXERCISE 9. *Make a Gradation with All of Your Pencils*

See how smooth you can make your gradation by only using pencils. When you are done, take your blender and gently push your lightest lights off to the right to lighten them even further. I can always get a lighter and smoother value using my blender than I can with a pencil. Here is my final result:

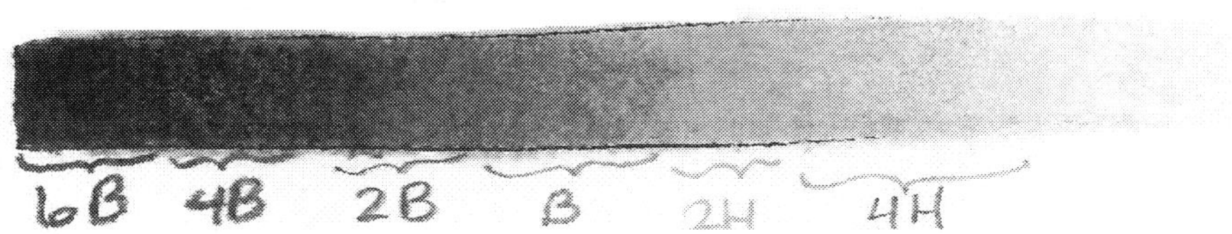

FIGURE 13. *Multi-pencil gradation plus blending tool.*

Blending Multiple Pencils

Because different grades of pencil have differing amounts of graphite, they blend differently. Experiment in this workbook to get to know these differences so you won't be surprised when shading your artwork. After getting used to shading only with my Zentangle pencil, the first time I used a 2B pencil, I was surprised by how far it blended. At the time, I was working on shading a Zentangle tile, and instead of ending up with some nice, smooth shadows, I had a very gray tile.

TIP: *I find it easy to "over-shade" when working with super soft pencils, especially when I first started using them.*

Soft pencils, because they deposit more graphite, can be blended further and more easily than hard pencils. When I am shading, I usually don't even attempt to blend "H" pencils because I don't put down enough graphite. I use a tool to blend any pencil HB or softer.

Here is a chart I made to see how far I could blend each of my pencils. I filled the box with a much harder pressure than I usually do, so that I would be able to blend the harder pencils, but I tried to use the same consistent pressure with each of my pencils.

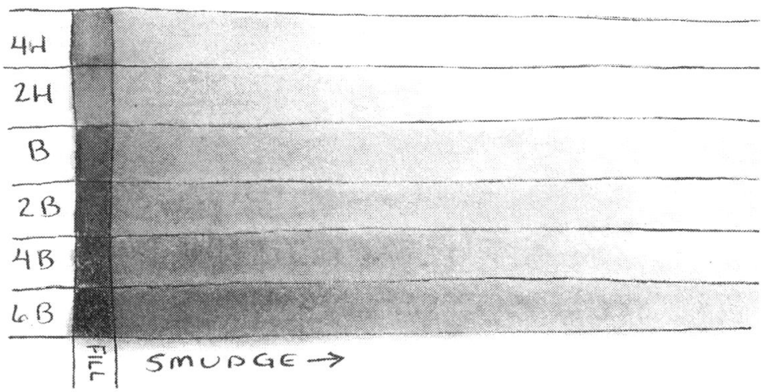

FIGURE 14. *Look at how much further soft pencils can be blended than hard ones.*

Fill in the chart below to see how far you can "stretch" each of your pencils. Use your regular pressure to fill each "fill" box, then use your blender to see how far you can push that graphite. Start with your hardest pencil and work towards the softest and clean your blender between pencils for a more accurate result.

✎ **TIP:** *The amount of graphite laid down by your pencil determines how easy it is to blend it. If you have a naturally heavy hand, you may be able to blend H pencils that I cannot.*

PENCIL	*fill*	***SMUDGE ->***

EXERCISE 10. *See how far each of your pencils will blend.*

✎ **TIP:** *You can quickly clean your blender by rubbing it over a piece of scrap paper until it stops leaving a mark.*

PEN SHADING

NOTE: *Pen shading sounds intimidating to many, but the marks you make are so small that you cannot make a "big mistake."*

NOTE: *You can compare pen shading with digital photographs. Usually, the photo looks identical to a photo from a film camera, but zoom way in and you can see the squares or dots of the individual pixels.*

TIP: *It is also possible to create subtle shading by changing the pressure of your strokes. Pressing harder, especially on cushioned paper, can give you a little thicker line. Just be careful not to press too hard and ruin the delicate tip of your pen.*

Another shading technique is **pen shading**. Knowing how to shade with a pen gives you the option of shading when using a pencil will not work. For instance, if you are tangling on ceramic or jewelry, you can't use pencil. It is also just fun to try when you want a different look.

Of course, you can't change the lightness or darkness of your pen by changing the pressure of your stroke as you can with a pencil. Instead, you vary the amount of ink you use to fill up the space. Your eyes will read the density of the pen marks as shades of gray. Leave a lot of white space between your marks and the area will appear light gray. Fill the area densely to develop a darker shade of gray. Upon close inspection, you will see the individual marks, but from a distance, it should look smooth.

There are three main techniques used in pen shading: stippling, hatching, and scumbling.

- **Stippling**: creating a shadow by covering the area with small dots.
- **Hatching**: a shading technique using a series of straight lines
- **Scumbling**: filling an area with tiny circular or squiggly lines, like controlled scribbling.

Stippling

Stippling is the most popular method of pen shading. It fits well with the Zentangle philosophy:

- Every mark is deliberate.
- Focus is required to achieve good results.
- There is no eraser involved.

To stipple, hold your pen straight up and down and gently touch the tip of your pen to your paper. This leaves a nice circle, rather than a check or slash. Keep your dots uniform in size for a smooth look.

Filling an area with stippling is done in several steps.

1. Start by outlining the area you want to shade with a dots. Place the dots close together on the darker side and further apart on the lighter side so you can use your outline as a guide for spacing.
2. Fill the entire area to be shaded with random, widely spaced dots. Always start lighter than you think you will need. You can always make it darker, but you can't go back and lighten an area that is too dark.
3. Gradually build up the shadow areas deliberately.

TIP: *Take frequent breaks and step back to look at the big picture. It is easy to get so focused on your dot-making that you keep making dots long after the area is dark enough.*

Stippling Tips

- Keep the dots the same size by using a consistent speed and pressure.
- Take your time. The faster you work, the more likely you are to end up with dashes rather than dots. There is no question that stippling takes time. This can either be "tedious" or "meditative." It all depends on your expectations and attitude.
- Use the smallest pen tip you have. The smaller the pen tip, the more subtle are the variations that are possible.

Before shading anything with stippling, take a few minutes to learn the technique. Hold the pen straight up and down and gently make some dots. If you have different sized pens, try using them all to see which you prefer. Don't tense up and take a break if your hand gets tired.

EXERCISE 11. ***Go dotty with stippling.***

Now try your hand at making a value scale using stippling. Here is mine as a guide. Remember when I said that stippling takes a long time? The tiny sample took me almost 15 minutes. It is enlarged below to show detail.

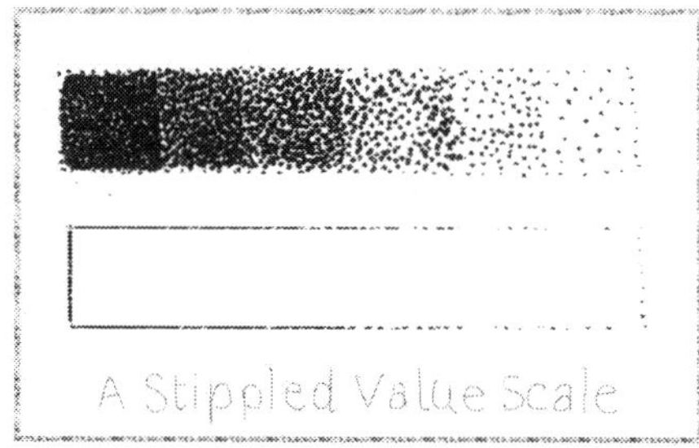

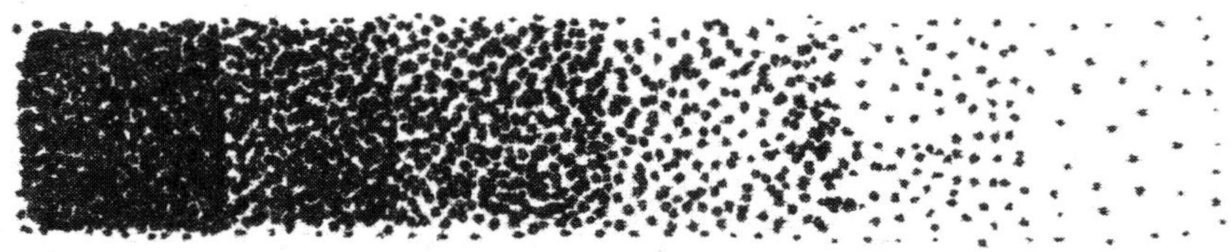

EXERCISE 12. ***Make a Value Scale with Stippling***

FIGURE 15. *Stippling, up close.*

If you are up for a challenge, try to make a gradation with stippling. Start with the value scale you made in the last exercise and work on eliminating each line by carefully darkening the area just to the right of it, dot by dot, to blend it seamlessly into the next value. Making a stippled gradation shows you have great pen control, and you will be able to add some beautiful details to your Zentangle artwork using stippling.

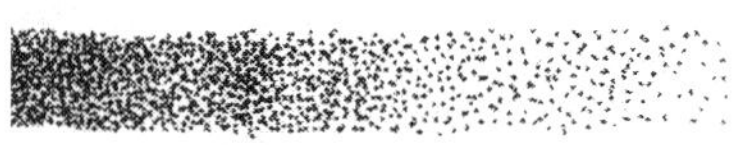

FIGURE 16. *A stippled gradation.*

Hatching

You've already practiced hatching when you filled the boxes with straight, parallel lines in Exercise2. As in stippling, the finer the lines, the smoother the result you can achieve. For dark areas, use thick lines that are close together. Thinner lines that are farther apart make lighter shades of gray. There are three types of hatching:

- (Regular) hatching - using a series of straight, parallel lines.

- Cross hatching - using a series of criss-cross lines.

- Contour hatching - using curved lines that follow an object's form.

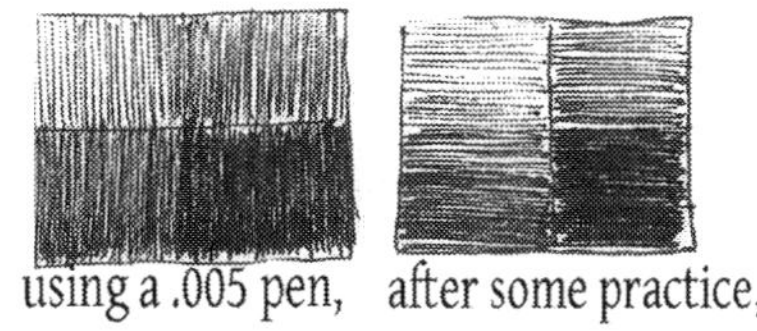

Figure 17. *Hatching.*

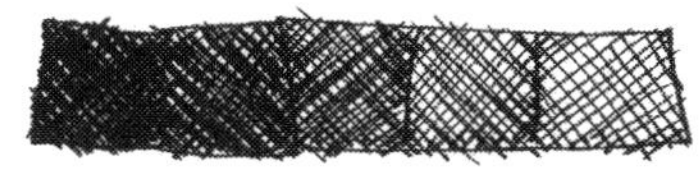

Figure 18. *A cross-hatching value scale*

For me, hatching is the most difficult of the pen shading techniques. My first attempts were very uneven and rough. Here is what I learned as I practiced:

Hatching Tips

- Keep a consistent speed when drawing your lines,
- Pay attention to how you start and stop your lines. I tend to leave thick marks when I start and they fade off as I finish. If you have this problem, lay down some scrap paper so that you start and end of your lines on the scrap and draw only the middle of the lines on your art.
- Slower speed makes thicker lines than quicker speed.
- Perfection is not necessary! Uneven hatching can add interesting texture.

Use the space below to get a feel for hatching and try it on some of the pieces in the Shading Playground chapter.

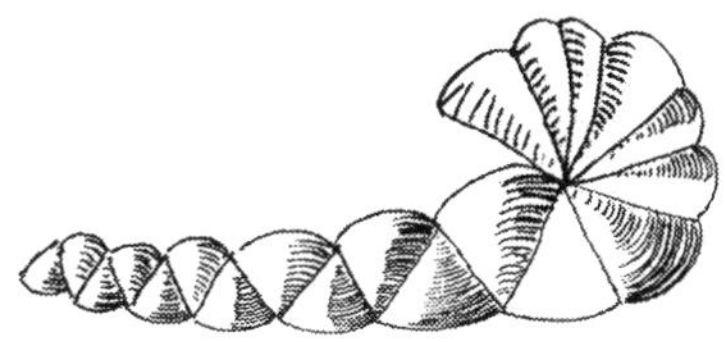

Exercise 13. ***The shading on the first 4 cone shapes are done using straight-line hatching. The rest uses contour hatching which adds a bit of dimension to the curves. Add some contour hatching to the empty one.***

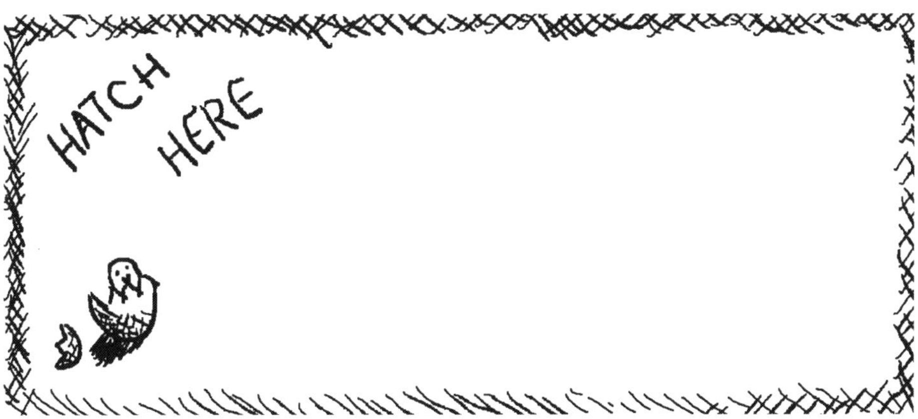

Exercise 14. *Try your hand at hatching.*

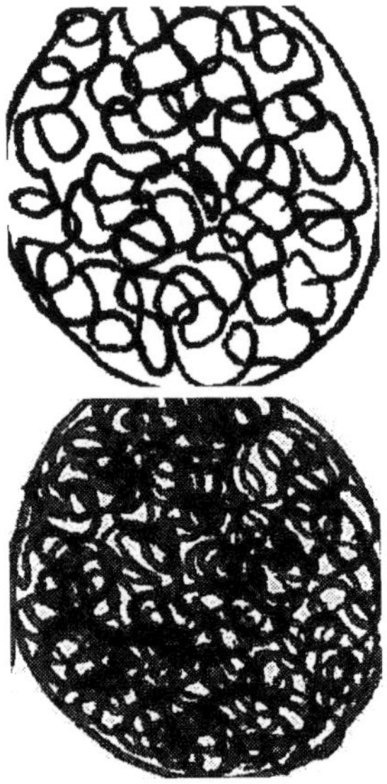

FIGURE 19. *Scumbling details: light value (top) and dark value(bottom).*

Scumbling

I remember being taught this technique as a child to make my crayon drawing smoother, but my mom didn't call it that. All she said was, "don't use straight lines to color because it will look messy." As a child, I didn't yet have the muscle control necessary for smooth hatching and whenever I'd change direction or overlap lines, I would get frustrated because it looked messy to me.

Instead of drawing lines or dots with your pen to shade, just put your pen down and start drawing squiggles. I like it because you don't have to lift your pen until you are finished with the area. You don't have to worry about starting and stopping as you did with hatching. If you don't have enough pencil control yet to make the parallel lines needed for smooth hatching, then perhaps scumbling is the technique for you. The lines are freer and more relaxed. It can add a soft, loose feeling when you shade with scumbling.

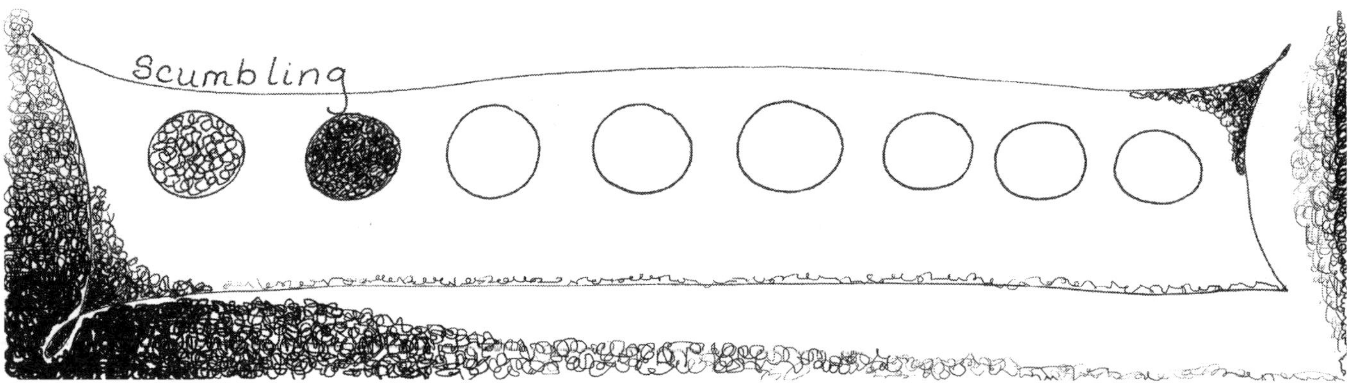

EXERCISE 15. ***Practice scumbling in the circles, making some light and some dark.***

BEYOND THE BASICS

As you can see, each of these techniques adds a different texture and feel to your artwork, but it doesn't have to stop there. You can use the same technique of making tiny shapes as fillers, but there is no rule that says you are limited to dots, lines, and circles. Go wild; use all three or use something entirely different, like swirls or stars or even letters. Have fun with your pen and add some sparkle to your shading.

Also while you are "going wild," I wanted to point out that these three techniques listed under "pen shading" can also be done with your pencil. When stippling with a pencil, instead of just touching the tip of your pencil to the paper, give it a twist before lifting it. Stippling works best with an HB or softer pencil. To see pencil scumbling, look at the Seahorse ZIA on page 99. There, I did some dark scumbling with a soft pencil and added more rows to make a scumbling gradation.

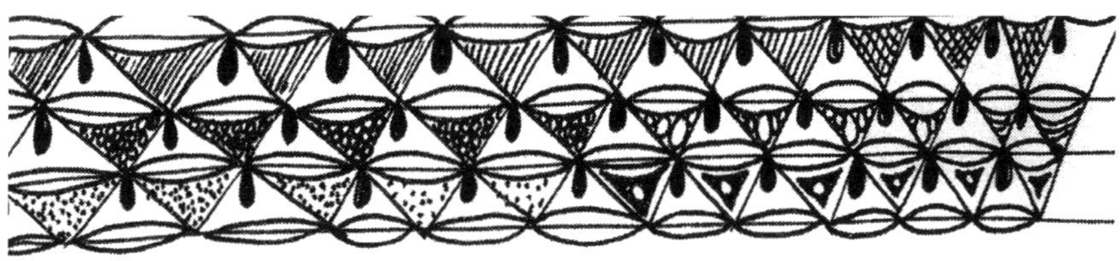

FIGURE 20. *A variety of penwork enhances this pretty piece by Sonya Yencer. I love the combination of techniques.*

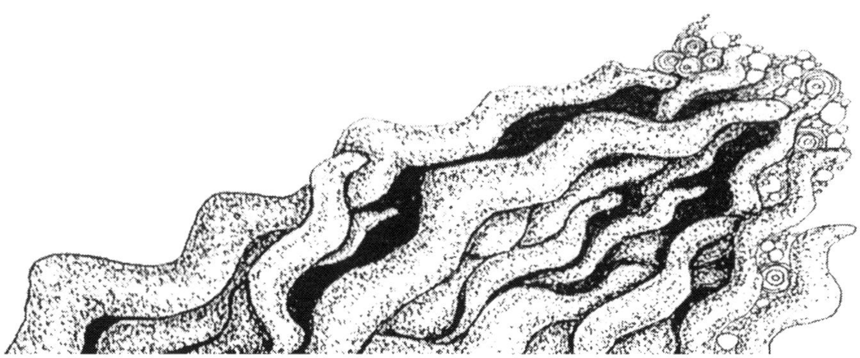

FIGURE 21. *Beautiful stippling by Brinn McFetridge.*

Not So Simple Squares

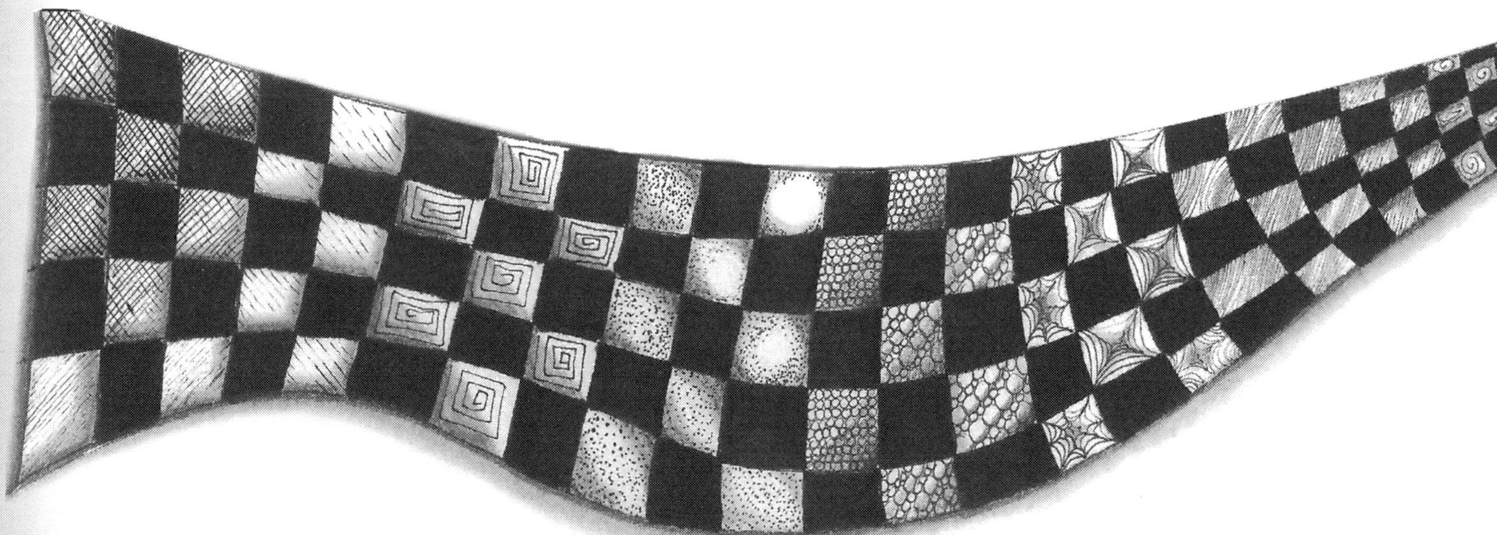

Tangles Used: **KNIGHTSBRIDGE**, *filled with* **EMINGLE**, **TIPPLE** *(and tangleations)*, **BALES** *(tangleations) and different shading techniques*

CHAPTER 2 SHADING SIMPLE SHAPES

Now that you have had some time to learn and practice basic shading skills, you are ready to put them to use. Before shading tangles, which are often complex and have a number of different shapes, you will start with the learning to shade individual simple shapes.

You will learn how to use shading to add the illusion of dimension to transform a flat shape into a form with depth. Once you know how to change a circle into a sphere or a square into a cube, you will be able to add that same 3-dimensional quality to the tangles that contain them and make your art pop.

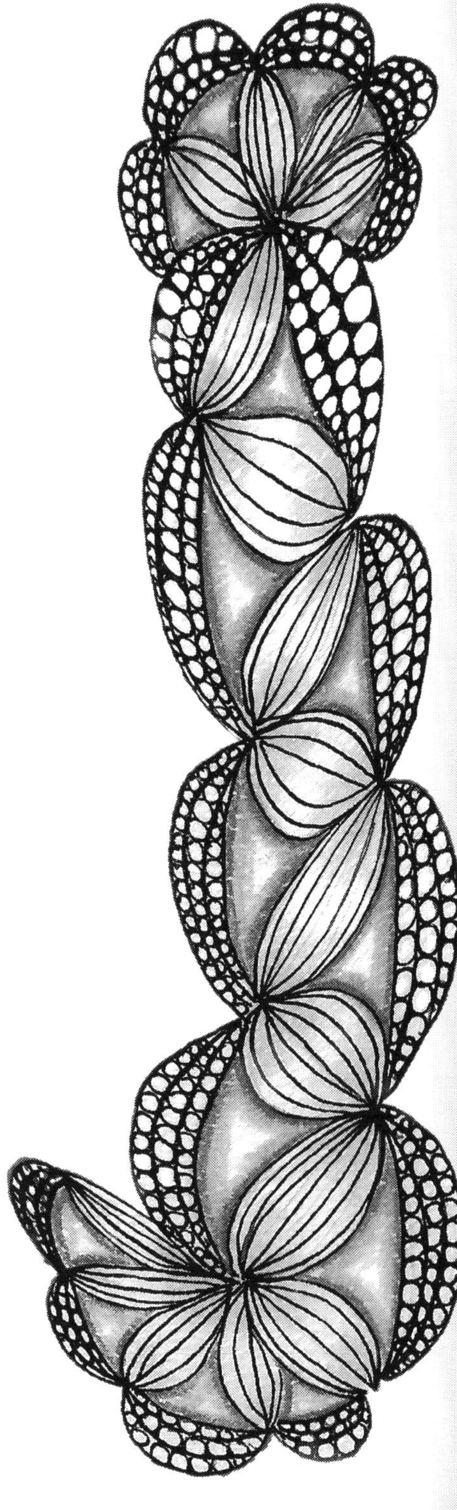

FORMS

When you shade simple shapes, you can turn them into **forms.** A shape is a flat, 2-dimensional object having only length and height. A form is a 3-dimensional geometric figure that has length, height, and depth. Of course, it is impossible to draw an actual 3-dimensional shape on a 2-dimensional piece of paper, but you can create the *illusion* of three dimensions.

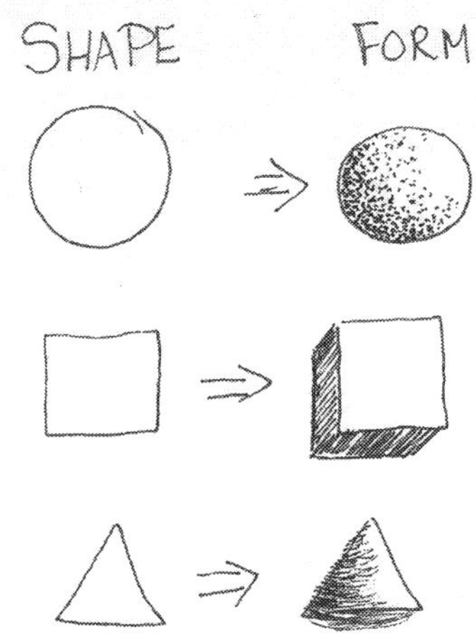

FIGURE 22. *Shading can give the illusion that the circle, square, and triangle now have depth and have transformed into a sphere, cube, and cone.*

See how the shading makes the form seem to be something tangible while the shape just lie there on the page?

You can use light and shadow to add dimension to your art. Darkness tells your eye that something is deep, and lightness tells your eye that it is elevated. Use the brightest highlights on the parts you want to appear highest, and the darkest shadows on the lowest. If you want something to appear flat, make sure it has the exact same value throughout. If a part becomes darker, it seems to slope down. If it lightens, it seems to float up. When you shade the simple shapes in your tangles to turn them into forms, your art will pop.

But before I show you how I shade forms, I need to take a moment to talk about erasers and erasing.

To erase or not to erase, that is the question.

Erasers aren't part of the Zentangle kit because there are "no mistakes" in Zentangle. I totally agree with this philosophy. As you are tangling, allow yourself to get into the "zen zone" and not stress about the results. However, I am assuming that you are reading this book because you want to make your finished tangling more artistic. An eraser is a valuable tool in an artist's toolkit. I often use it when shading, not to remove mistakes, but to add highlights, as if it were a white pencil. I also use it when my smudging goes too far. I would rather have the option to "clean up" stray marks rather than to have to worry about staying inside the lines when I am blending soft shadows. Note that just because I am an eraser advocate, I don't feel you should erase every time something does not go as planned. Often the results you did not intend to produce can be as or more beautiful than the one you were trying to create.

TIP: *If you really do not want to be tempted by having an eraser around, you can try adding highlights by using a white charcoal pencil or a white colored pencil, but you will then have to be extra careful when blending to stay inside the lines.*

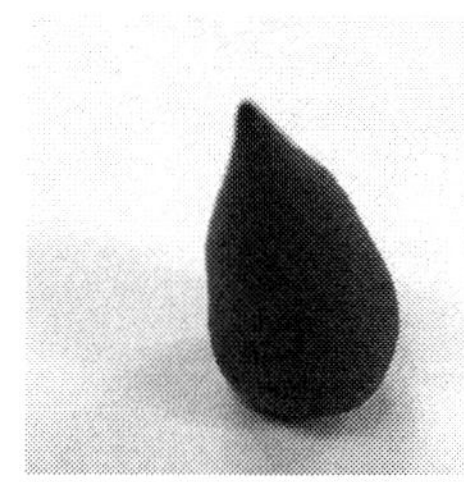

FIGURE 23. *Kneaded eraser shaped to a point.*

A kneaded eraser is a great addition to your shading toolkit because you can form it into a small point and use it to add highlights. Gently touch an area to remove a bit of your shading and you have an instant highlight. You can't press hard with your eraser or you will lose the point you created. Instead, gently tap your eraser onto the area to be highlighted and repeat until the highlight is just how you want it. If you want to use a kneaded eraser to create highlights, shade lightly or you won't be able to completely erase your highlights and the technique will not be as effective.

NOTE: *Anything written in small capital letters:* LIKE THIS *is the name of a tangle.*

Circles

Circles are a basic shape that has endless possibilities.

Circles are also used in many tangles, such as NIPA, PURK, and JETTIES.

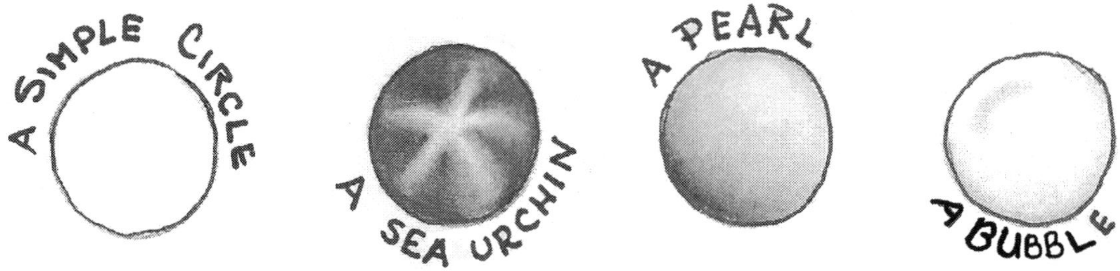

FIGURE 24. *Look at all a circle can become with a fresh coat of graphite.*

Take a look at this humble circle and all that it can become. I hope you use this page to spark your imagination. Look for circles that you see every day and pay attention to how the light and shadows play across their surfaces. Careful observation is the first step to being able to recreate objects in your art.

You can see that the rays on the shell seem to be elevated from the rest of the shell. This is because the lightest part of the object appears to be the highest. The rays appear to have width in addition to height because I used a lighter shade on the downward slope. I reserved the darkest values for the base of the shell.

On the pearl, I used a gradation to create a spherical look. I left a highlight on the side opposite the shadow to show where the light is hitting the object.

When creating a realistic pencil sketch, an artist will have a single light source and make sure all of the highlights and shadows are consistent with this lighting source. For shading tangles, I find this unnecessarily complicated and let each tangle shine with its own light.

If you want just a quick suggestion of form, use a soft arc and a hint of shadow. I used my dirty tortillion to create this effect. It allows me to get a very light, soft mark, which is perfect for this hint of shading.

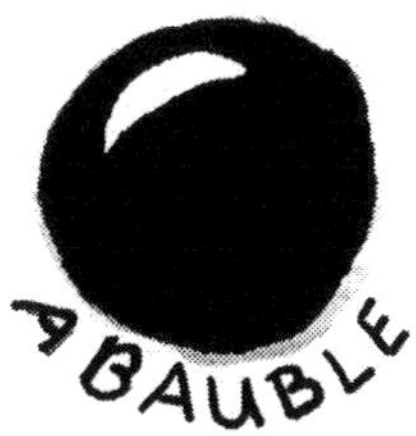

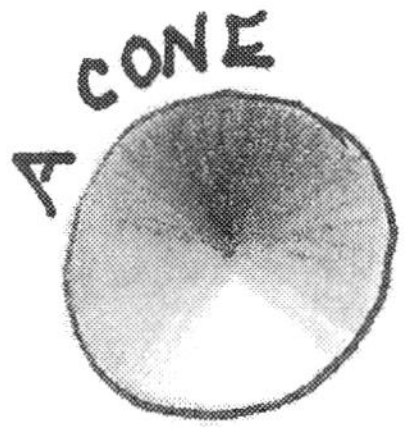

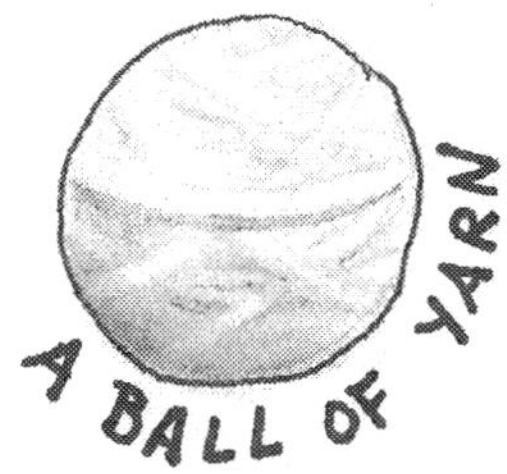

This bauble or bead looks as if it is made of shiny jet. It is almost the inverse of the bubble. I use my pen to fill in the entire circle except for leaving a white highlight on one side. Then I use my pencil or tortillion to create a soft, subtle cast shadow.

Adding a few baubles to your art can create a dramatic focal point when placed next to a light area because of the high contrast.

I transformed this circle into a bird's eye view of a cone. To create this look, I stroked from the center of the circle to the edges. I used a 4B pencil to make the darkest shadow area and a 2H for the medium gray. Then I used my blender to smooth everything out, stroking from the center point out towards the circumference. I used my kneaded eraser to clean up the stray smudges outside the circle.

Each strand of yarn casts a shadow, but the whole ball itself needs a shadow. I started by using my 4H pencil to place some fine detail shadows behind individual strands. Then I added a shadow to the whole ball on the bottom left with my B pencil and blended it with my tortillion. I kept it light because I didn't want to lose the yarn texture. The final step for the yarn was to use a kneaded eraser to add back some of the highlights that were lost by blending the shadow. You can see two strands in the shadow area that I erased to make them look as if they were lying on top of the ball. I formed my eraser into a fine point so I could erase inside each strand.

NOTE: *Take a look at the pencil on page 1. See how the shadows curve around the contour?*

One thing to notice is that shadows always follow the form of an object. So if you want a circle to look like a ball, your shadows need to be curved. Look at the circles on the previous page. Notice that the shadows seem to wrap around the edges of all of the spherical objects. This is especially true of the strands of yarn. Despite going in many different directions, they all curve as if following the ball shape.

NOTE: *The cone uses straight line shadows because the intended illusion was pointy instead of spherical.*

Take a look at what happens if the shadows are straight lines. Since your mind knows that shadows follow the shape of an object, the circle on the left gets interpreted as a flat circle that is colored gray and white. It doesn't matter how perfect your gradations are, if your shadow does not follow the form of the object, you will lose the ability to trick the eye into seeing a 3-D shape.

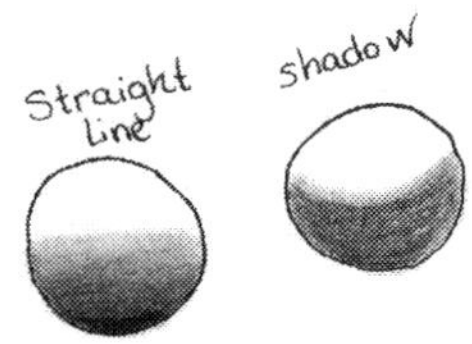

FIGURE 25. *A shadow that does not follow form is no shadow at all.*

Practice shading in the circles below using one or more of the techniques that you practiced on the previous pages. Use both your gradation skills and your blender to add soft shadows. Which do you prefer?

It doesn't matter where you place your highlight; just put the darkest shadow on the opposite side. If you have a kneaded eraser, you can practice using it to create highlights. If your eraser pulls too much graphite and your highlight is too big, just use your blender to add more shadow. If you use a light hand on both your blender and eraser, you will be able to repeat this process until you get the look you want.

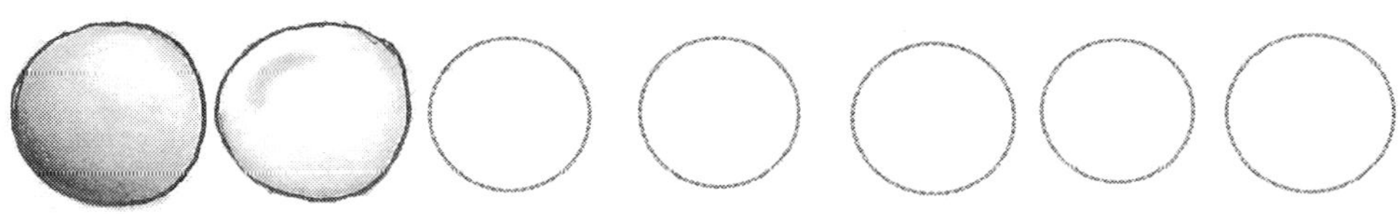

EXERCISE 16. ***Turn a circle into a sphere using shading.***

Squares and Rectangles

Squares are found in a multitude of tangles, from KNIGHTSBRIDGE to W2. And don't forget about all of those tangles that start with a grid. When you can make simple squares interesting, it is like having a magic wand that can transform your tile from simple to extraordinary.

NOTE: *In Zentangle-land, squares are different than they are in geometry. They don't all have to have straight lines and 90-degree angles. Anything with four somewhat equal sides counts.*

Squares and rectangles start out simple, but just like circles, they can be transformed into a variety of interesting forms with a little imagination. In shading the circles, we used curved shadows that wrap around the form of the sphere, but that does not mean that squares and rectangles must be shaded with straight vertical and horizontal lines. On the contrary, using different lines will trick the eye into thinking that the square is not just a box, but an object with interesting dimensions.

Look at this photo. Clearly it is just a square, but the way the light and shadows play on it tells you that it is something more. Can you envision shading KNIGHTSBRIDGE with these instead of black squares?

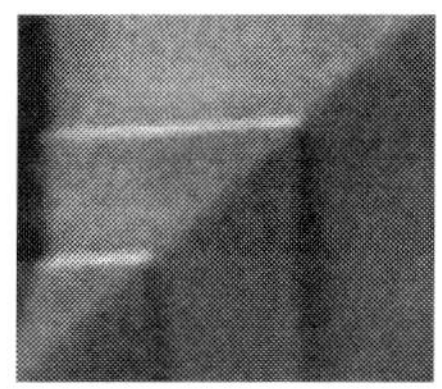

FIGURE 26. *Interesting squares are all around you. This is a carved wooden decoration at the end of a pew.*

I can easily recreate that shape by paying attention to the way the light is reflected and the shadows follow the planes of the wood. While this is not a tangle, I wanted to show you a process you might use for taking objects you see every day and use them in your tangling.

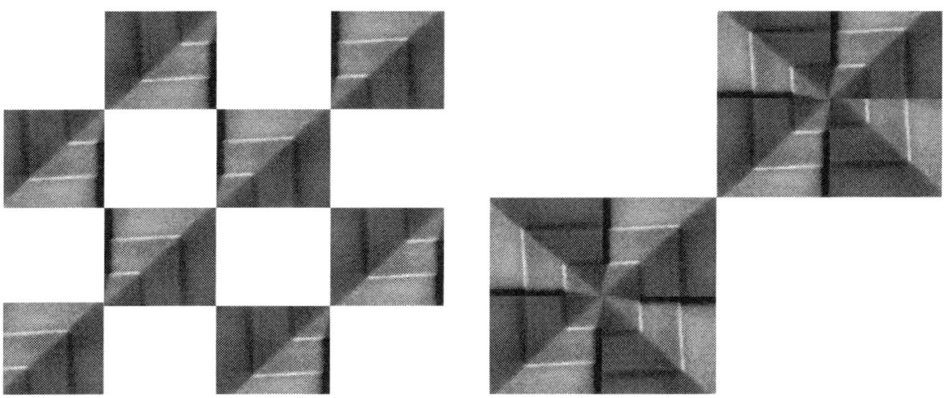

FIGURE 27. *Just imagine what you can do if you could make light shine wherever you want...Wait, it is YOUR art. You can!*

FIGURE 28. *Step-by-step illustration showing how I copy light and shadows.*

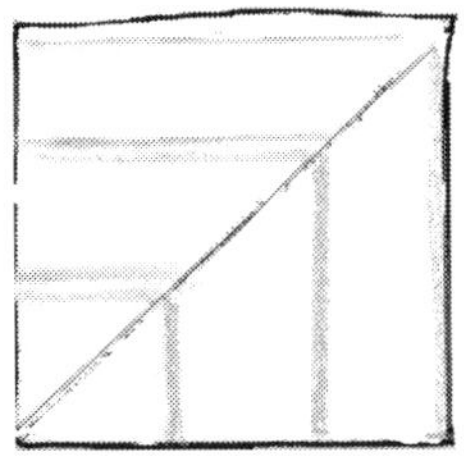

Lightly outline the highlighted areas. I used my 4H pencil here because I wanted to make sure my outlines would disappear after I shaded it.

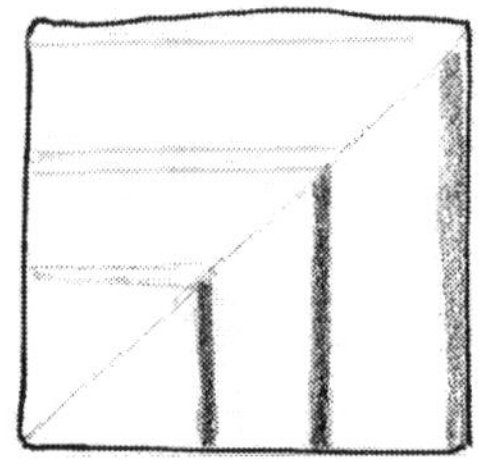

Shade the darkest shadows with a soft pencil. I used a 6B so I would have extra graphite for blending.

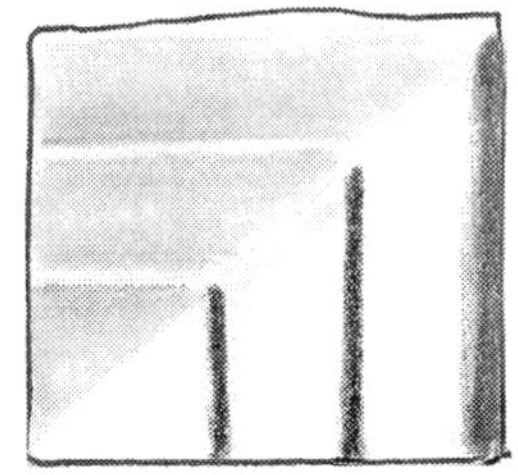

Shade the side that is in the light, carefully leaving the highlights white. Notice the subtle gradation within the shadows.

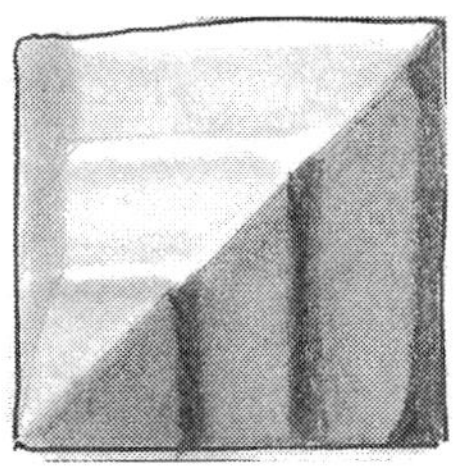

Add the darker shadows and blend them. See how the left-side shadow helps define the form? Otherwise, I may have used artistic license and left it out.

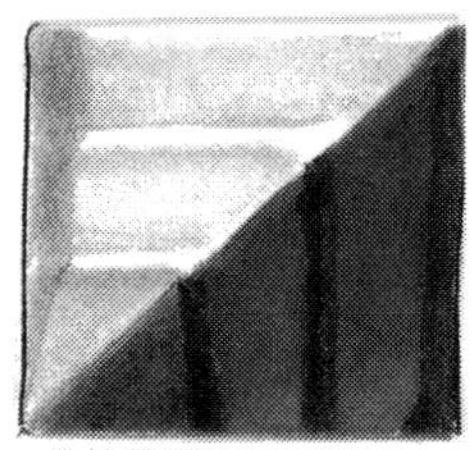

Now that I know I have the shadows and highlights placed correctly, I went back and darkened darkest shadows. The increased contrast makes the form more interesting. Compare this with the previous. See how much the darks contribute?

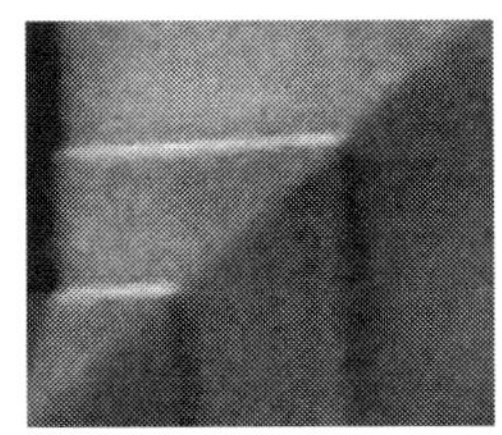

Compare my drawing to the original. I think I captured its essence even though it is not an exact copy.

It isn't necessary, or even desirable to try and replicate a photograph exactly. Allow yourself freedom to express yourself through your art.

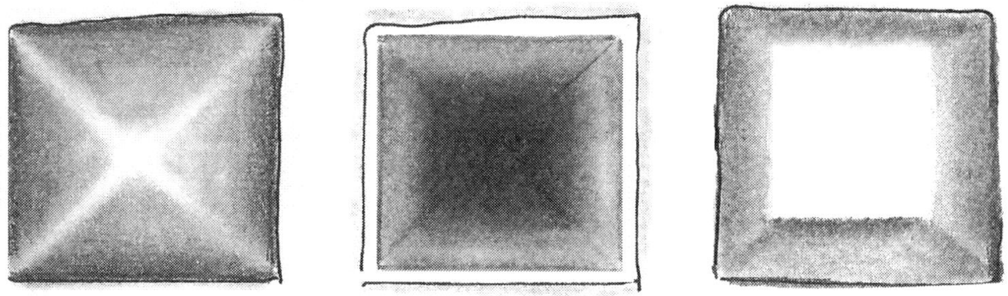

Figure 29. *Three more plane squares transformed by shading.*

Turn your square into a bird's eye view of a pyramid by making 4 smooth triangular gradations, leaving the tip and ridges highlighted. Here, the light is shines down.

Contrast this with the cone on page 39 where the viewpoint is the same, but the light is coming from the front.

This form could be that same pyramid viewed from underneath or looking down into an empty box. The deepest part is in the center. I left a small white band around the edge as a lip. I also added some light shading outside the lip to add even more depth.

Finally, see how a little shading can turn this square into an open window or a key on a keyboard. The top is the darkest, and the other 3 sides have gradations.

Shading these shapes is an iterative process for me. I lay down a little graphite and blend it smooth. Then I put more pencil down in the deepest shadows and blend it into the existing shadows. I keep adding more in the shadows until the dark is dark enough. Then I go back and clean up the edges by using a kneaded eraser if you have one.

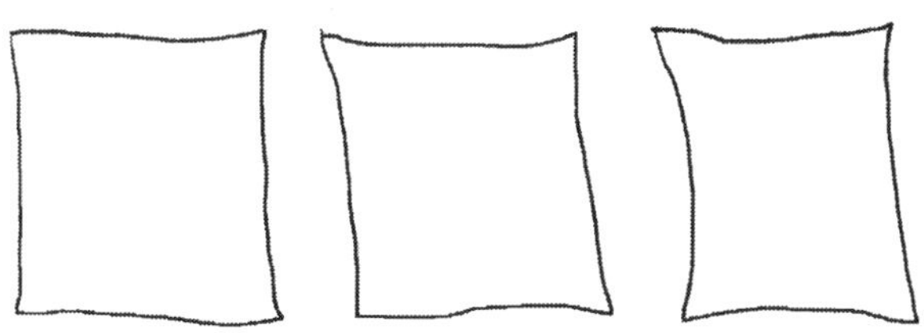

Exercise 17. *Shade these squares to make interesting forms.*

Miscellaneous Shading Advice

Three simple principles to make your shadows more realistic and thus more pleasing.

- Shadows always follow form.
- Form shadows must be soft.
- Lower places are darker than higher ones.

Great Spots to Shade

- Anywhere lines converge or intersect.
- Anywhere a shape tapers.
- Anywhere one shape appears behind another.
- Opposite any highlight.

FIGURE 30. *Shading in an arc turns parallel lines into a row of pipes. The curved bands also follow the form and emphasize the roundness.*

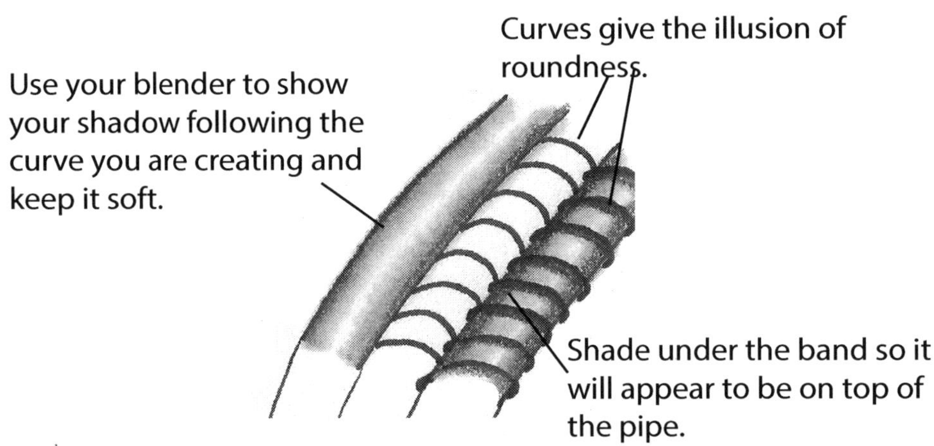

FIGURE 31. *Shading at the tips where the teardrop shapes come to a point emphasizes the roundness of the centers.*

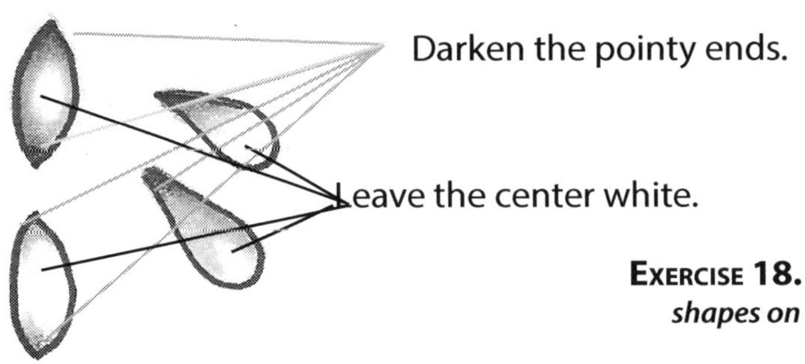

EXERCISE 18. ***Practice shading the simple shapes on the following page.***

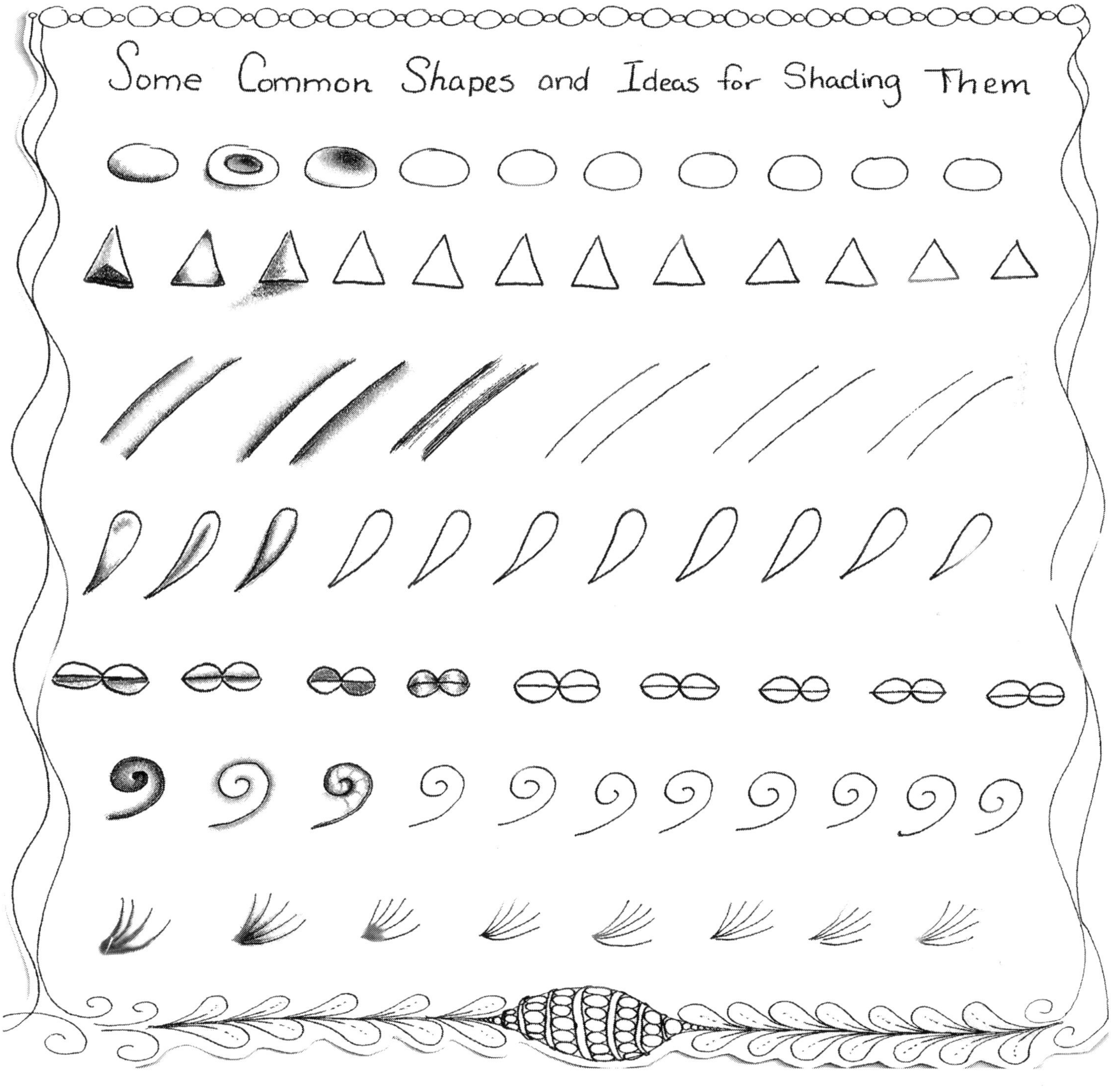

Nara

©Michelle Beauchamp, 2012

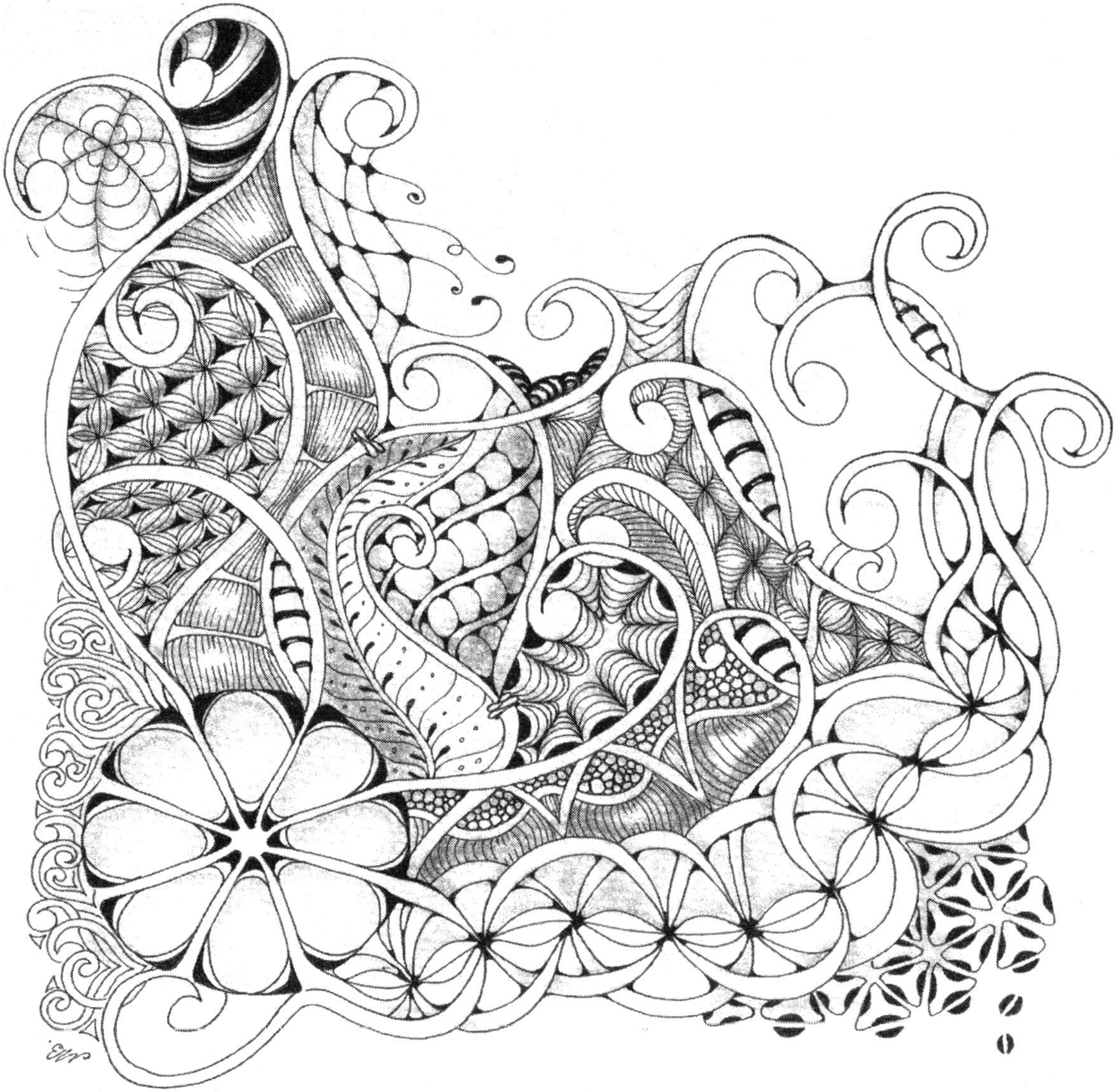

Tangles Used: STEPH-AH-NI, TRIPOLI, MOOKA, TWING, CRESCENT MOON, FINERY, ZANDER, BALES, MEER, DYON, FLORZ, BETWEED, PURK, BUNZO, YINCUT

CHAPTER 3 SHADING TANGLES

This chapter contains ideas for shading twenty individual tangles. Since I couldn't possibly show every tangle that exists, I have categorized the tangles into groups based on shading ideas. These groups are different from ones you may have seen because they are based on structure, not appearance. For example, many tanglers classify **CUBINE**, **HUGGINS**, and **BALES** as grid based on their appearance, but they are usually shaded differently. Classifying tangles is not meant to imply that there is only one way to shade each tangle, but as a starting point to give you ideas on how to shade new tangles.

Keep in mind that these ideas are just suggestions. Use them to spark your own creativity. I have given you plenty of room to try out lots of different ideas. Have fun in this chapter and let your imagination run free. When you have filled in the blanks with your own shading, use it as a reference when you are shading your own work.

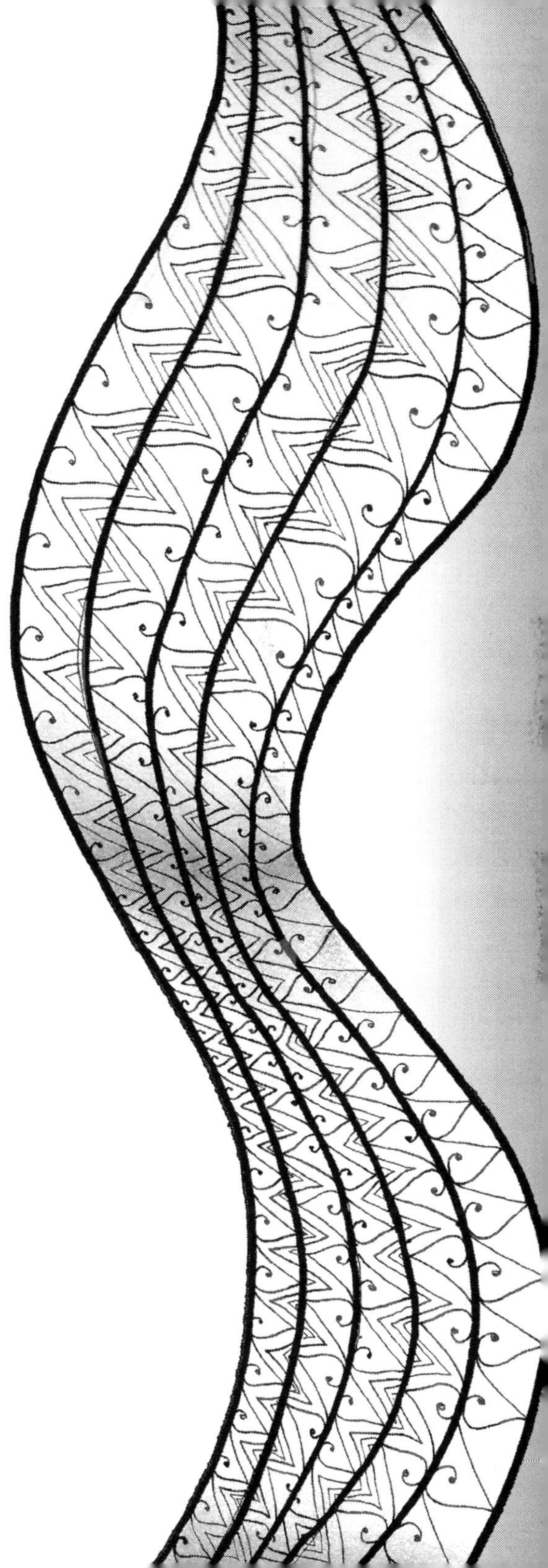

TANGLES THAT BEG TO BE SHADED

Certain tangles are never seen without their shading. It is such an integral part of their design that if you see them without any shading, you might not even recognize them. The tangles in this group are usually shaded similarly by tanglers everywhere. See how naked this poor tile looks without any shading?

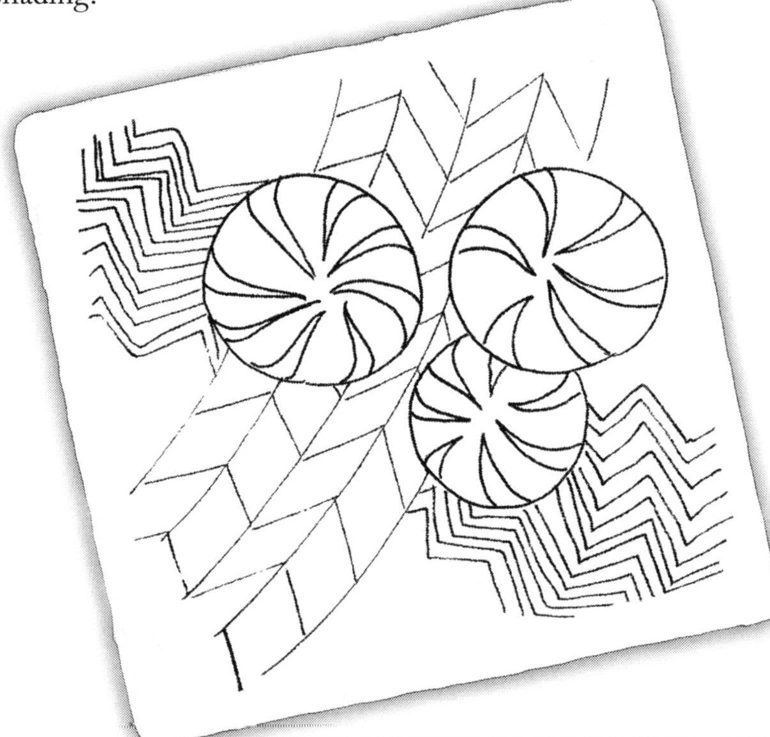

EXERCISE 19. ***Shade this tile after you practice shading the individual tangles in this section.***

BRAZE, RADDOX, GNEISS, And **BEELINE** are also in this group and can also be shaded similarly to **STATIC**.

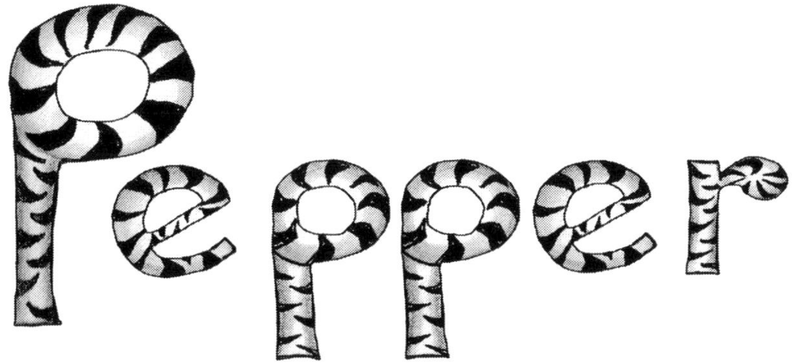

PEPPER

NOTE: *Unless otherwise noted, all of the tangles in this book are "official tangles," meaning they were created by the people at Zentangle, Inc.*

The first tangle that comes to mind in this group is the official tangle PEPPER. The shading is so important in this tangle that I find it helpful to actually do the shading first. I know this would be "against the law" if there were laws. But, there are no Zentangle police, so if you have trouble drawing PEPPER, give this a try.

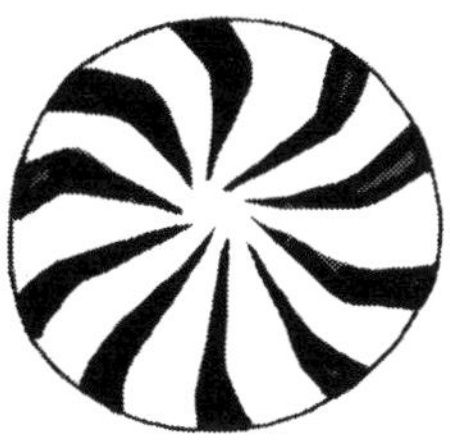

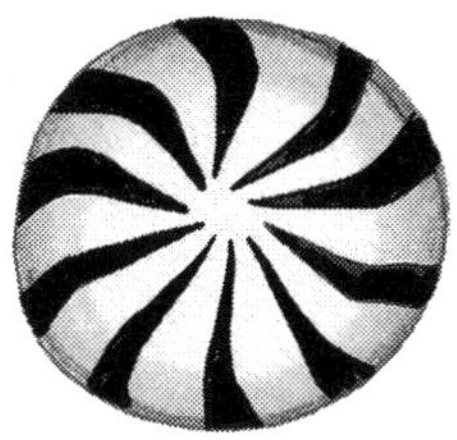

Unshaded PEPPER. PEPPER *is designed to be three-dimensional. It looks like a peppermint candy. In order for it to look three-dimensional, the candy stripes must follow the contour of the candy. Since the shading defines the contour of the candy, it is easier for me to start there. To draw the stripes, start from the center and when you reach the shading, curve your lines so it appears to go around the edge.*

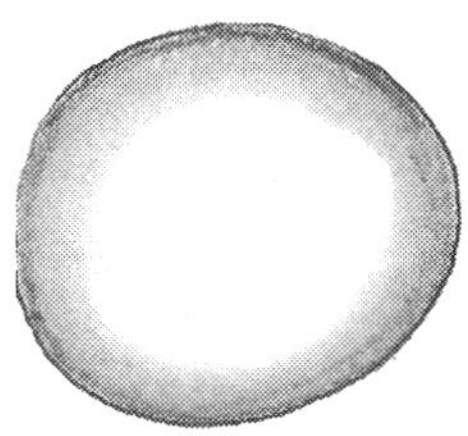

EXERCISE 20. ***Now, you draw the stripes..***

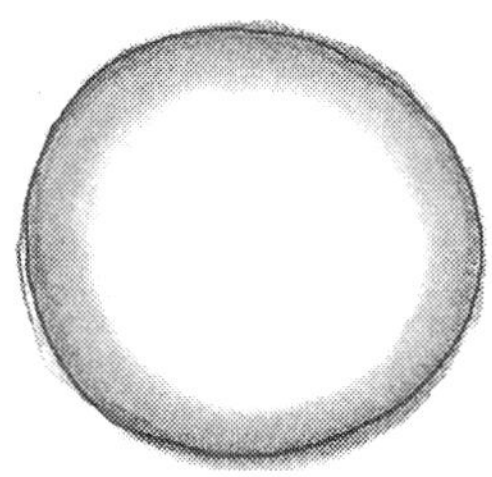

EXERCISE 21. ***Here is another one. Rather than simply coloring your stripes black, why not do something different, like stripes, or filling them with circles?***

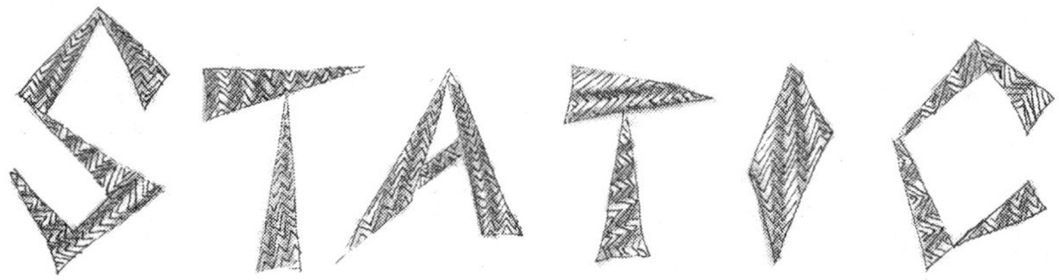

STATIC

Another tangle that just wouldn't be the same without its shading is STATIC. Without its shading, it is rather flat. The shading gives it its characteristic hills and valleys.

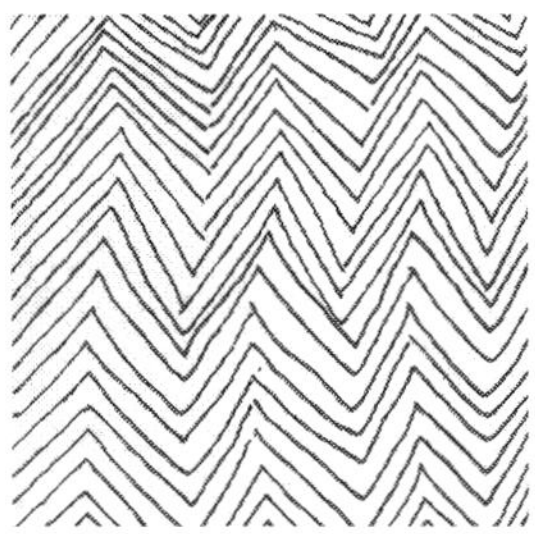

Unshaded static.

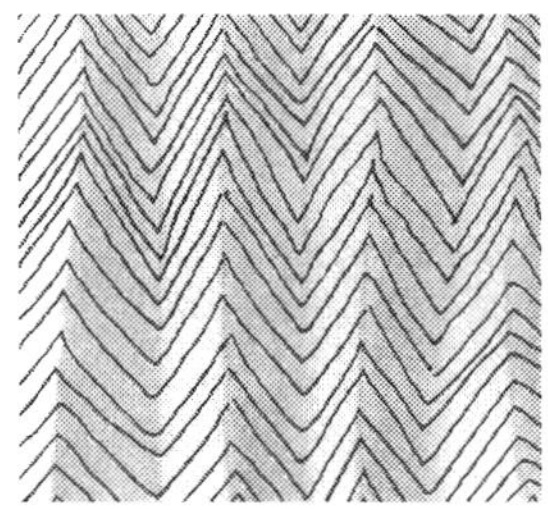

A simple way to shade STATIC *is to shade alternating bands of color. I find it easiest to draw a light line connecting hills to hills and the valleys to valleys. Then there are guidelines for placing the shading.*

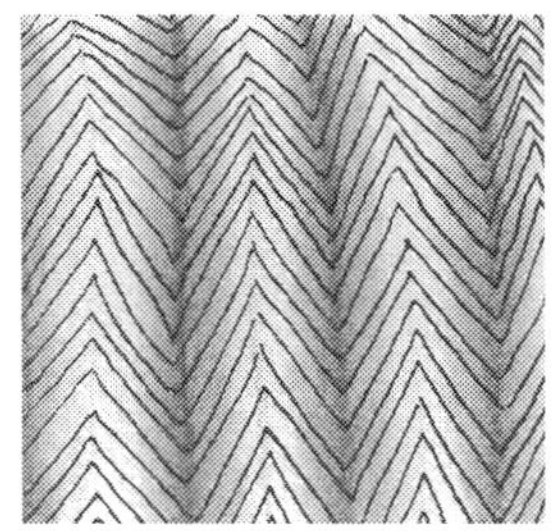

To really make the hills and valleys more pronounced, you can shade the valleys darkly, leave the peaks white, and make a gradation up and down the hills.

Exercise 22. ***Try shading these two differently as I did above.***

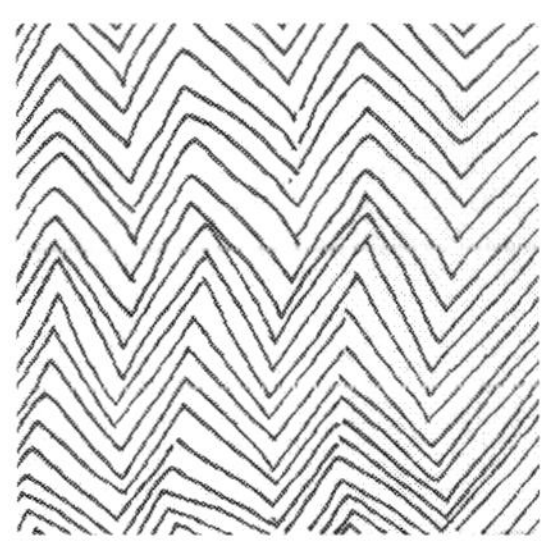

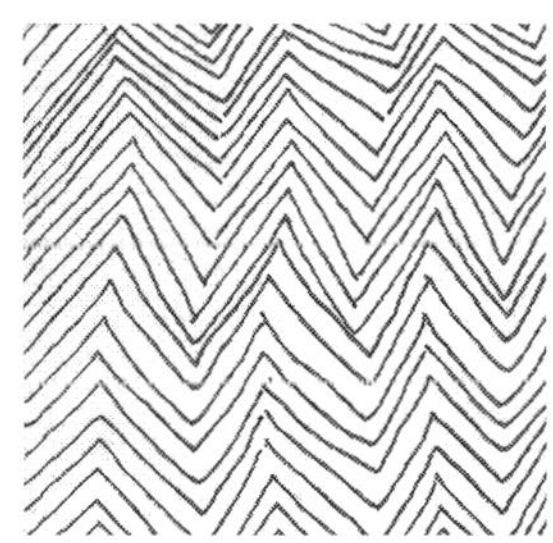

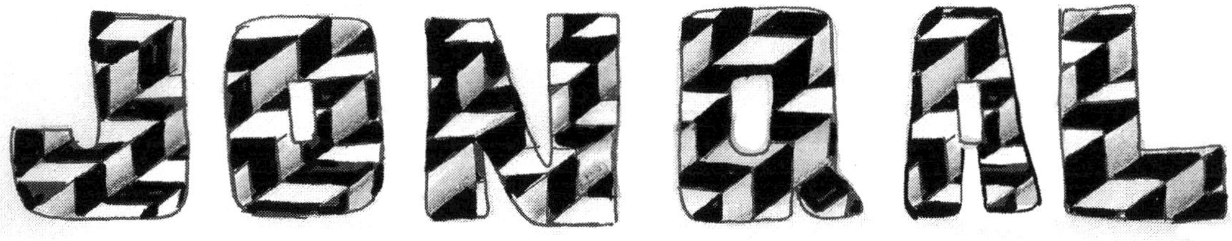

JONQAL

JONQAL is like a well-behaved cousin of STATIC. Where the lines in static are flowing and close together, JONQAL has more evenly spaced lines. JONQAL makes a bold statement and is a great tangle to use as a contrast to more light and airy or organic tangles.

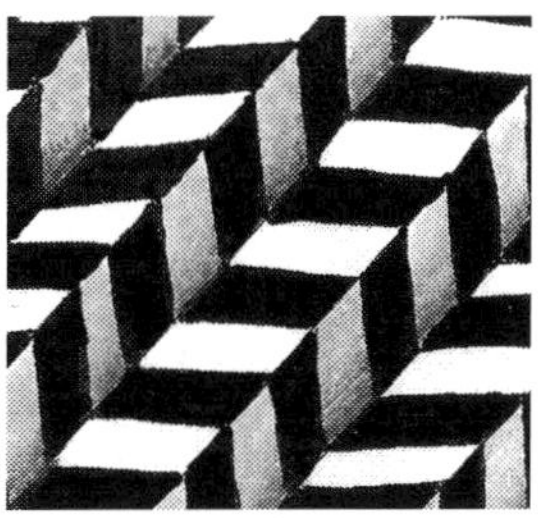

Usually, the vertical stripes are shaded. I like to use a gradation.

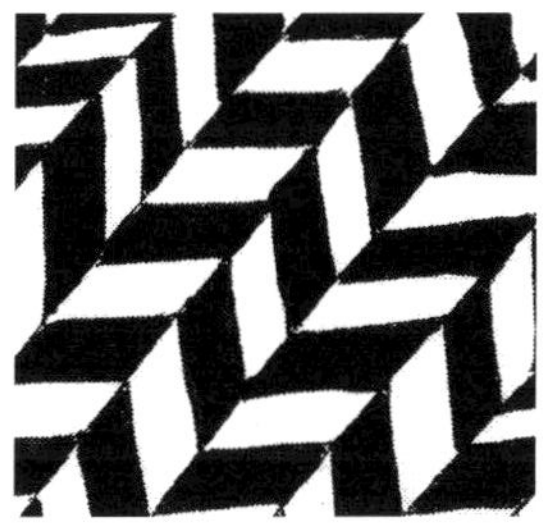

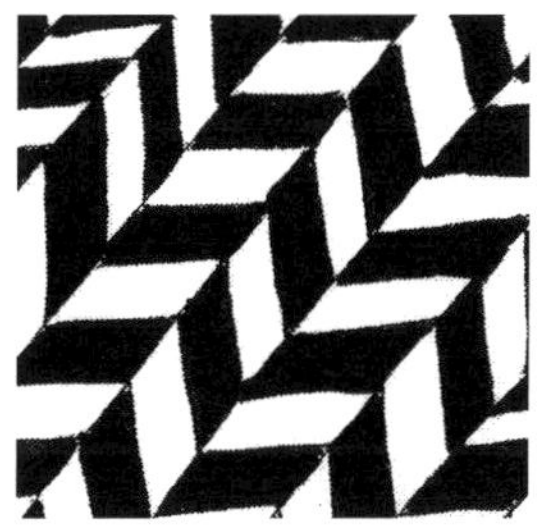

EXERCISE 23. ***Try your gradation skills on these two blank ones.***

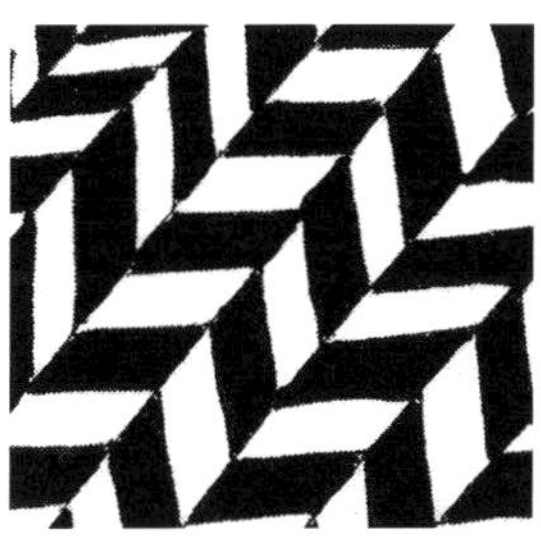

Unshaded JONQAL.

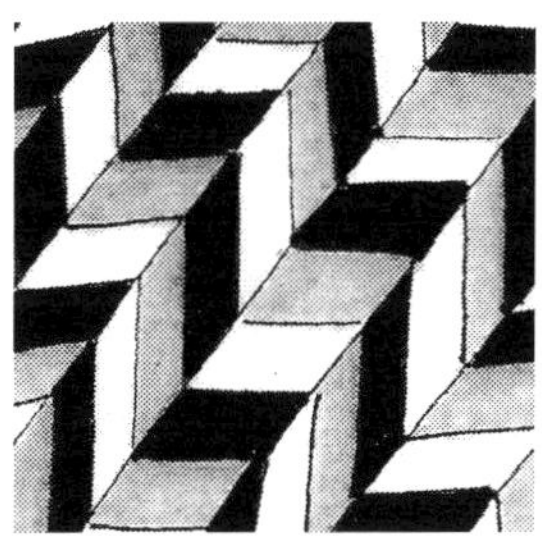

Here is one that is decorated with pencil rather than shaded.

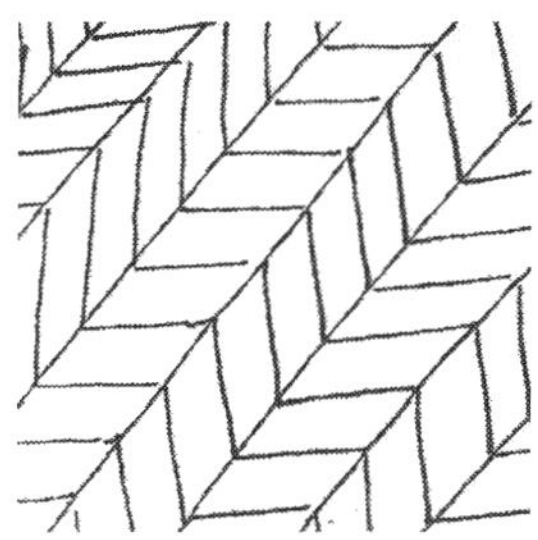

EXERCISE 24. ***Try something different on this one than you did in Exercise 23.***

SHADING LAYERED TANGLES

One of the things you learn in a beginning Zentangle class is that many tangles have components that are drawn behind one another in HOLLIBAUGH style. Some of these start out with a few elements and then everything else is drawn behind them. These tangles are built layer by layer and the end result has layer upon layer of components.

Any time one component is drawn behind another, it will appear as if one is on top of the other. Shading will enhance this structure. To shade layered tangles, simply outline each of the elements and blend outwards, over the top of anything drawn behind it. To make things really pop, color the background black and make sure to leave some areas white. I show you HOLLIBAUGH and PRINTEMPS, but you can use the same shading technique any time you draw one element behind another.

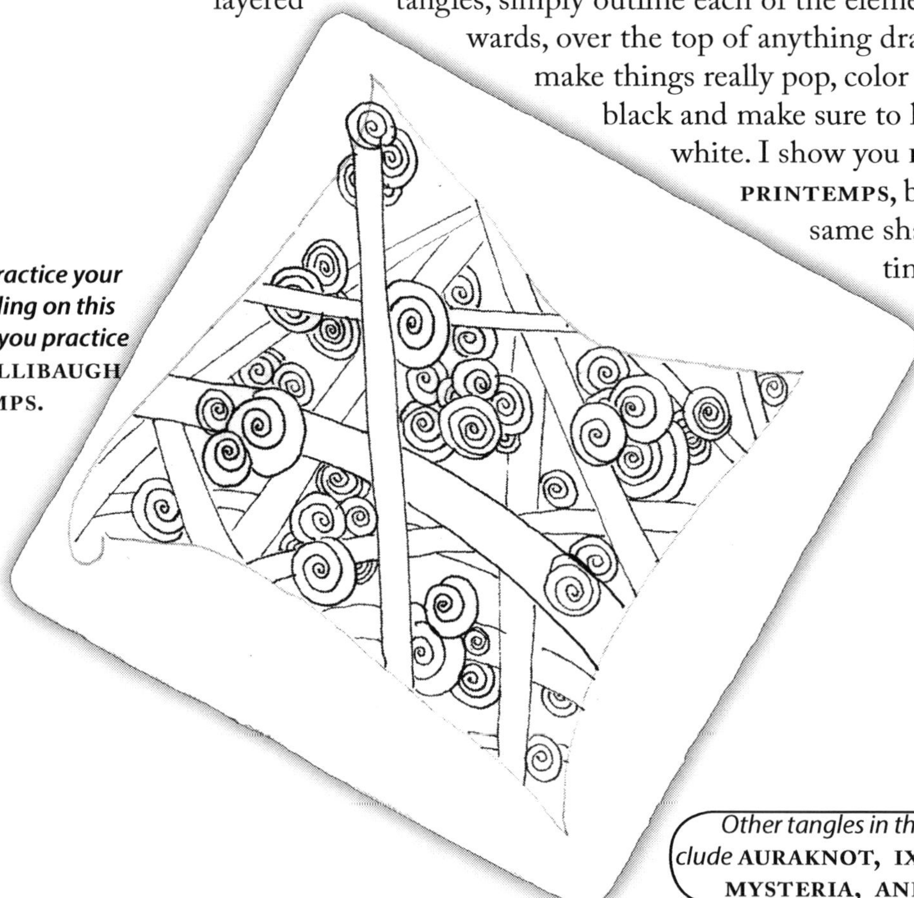

EXERCISE 25. ***Practice your layered shading on this tangle after you practice shading*** **HOLLIBAUGH & PRINTEMPS.**

Other tangles in this group include **AURAKNOT, IX, CIRQUITAL, MYSTERIA, AND UMBLE.**

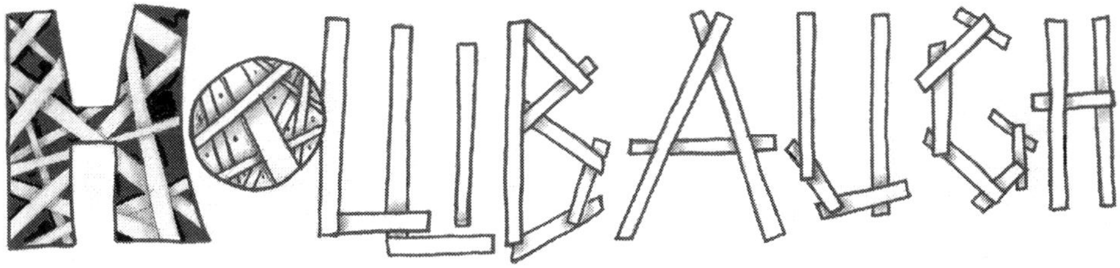

HOLLIBAUGH

When **HOLLIBAUGH** is drawn with straight lines, it can look like a pile of sticks, like in the game pick-up sticks. Where one stick is on top of another, it casts a shadow on the one below it. Shade to suggest this. Since these are cast shadows, they can be hard or soft. I prefer soft shadows.

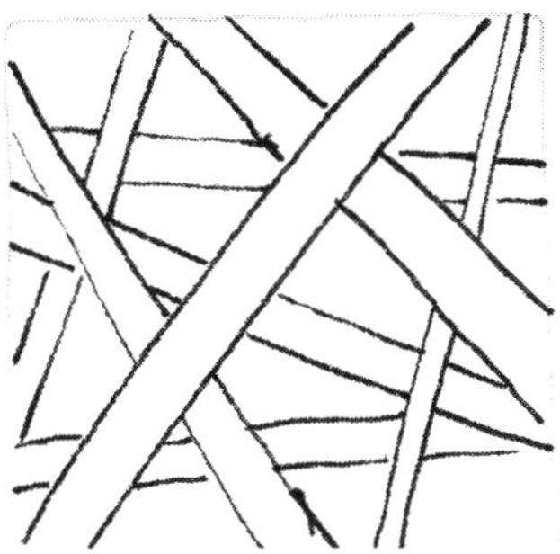

HOLLIBAUGH, *unshaded.*

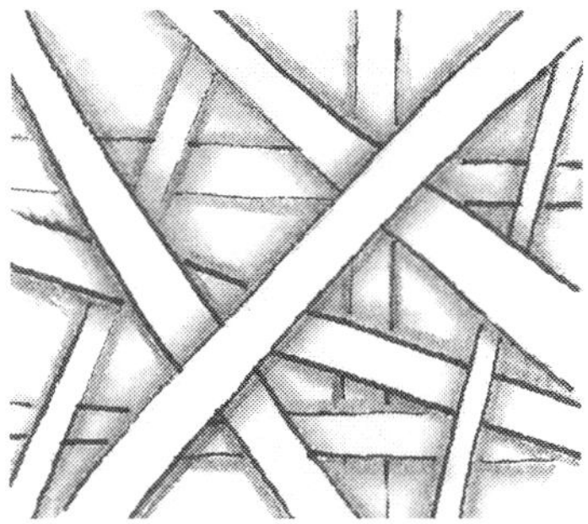

HOLLIBAUGH *is shaded outside each of the "sticks," right over top of the one behind it.*

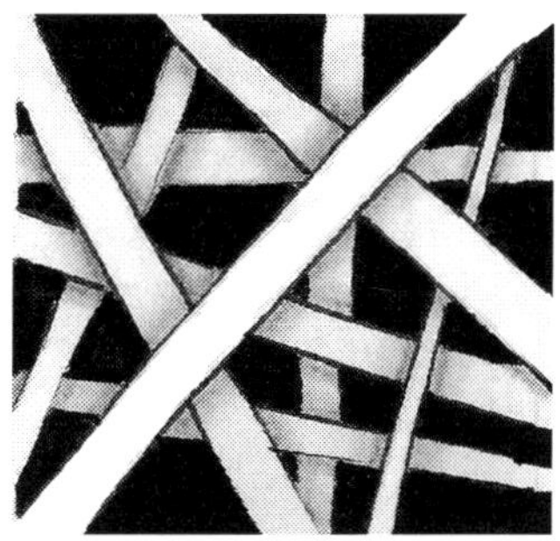

Coloring the background black increases the contrast and makes the whole tangle pop.

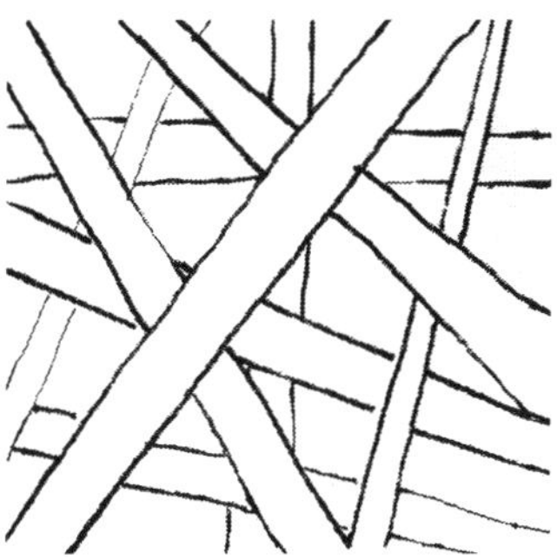

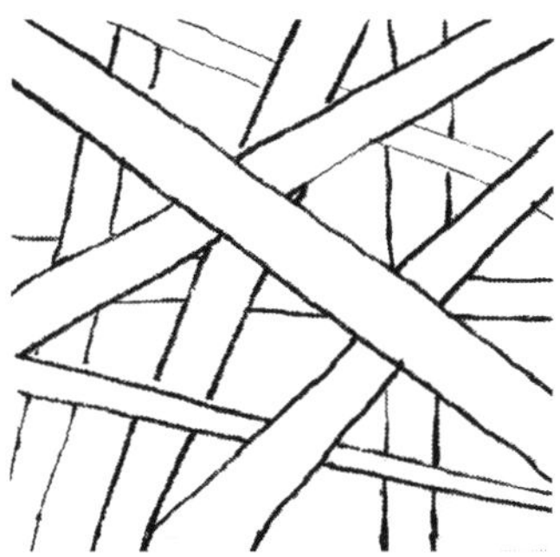

Exercise 26. ***Shade these two HOLLIBAUGH differently; maybe use hard shadows on one and soft on the other..***

TIP: *Sometimes it can be difficult in all of the lines to tell which is the background. Place a dot in the center of each area that appears to be a background. If you end up making a mistake, having a dot in the middle of one of your sticks looks better than accidentally coloring part of it.*

Printemps

PRINTEMPS

If HOLLIBAUGH is a pile of pick-up sticks, PRINTEMPS could be a pile of spinning tops. Again, shade around the edges of all of the tops, onto the ones below. If you want to get artistic, you could shade only on the side opposite the "sparkle," or highlight. I usually shade around the whole thing, but try both techniques below to see which you prefer.

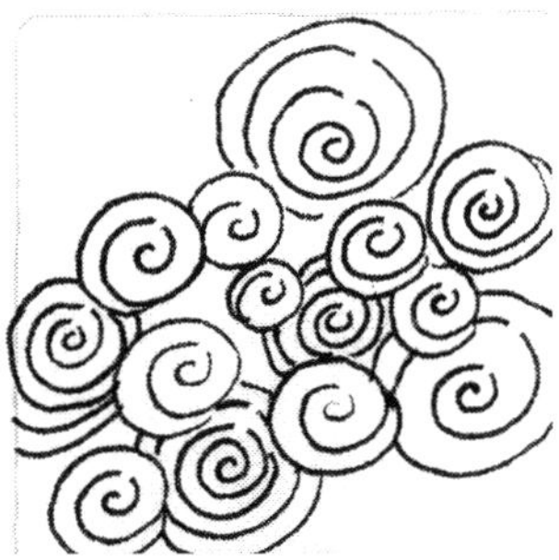

PRINTEMPS, *unshaded.*

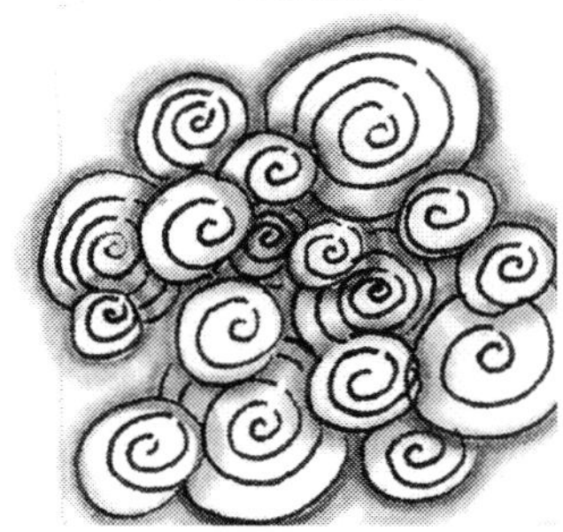

With just shading around the edges, some coils start to float.

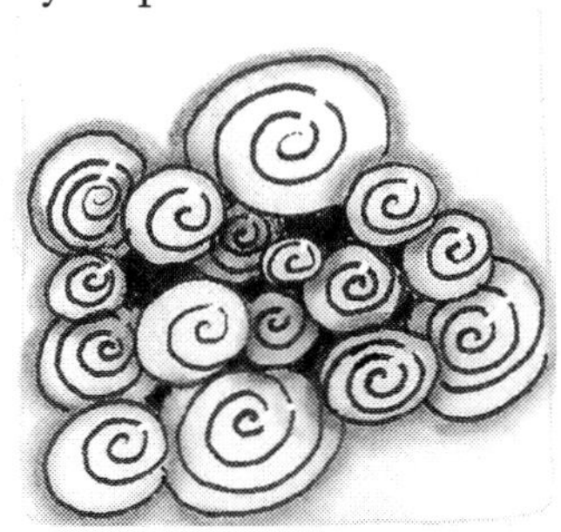

With the background black, can you see 4 distinct levels? On top are unshaded coils. Below those are partially shaded coils. Below those are completely shaded coils, and the bottom layer is black.

NOTE: *When shaded, there will be 4 levels: the top-most level where there is no shadow. The next level down where the coil will be in partial shadow. Below that are the coils in total shadow. The bottom layer is the black background.*

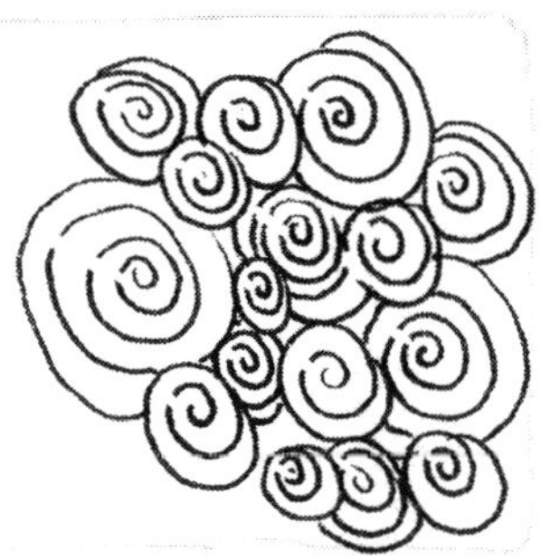

EXERCISE 27. ***Shade this one all around each coil.***

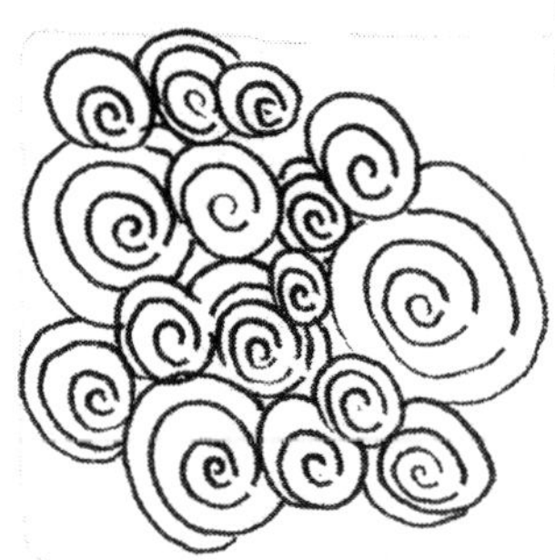

EXERCISE 28. ***Shade this one only on the side opposite the sparkle.***

SHADING WOVEN TANGLES

Shaded similarly to the layered tangles are those that look as if they are woven. Some look like woven fabric, like W^2 and HUGGINS. Others look more like woven rope or braids. These tangles look complex, but all they need for enhancement is some simple shading.

Just shade where one ribbon or thread looks as if it is going underneath another. This is similar to the layered tangles where you used shading to make one element appear to be above another. You can use this same "shade behind" technique on any tangle where you want one element to appear raised. It doesn't have to be a layered or woven tangle.

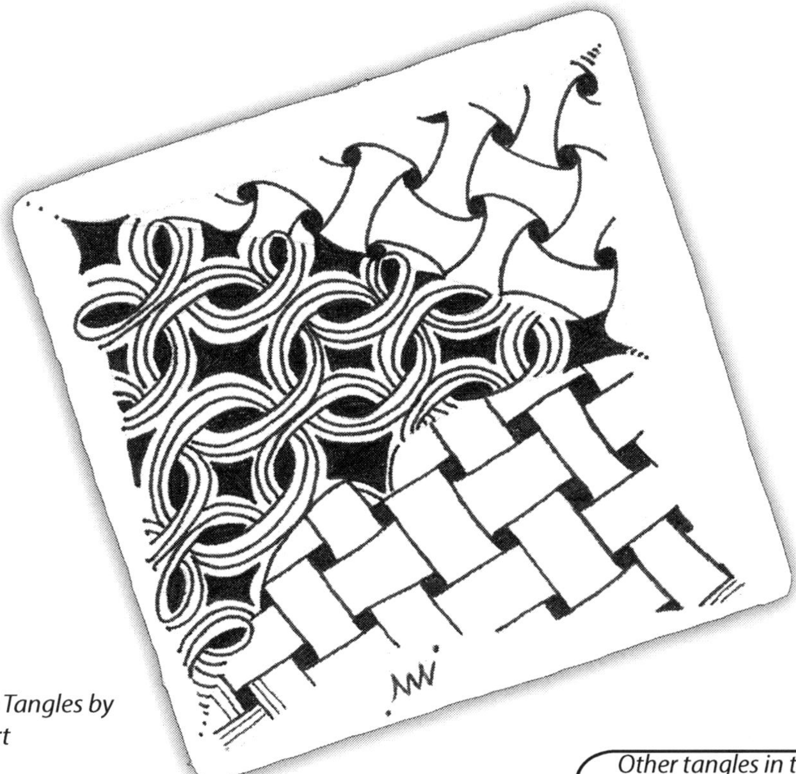

Three Woven Tangles by Mimi Lempart

EXERCISE 29. ***Practice shading these woven tangles after you've practiced on*** **HUGGINS.**

Other tangles in this group include **W^2, MI^2,** *and* **HIBRED.**

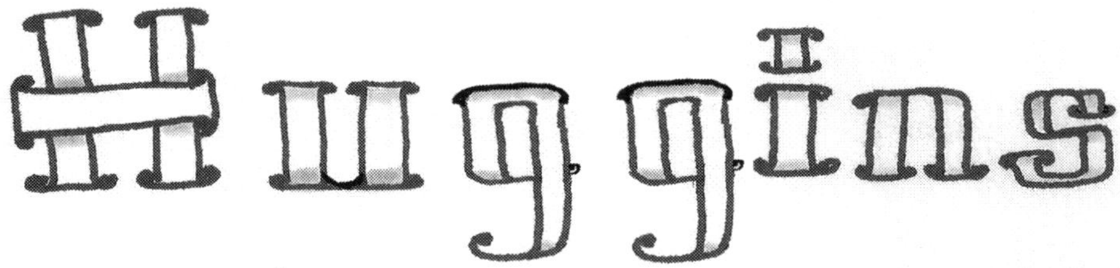

HUGGINS

HUGGINS is easy to shade because all you do is to connect the circle you drew to start your tangle, following inside the curve with your pencil. Use your blender to soften the line a bit if you wish and you're done. I love it when you can get such a big difference for so little effort.

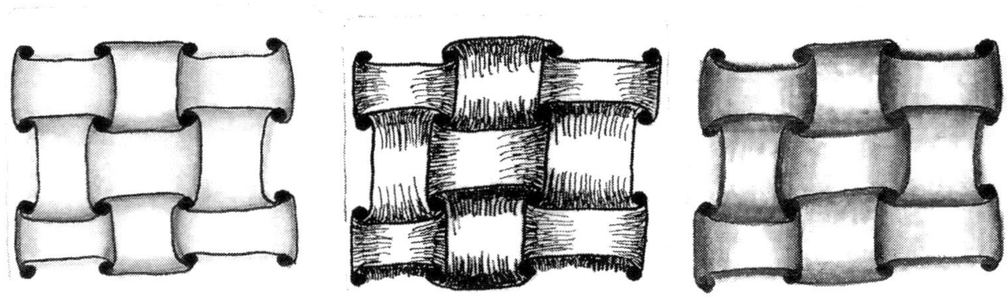

Top: Subtle shading, pen shading using hatching, heavy shading. I feel the highlights make it look shiny.
Bottom: Unshaded.

EXERCISE 30. ***Add some interesting shading to see the weaving come to life.***

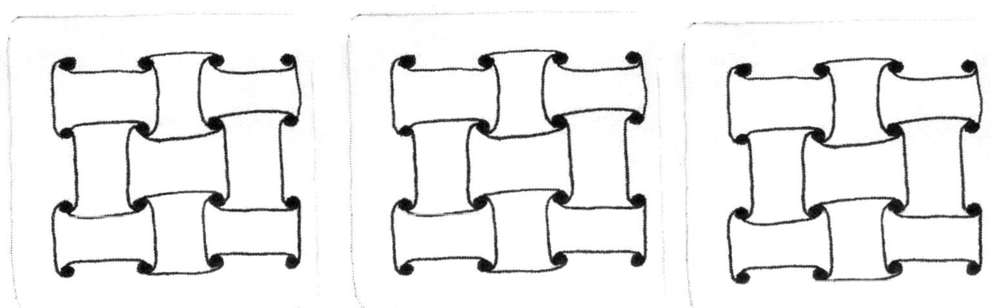

punzel & chainging

CHAINGING AND PUNZEL

These two tangles are woven like braids. **PUNZEL** is thin and **CHAINGING** is thick. Try adding something other than solid black in between the strands for a different look.

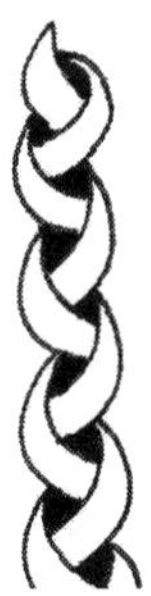

I *start by darkening the space between the ribbons. Use a pen or a 4B or softer pencil.*

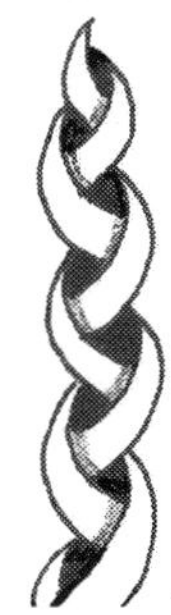

All you need is a line following the curve from one dark area to the next.

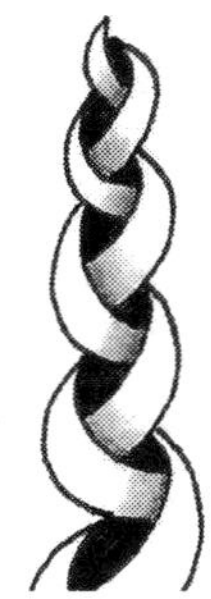

I feel it looks better if you smudge your shadow line.

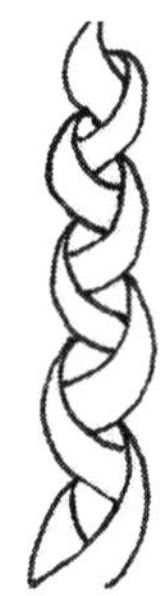

PUNZEL *for you to shade.*

EXERCISE 31. ***See how much shading can neaten up these braids? See what you can do on to tidy up the unshaded ones.***

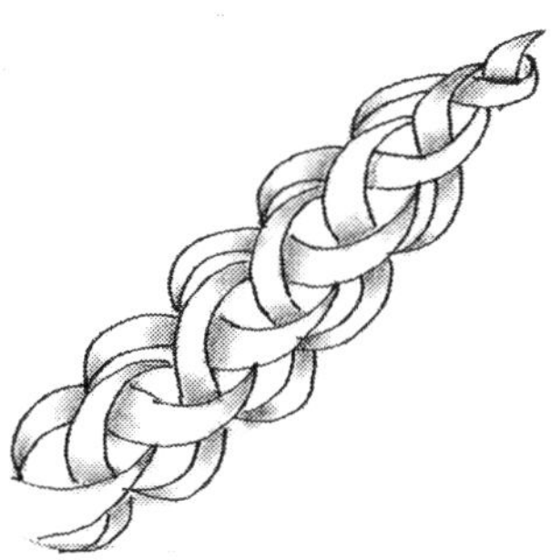

Just shadows.

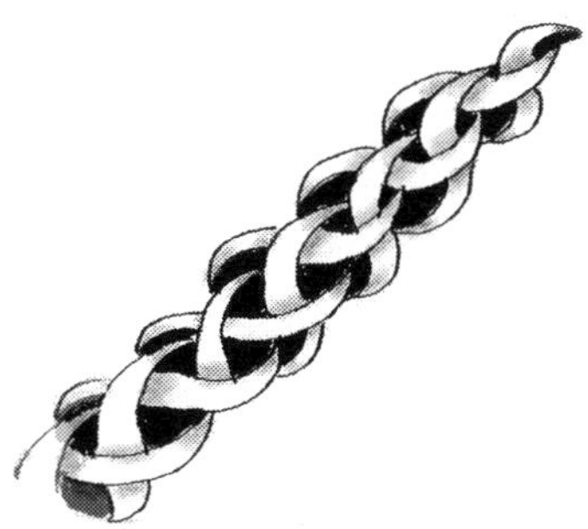

Shadows with a black background.

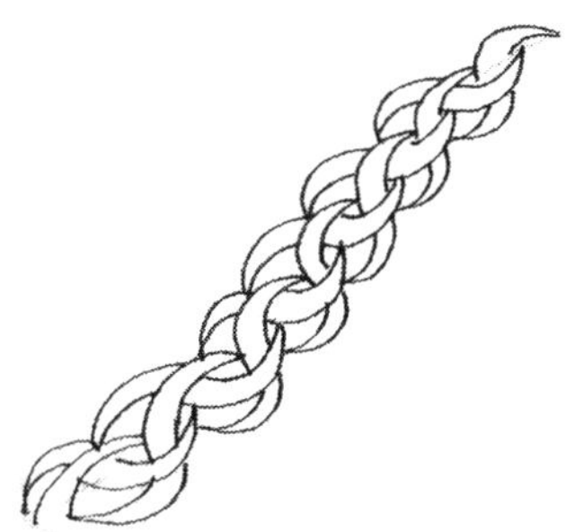

CHAINGING *for you to shade.*

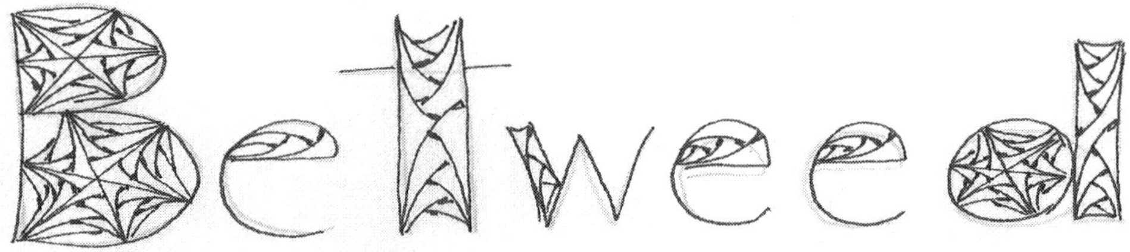

BETWEED is a tangle with simple drawing instructions and a complex-looking result. It is also like a chameleon. When drawn in a tube, it looks like a Chinese finger puzzle. When drawn inside a circle, it is something else entirely. Shade the overlapping pieces in the center to emphasize the woven effect or shade the edges where the lines converge, making it seem fuller.

Which do you prefer? Why not try them both?

NOTE: *This is actually 1/4 of a* **BETWEED***.*

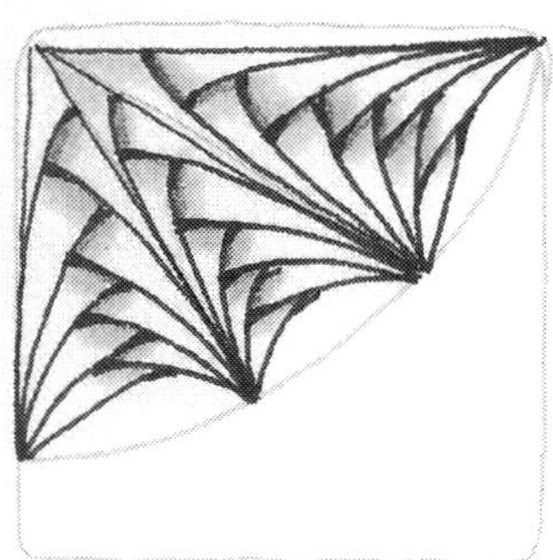

Shading the overlap.

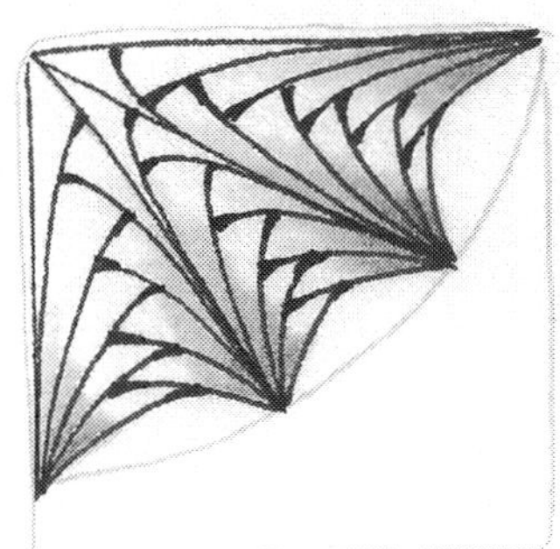

Shading the edges.

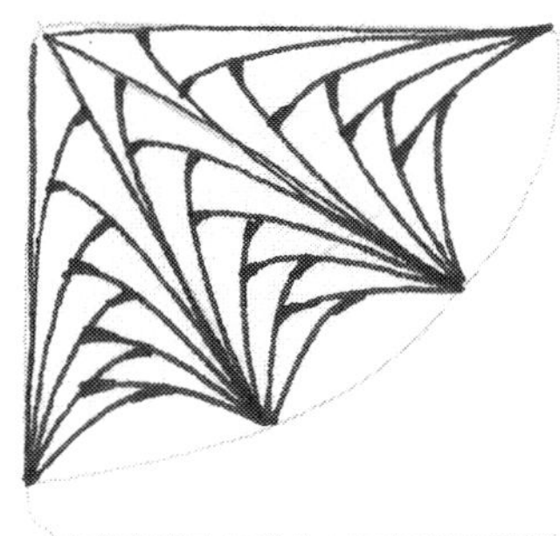

EXERCISE 32. ***Shade these two.***

TIP: *Try drawing* **BETWEED***, varying the pressure of your strokes to suggest subtle shading.*

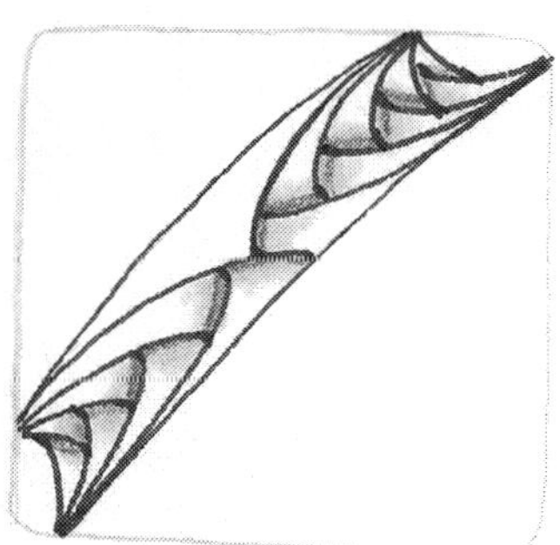

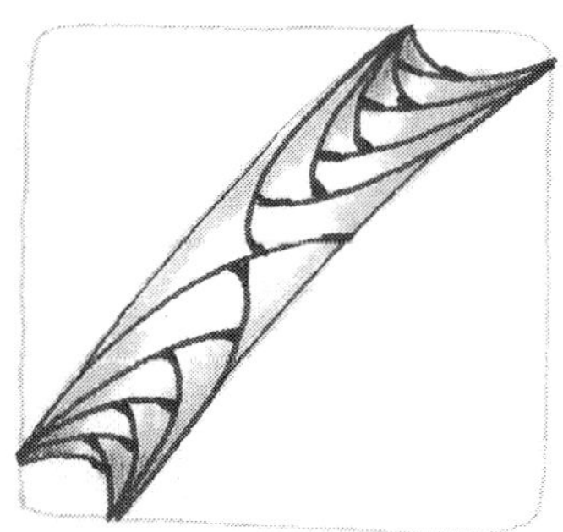

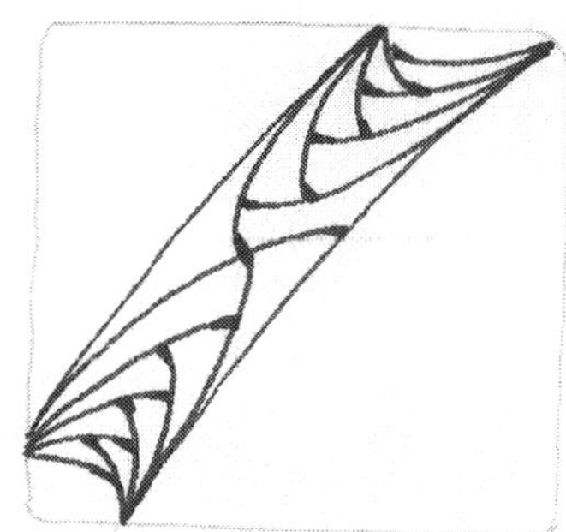

SHADING TO ADD DIMENSION

In shading the layered and woven tangles, your pencil work enhances the existing overlapping lines that already suggest depth. In many other tangles depth is not defined by the way they are drawn. In these tangles, you are free to create your own reality. When the tangle itself doesn't give an illusion of depth, you can use shading to decide for yourself which parts you want to be on top CUBINE, ENNIES, and NIPA are three tangles that fit this category well.

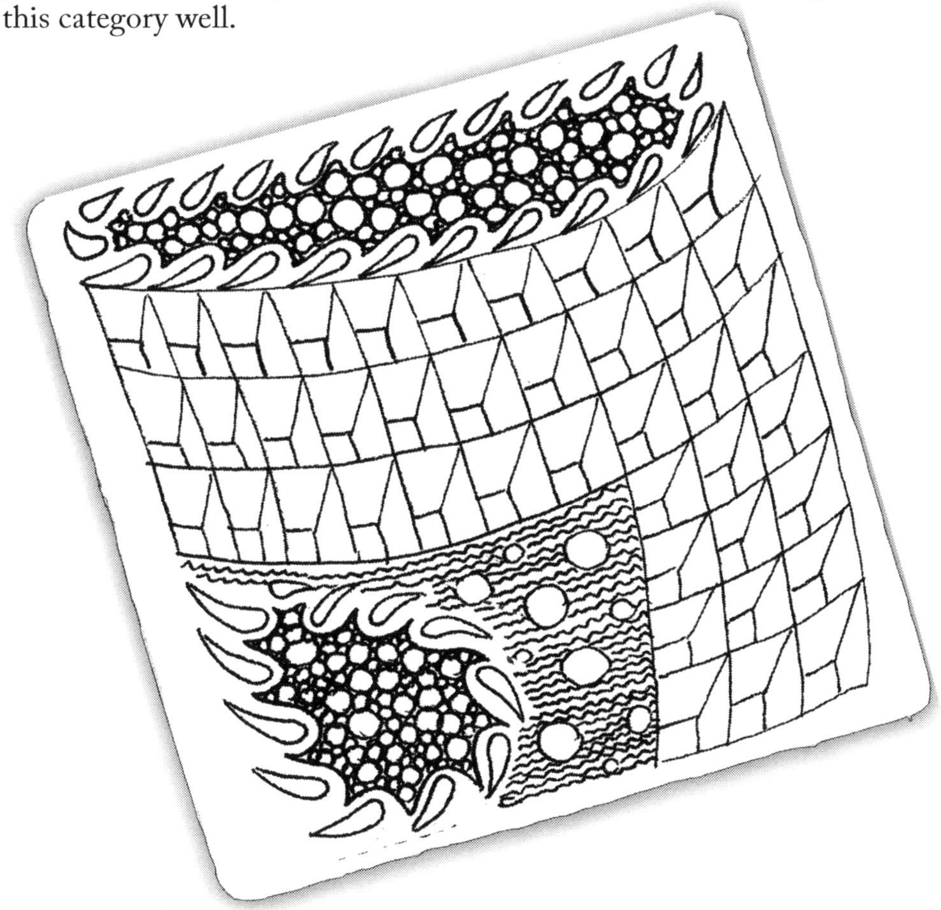

EXERCISE 33. ***Shade this tile after you practice shading to add dimension.***

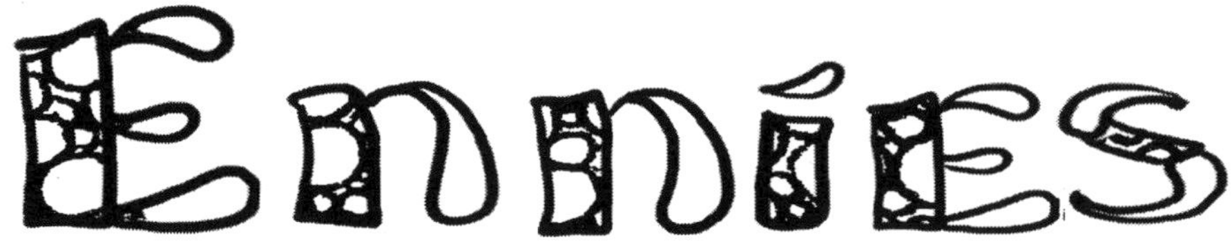

ENNIES

ENNIES is a perfect example of a tangle that just lies there like a rug. But, a little shading makes this a visually exciting tangle.

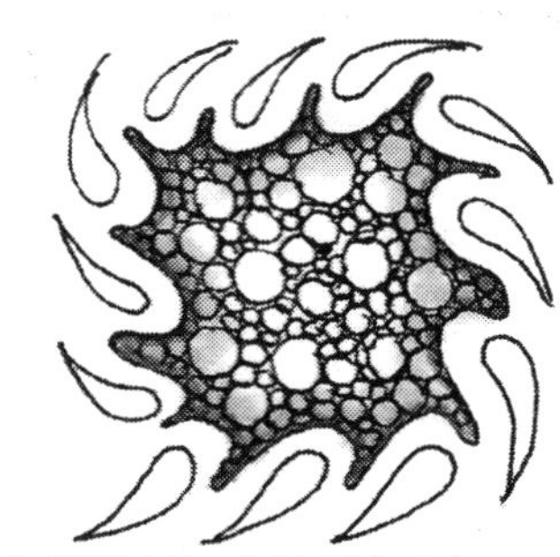

Shading around the outside of the circles makes the whole center recede, leaving a frame of teardrops. Shade darkest at the edges and blend inward. I used a 4B pencil to make this area look really deep. Lighter shading would produce a shallower look.

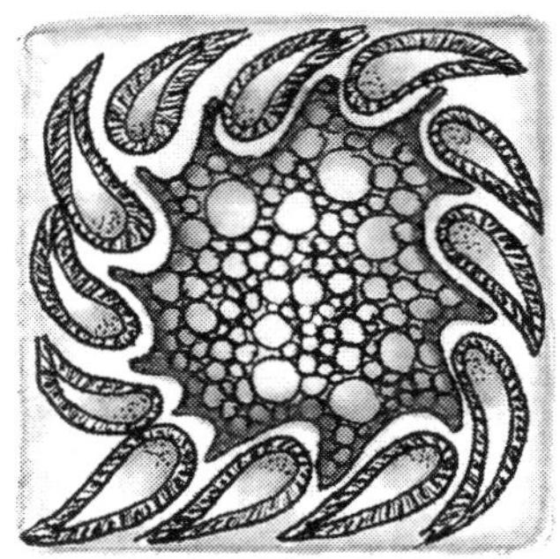

Here is something different. I added pen shading around the edges of the teardrops, shaded inside them to suggest shape, and then shaded around the edge of the square.

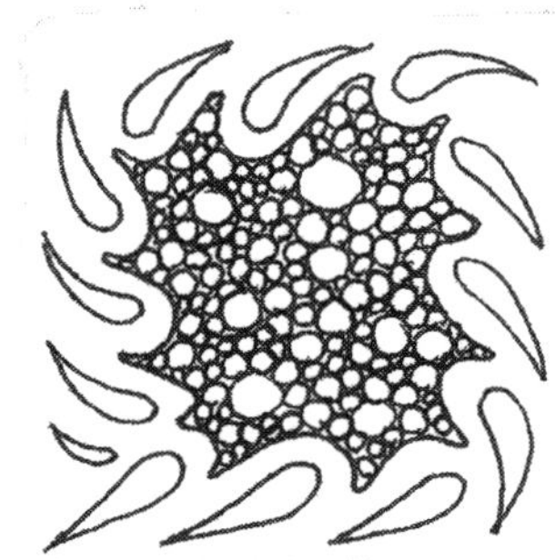

EXERCISE 34. ***See what happens if you add your gradation shade around the outside of the circles instead of the inside. Does it look as if they are bubbling up from underneath ready to ooze all over the teardrops?***

EXERCISE 35. ***Shade one of these with a gradation at the edge of the circles and do something creative on the other.***

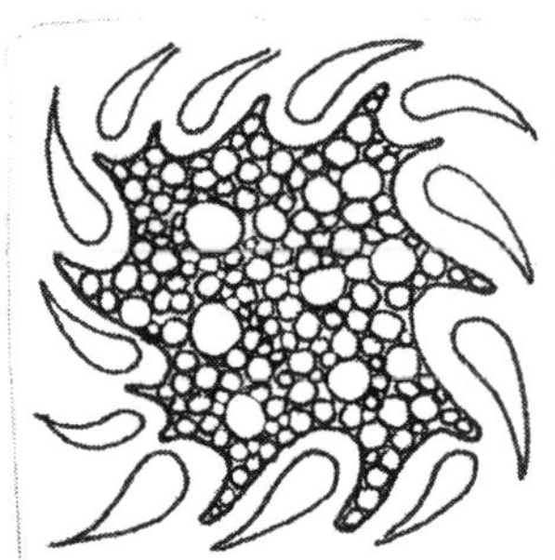

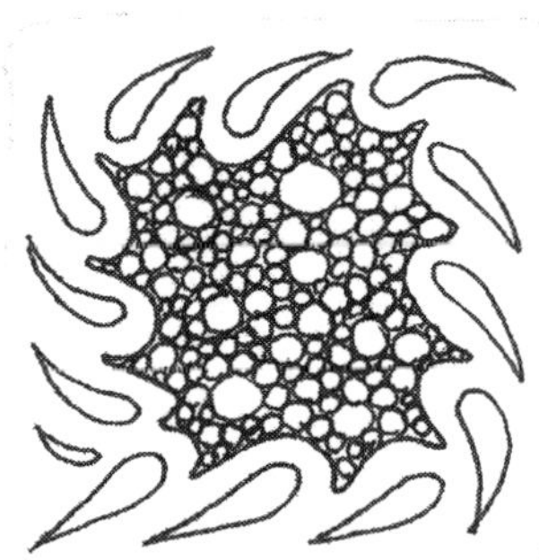

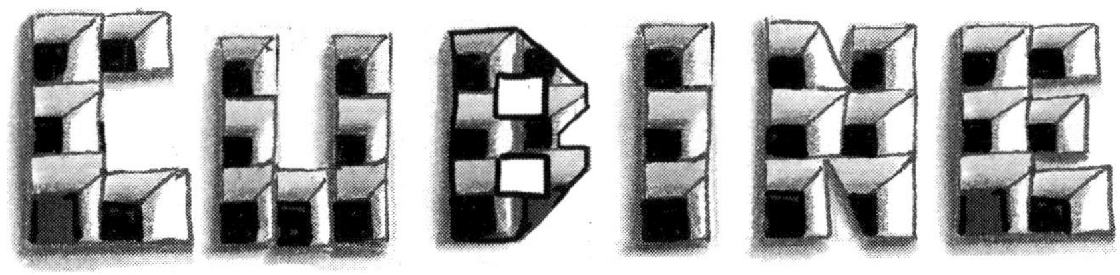

CUBINE

The optical illusion produced by shading **CUBINE** is so strong that shading it is almost as if you are performing magic.

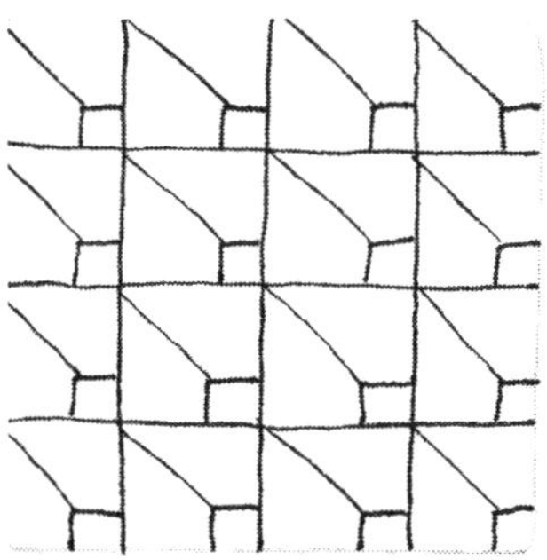

Unshaded, it is a little bland.

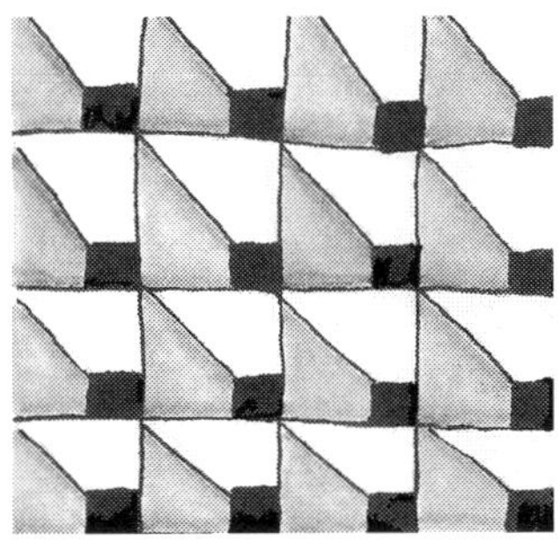

Usual shading - just color one triangle gray and the square black.

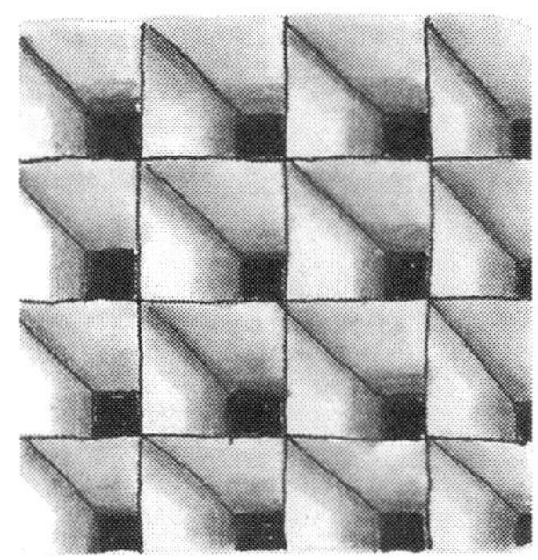

Shading kicked up a notch by using gradations.

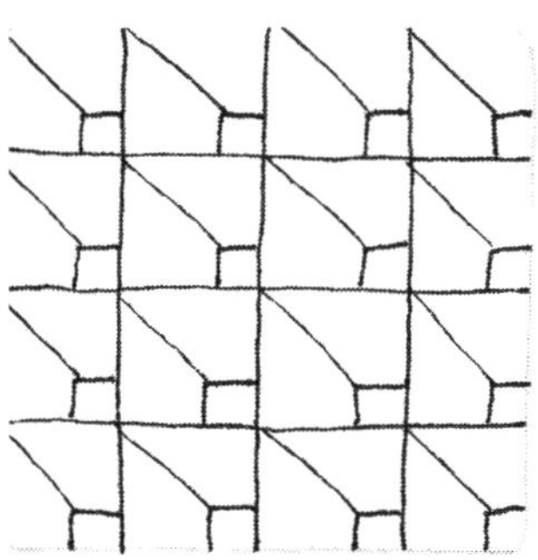

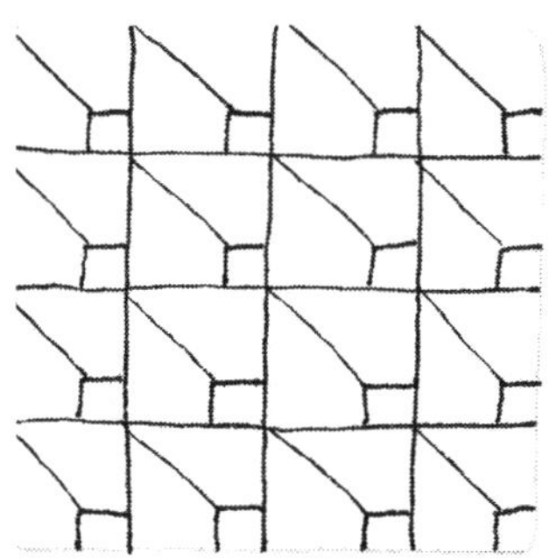

EXERCISE 36. ***Shade these two to see what kind of magic you can create with shading.***

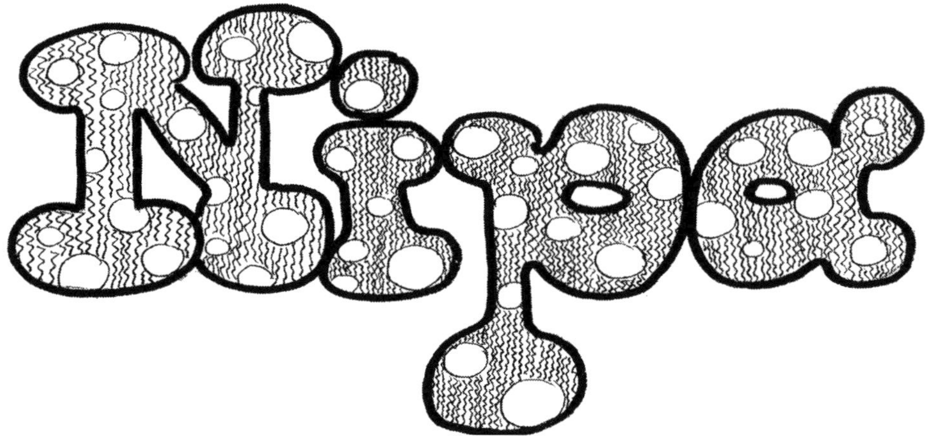

NIPA

NIPA technically could be considered a layered tangle since the lines are drawn behind the circles, but because there are so many lines so close together it is hard to see the connection between lines on either side of the circles. It doesn't appear to be layered until you add shading.

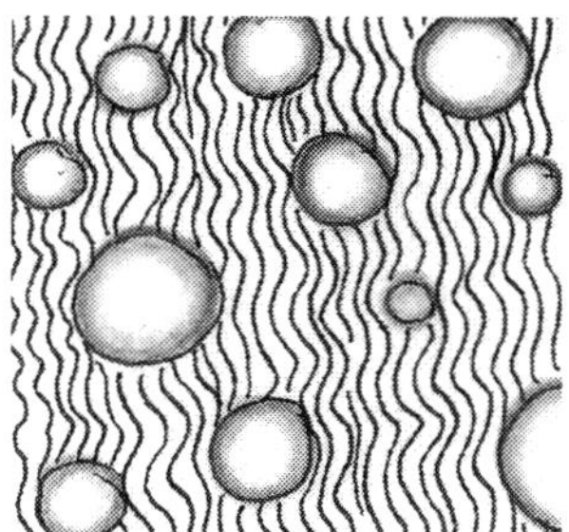

Shade inside the circles to turn them into holes.

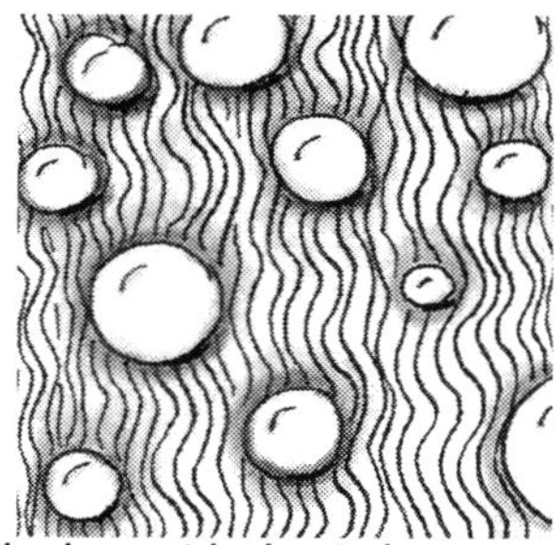

Shade outside the circles to turn them into pearls sitting on top of the lines. Add a small curved line to add interest to your forms

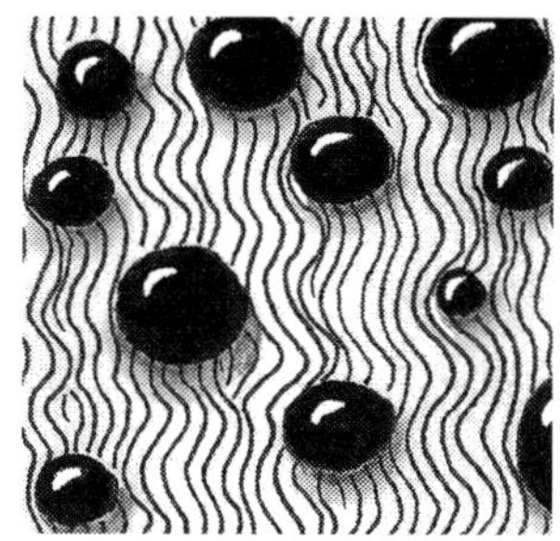

Or, use your pen to make some shiny black beads. I left a highlight on one side and placed the shadow on the other to give the illusion of light coming from the top left.

EXERCISE 37. ***Shade one version to make the circles look like holes and the other to look like spheres.***

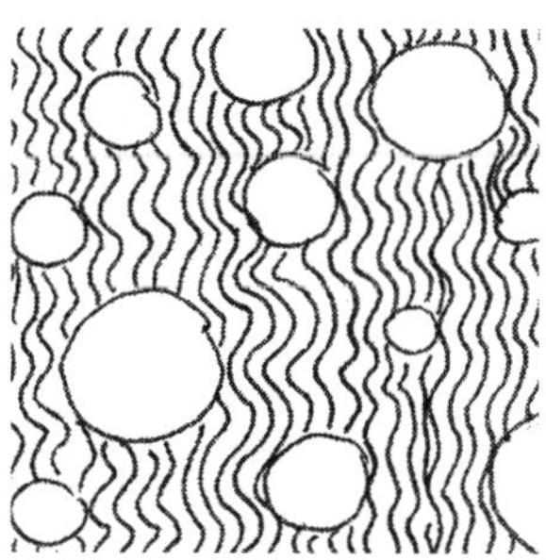

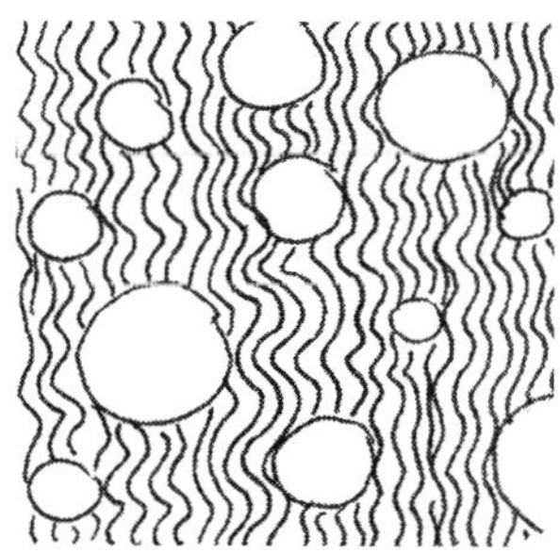

SHADING TO ADD PERSONALITY

Many tangles are flexible and often don't have a usual way to shade them. These tangles are fun to shade because they give you the most chance to show off your own style. You can change their whole look with creative shading. I will give you several ideas for shading these tangles. Use them as a starting point and explore your own ideas on these pages. Have fun and see how many different ways you can think of to shade these beautiful tangles.

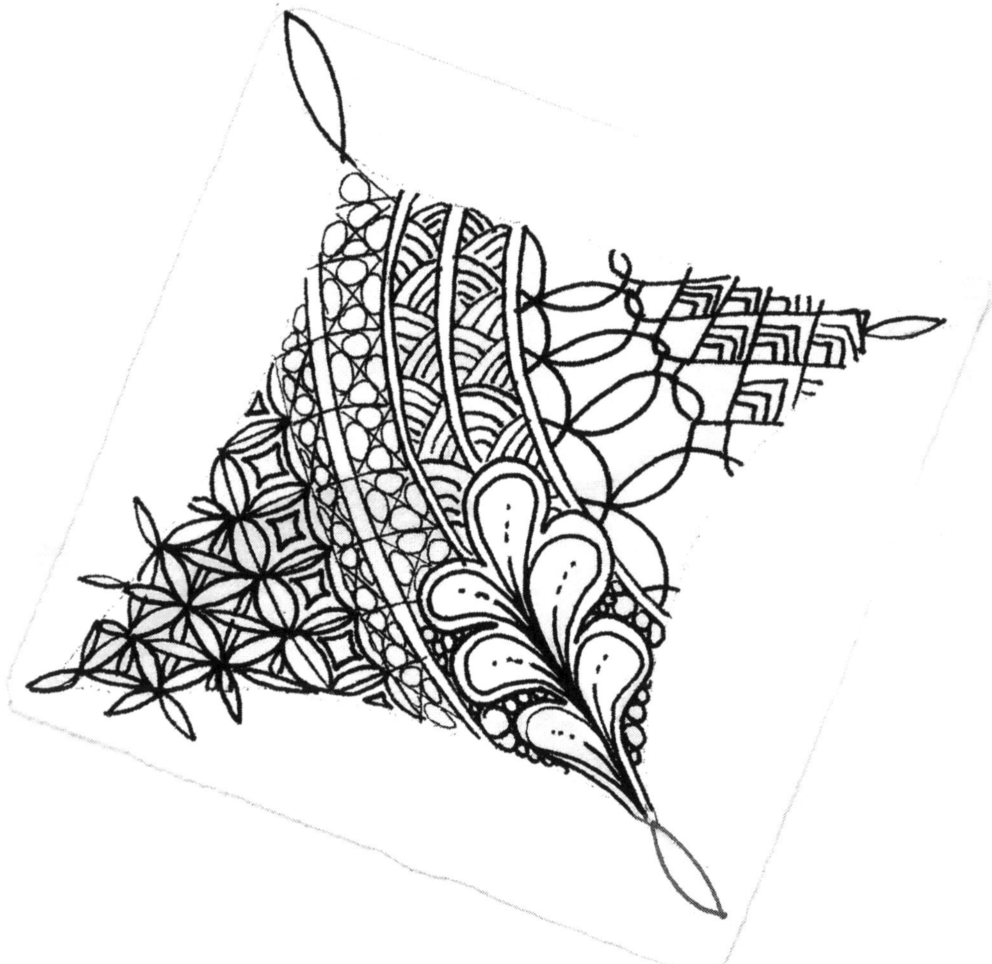

EXERCISE 38. ***After you practice shading*** FIFE, BALES, 'NZEPPEL, SHATTUCK, FLUX, OOF, ***and*** FLUKES, ***then shade this piece to give it some personality.***

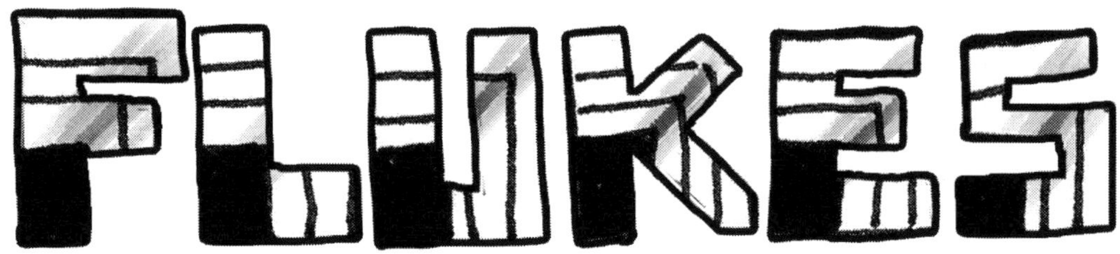

FLUKES

FLUKES is a bold geometric pattern that gets even bolder with some shading.

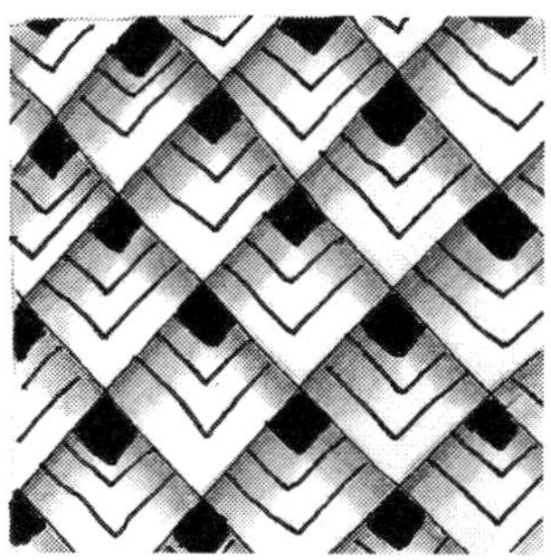

Shaded on two sides it looks like fish scales.

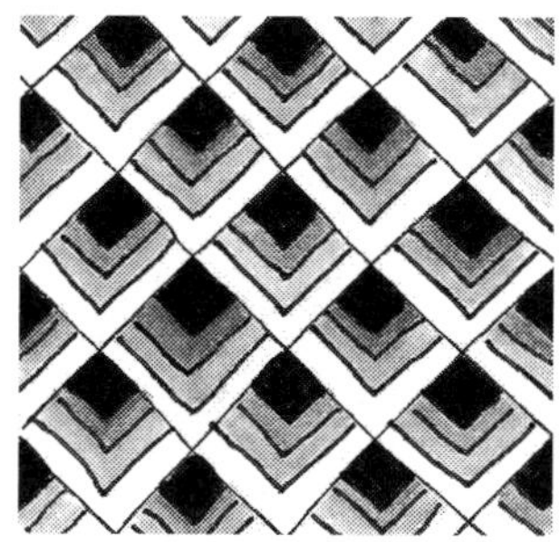

Shaded with a gradation down from the dark box adds an entirely new dimension.

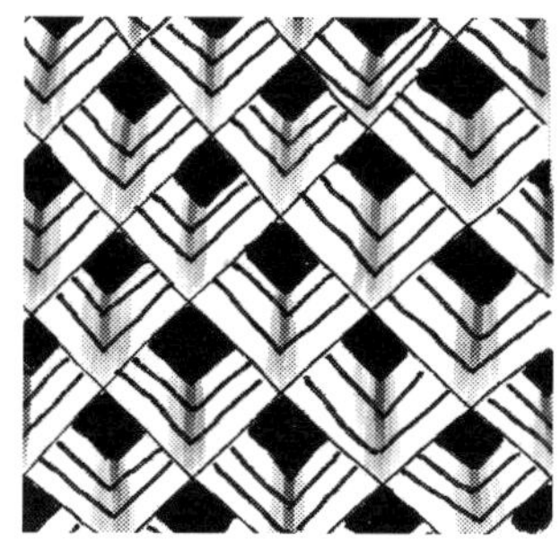

Shading straight down from the box creates yet another look.

EXERCISE 39. ***Shade the three unshaded FLUKES. Copy my ideas or try some of your own.***

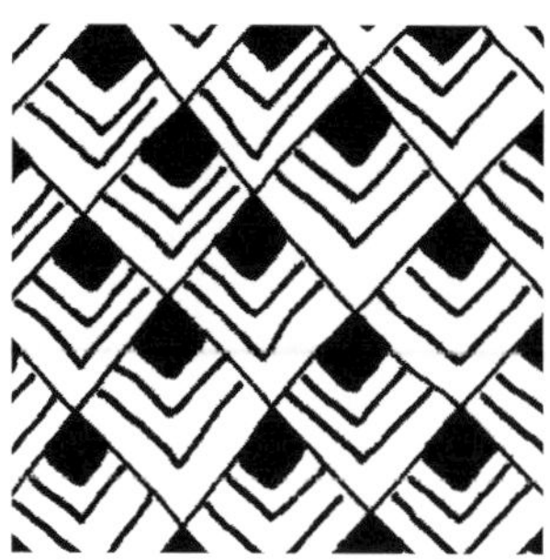

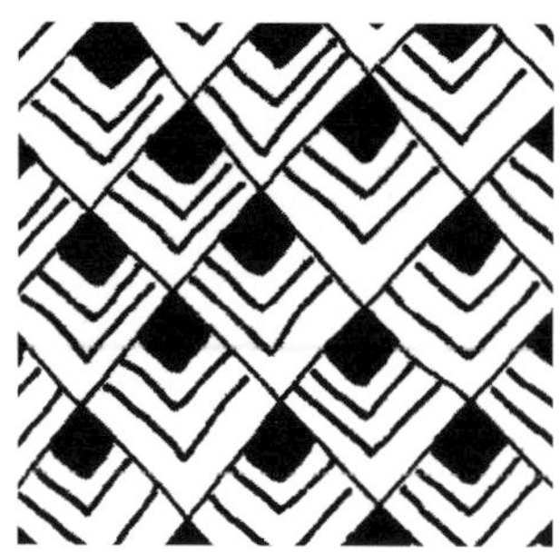

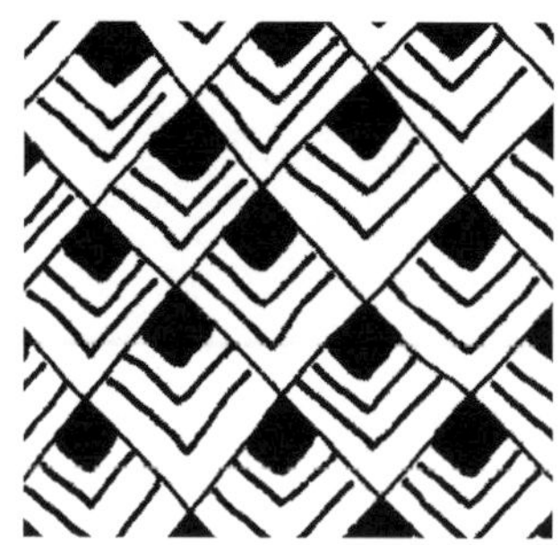

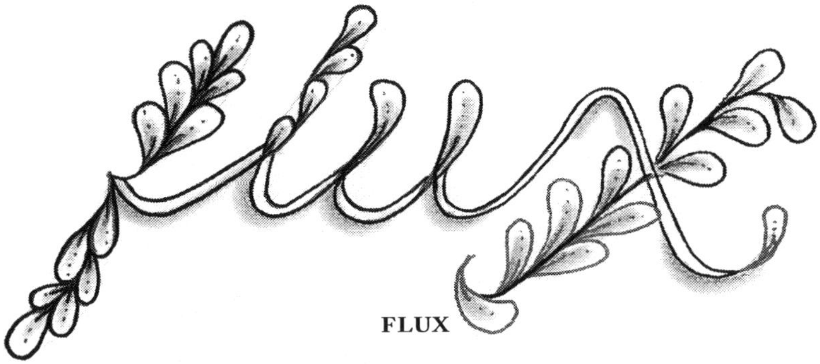

FLUX

flux is one of my all time favorite patterns to draw. Most of the time when I shade **flux**, the circles end up deep in shadow so you can barely see them, but sometimes it is fun to let them shine.

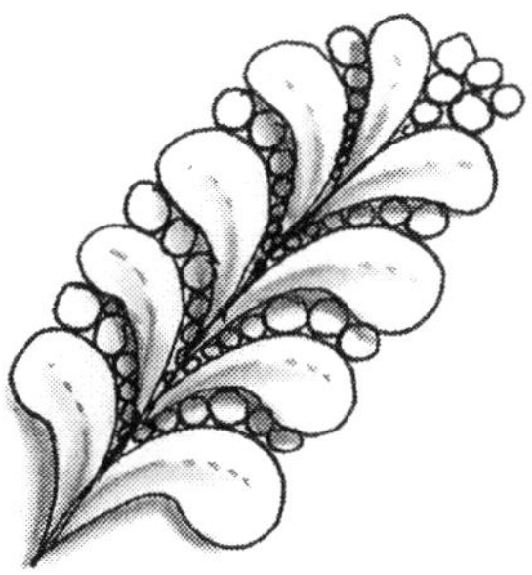

I usually shade behind lightly in the center of each petal and darker in the back of them.

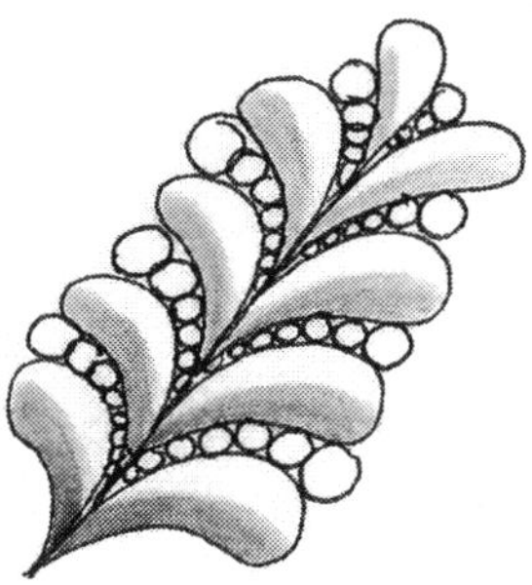

Just shading the bottom of each petal.

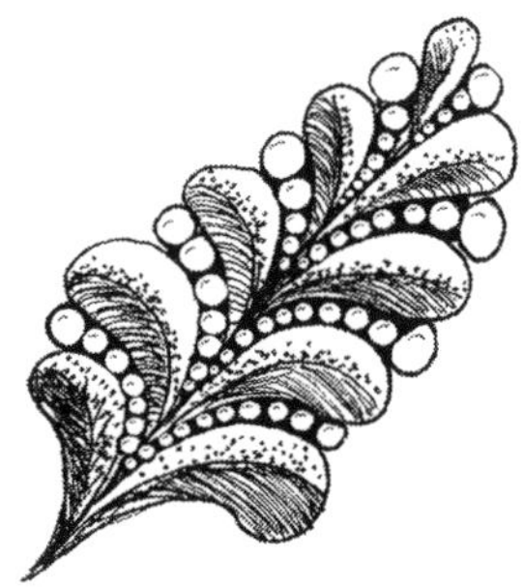

Hatching and stippling adds an entirely different look..

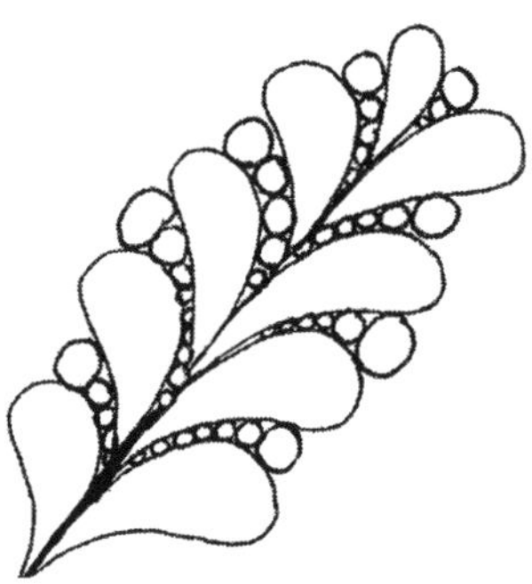

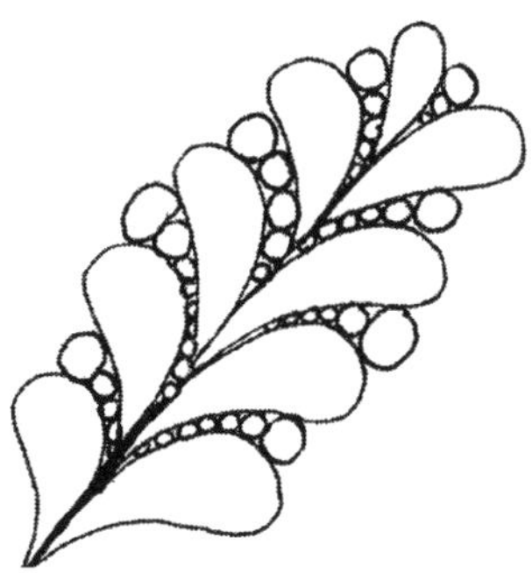

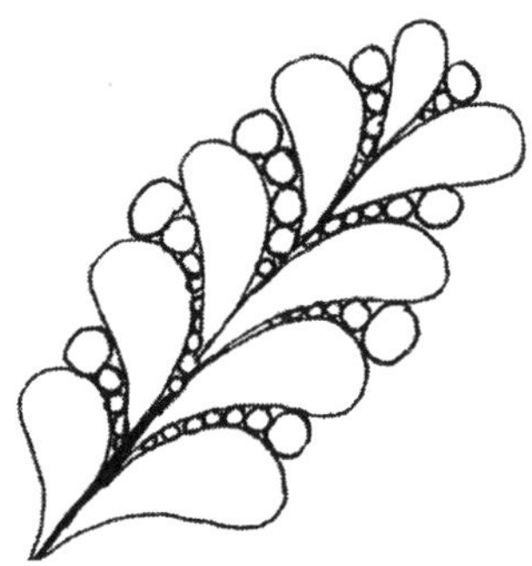

Exercise 40. ***Shade to give a different feel to each of these.***

Shattuck

SHATTUCK is a fun tangle to shade because there is so much room for creativity. I like it with both straight and curvy lines.

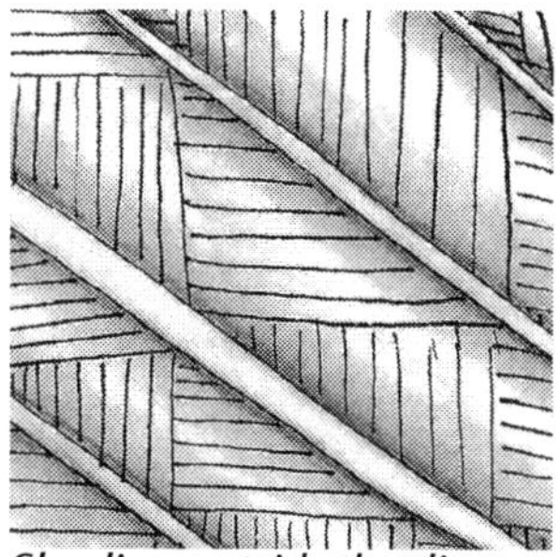

Shading outside the diagonals to make them pop up.

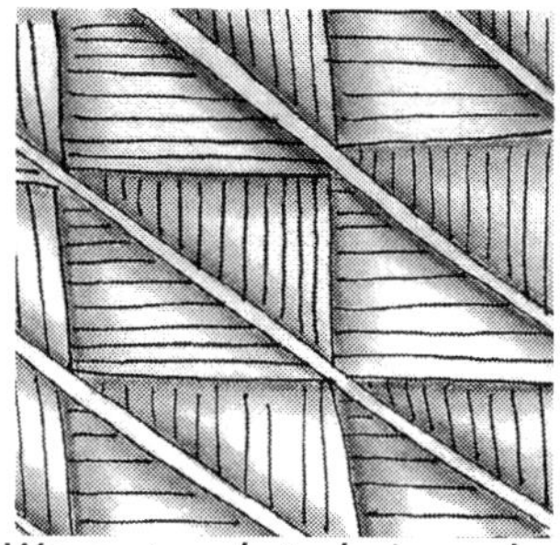

Woven tangle technique along with shading the diagonals.

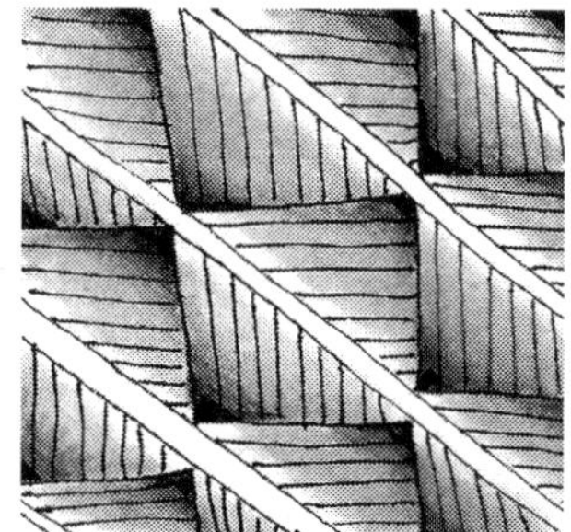

A heavy gradation on opposite corners.

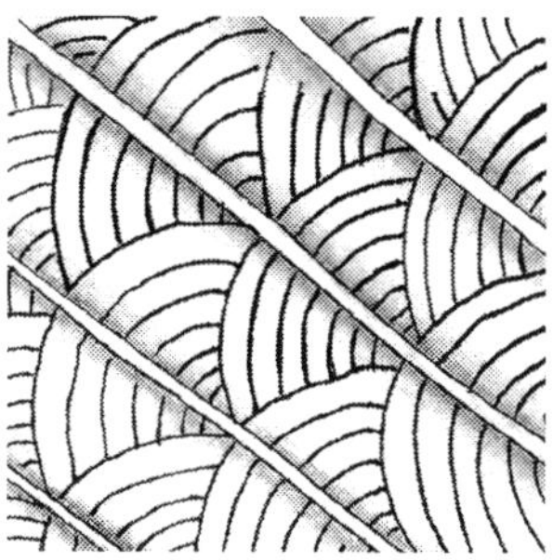

Shading the diagonals as above, but not blending as far.

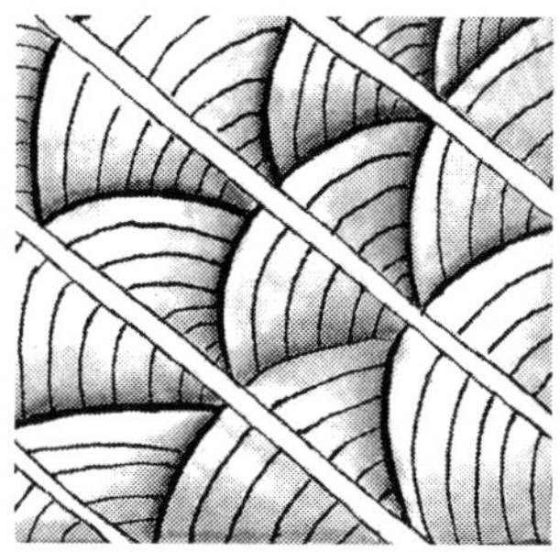

A dark gradation behind the arcs emphasizes the curves.

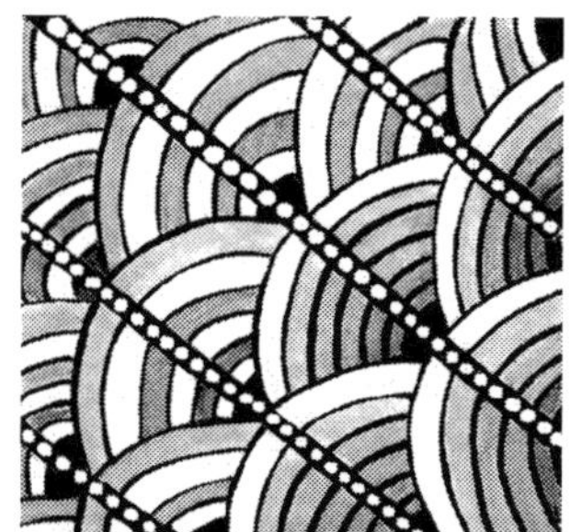

Wild shading! Notice the change from top to bottom.

EXERCISE 40. ***Copy your favorite of each and then make up one of your own on the blank tangles below.***

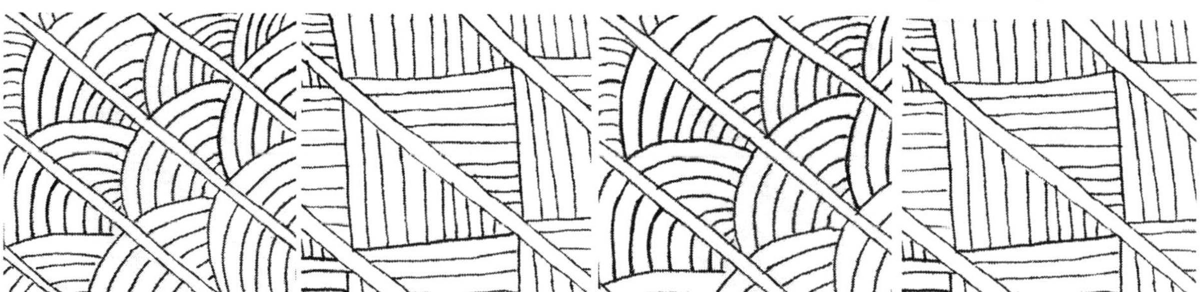

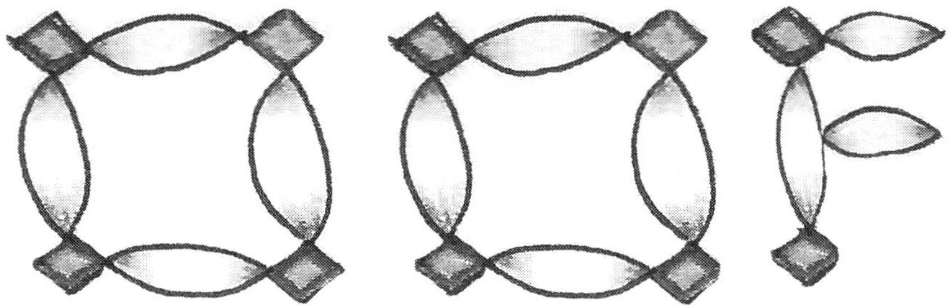

OOF

OOF is a pretty tangle with so many possibilities. You can shade just the "rice" shapes and diamond, the space in between, or all three with different values. Or you can really jazz it up by doing some more tangling in that wide open space. What can you think of to do?

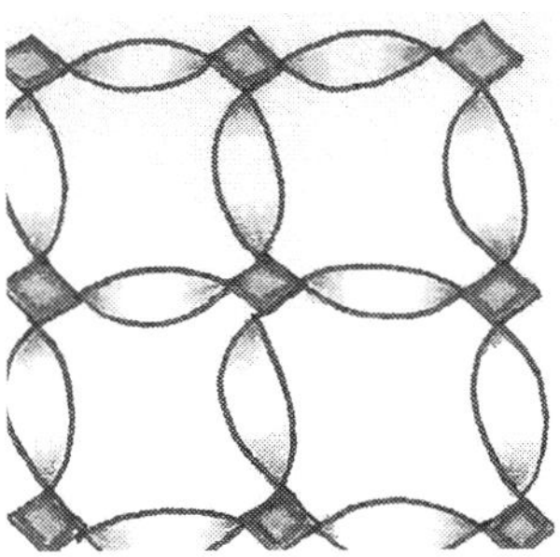

Simple shading in the diamonds and at the edges of the rice gives a lacy look

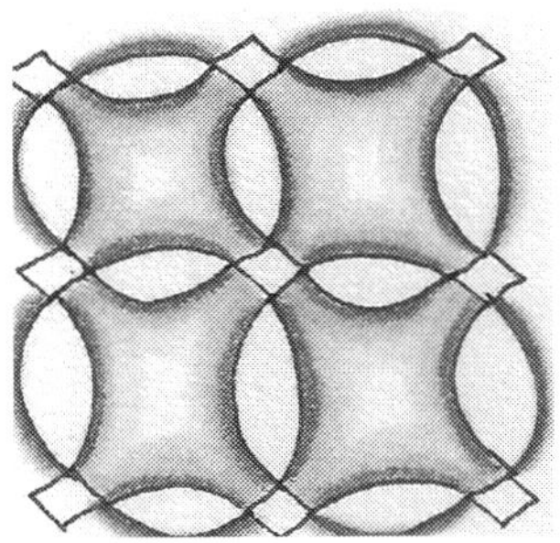

A light gradation in the open space shows off the rings.

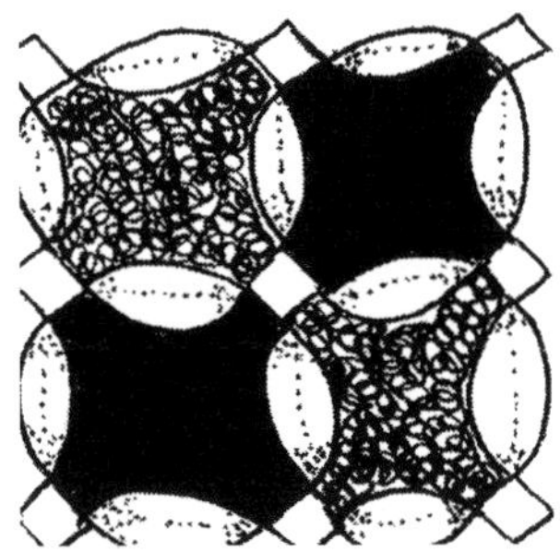

Shading alternate spaces differently makes a quilt-like effect while the dark scumbling hides a mistake.

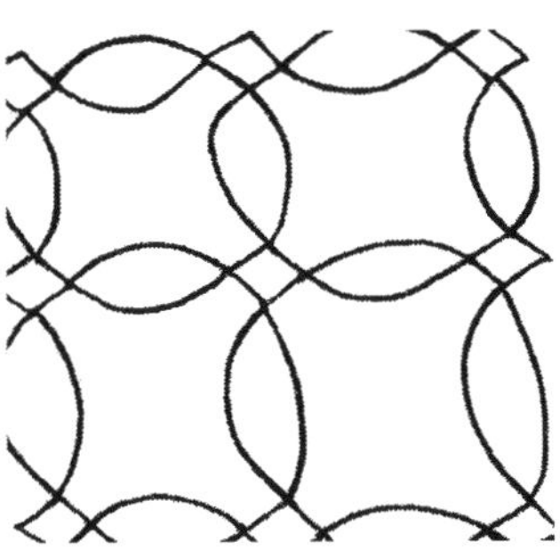

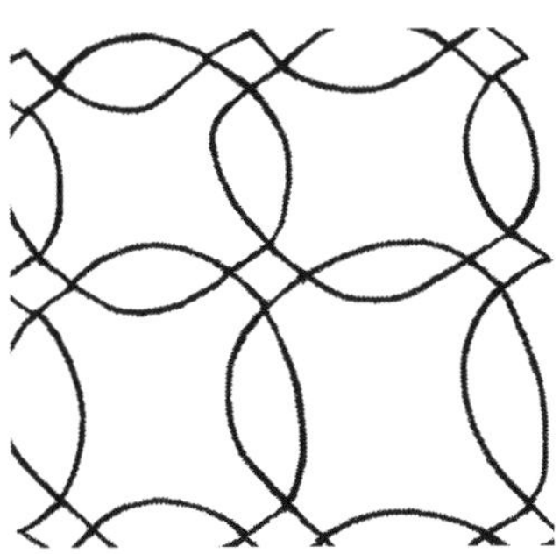

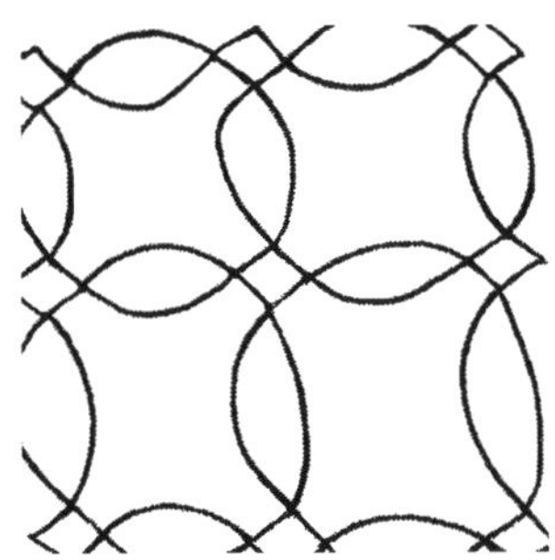

EXERCISE 42. ***Shade each of these differently to see what kinds of effects you can create.***

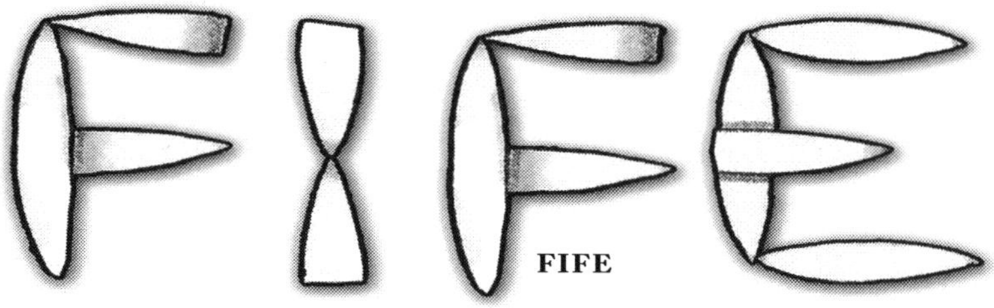

FIFE

FIFE is layered category, but there are so many beautiful variations, I felt it fit here better.

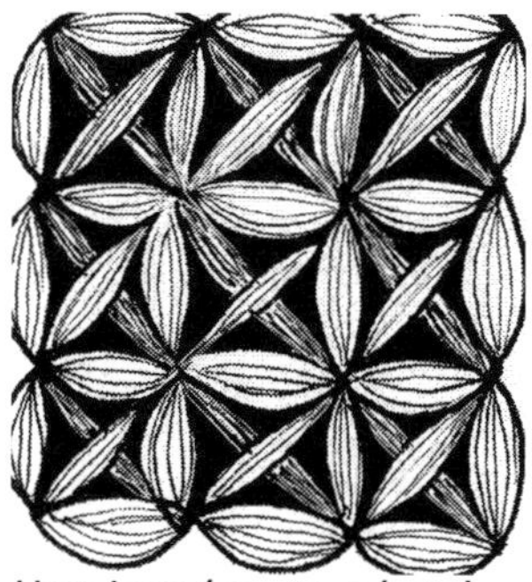

Here I used contour hatching with a tiny .2 mm pen to shade. Varying the distance between the lines causes some petals to recede and some to come forward. Coloring the whole background adds strong contrast.

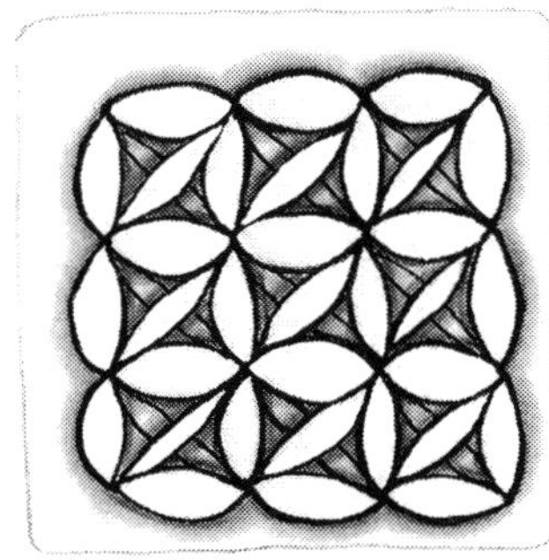

Shading around all of the petals. When you blend, be careful not to smudge too far as that highlight in the shadow area appears to glow.

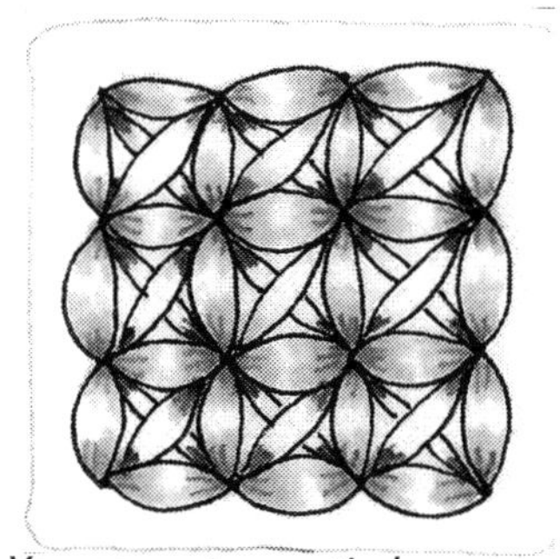

You can get an entirely different look by shading the intersections of the petals. I drew a light circle around the intersection and blended outward. Then I drew a few lines to indicate form.

EXERCISE 43. ***Shade each of these FIFE differently, emphasizing a different part in each for a different look.***

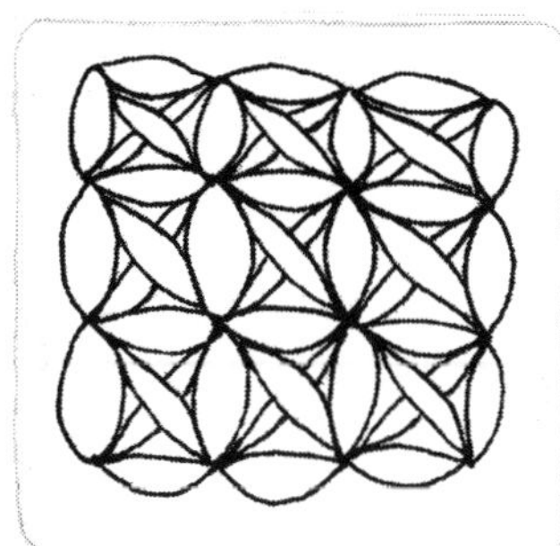

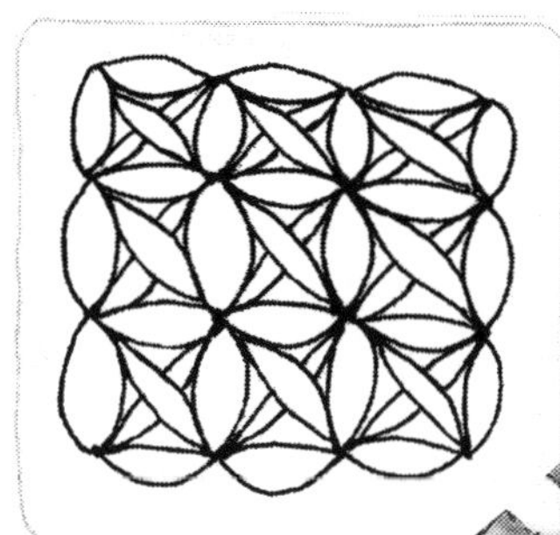

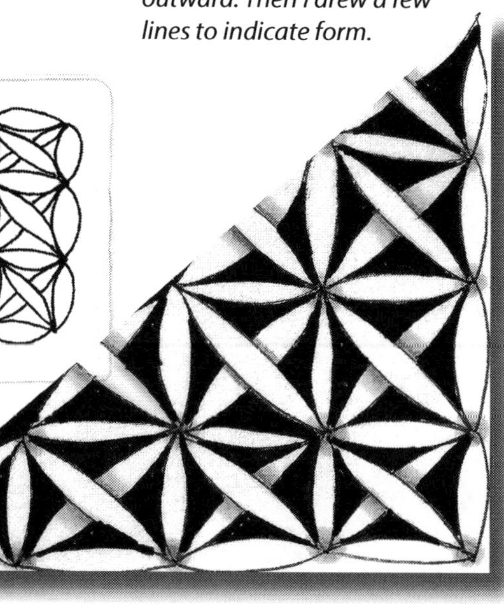

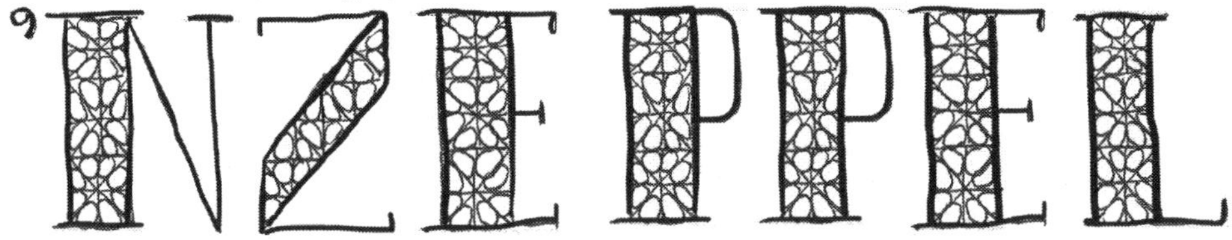

'NZEPPEL

I learned to draw 'NZEPPEL at my CZT training, and I've loved it ever since. It's a grid; it's a flower; it's a geometric shape. Enjoy the chameleon that is 'NZEPPEL.

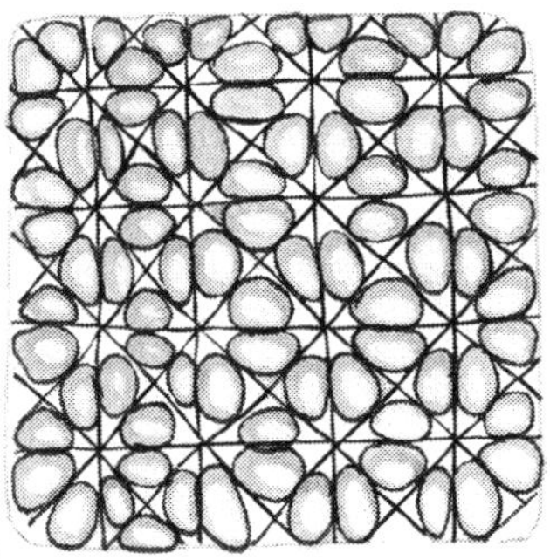

Shaded with a 2H pencil just inside the "squashed balloons."

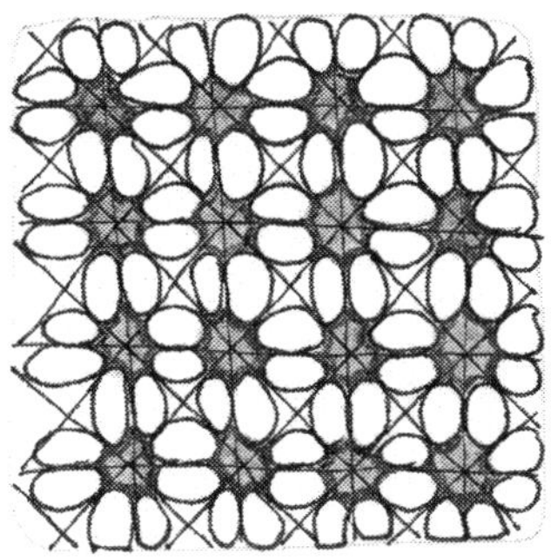

Shaded with a dark gradation only in the "spider web" section.

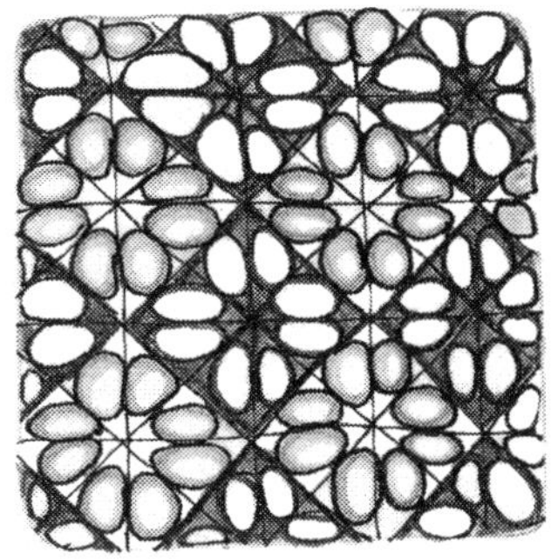

Alternating shading. Inside on one square and outside on the other.

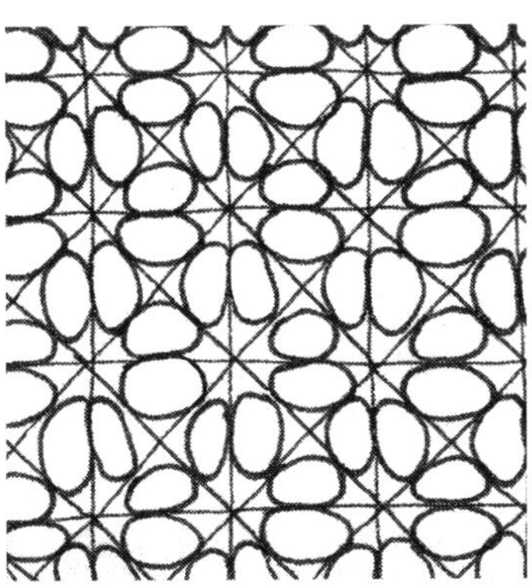

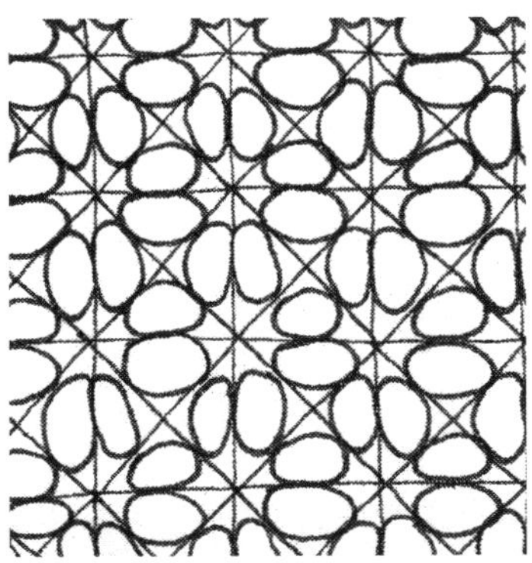

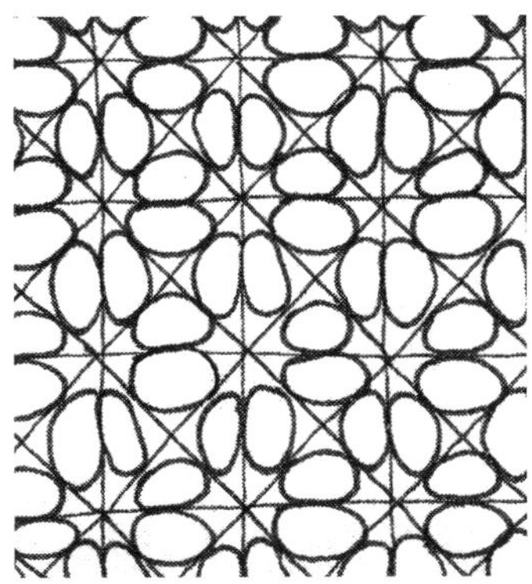

EXERCISE 44. ***Shade each a different way. Use my ideas or make up one of your own.***

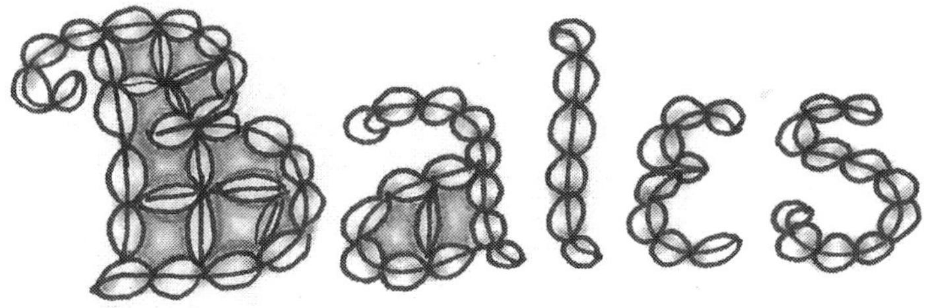

BALES

BALES and **OOF** look like close cousins and can be shaded similarly. My daughter Alexa and I both love shading **BALES**, so I've given you lots of examples and lots of room to play with this one. Enjoy.

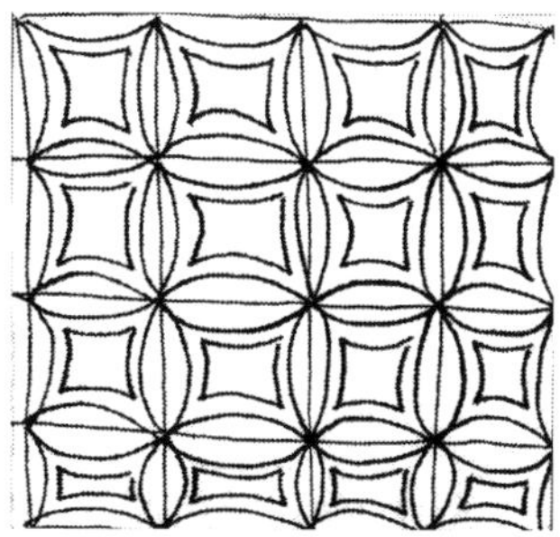

Unshaded, the auras give BALES *a lacy look.*

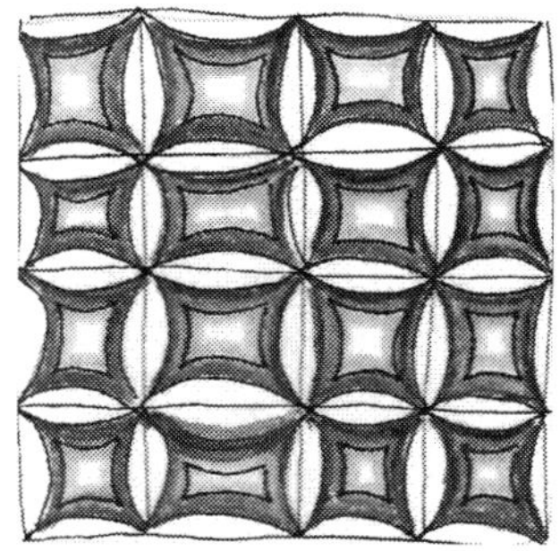

With a darker gradation the flowers and circles share the spotlight.

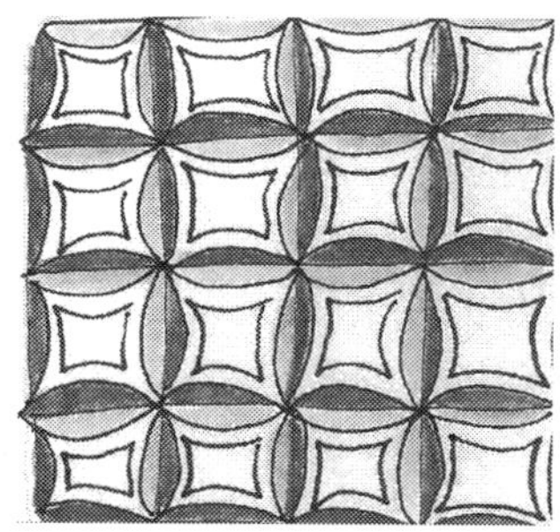

Dual-tone shading on the petals is an interesting choice and show off pinwheels.

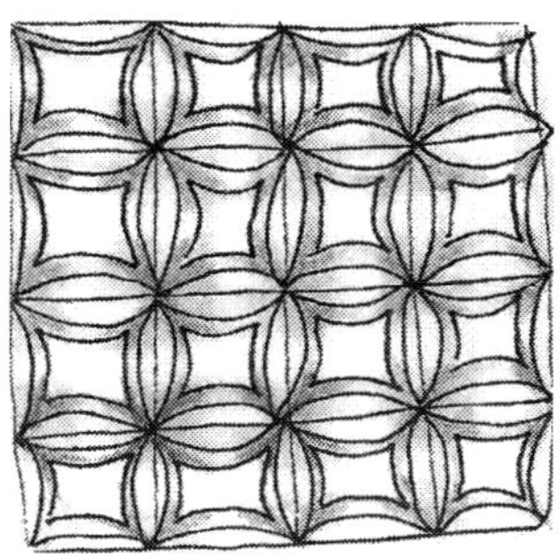

Just a little gradated shading on the inner aura brings out the flower shape.

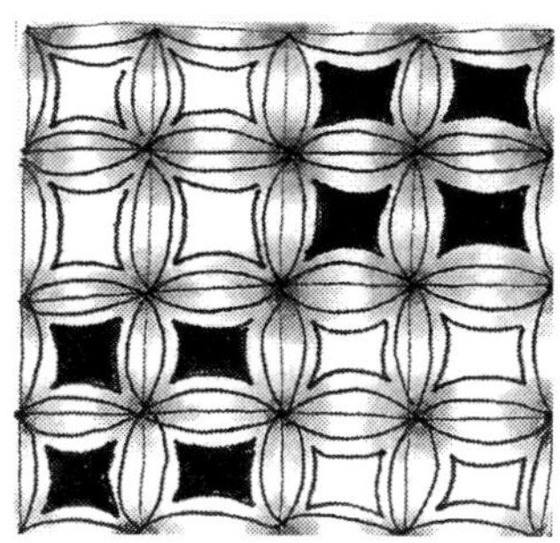

A circular gradation at the intersections of the flowers plus alternating black and white center fills creates a quilt-like effect.

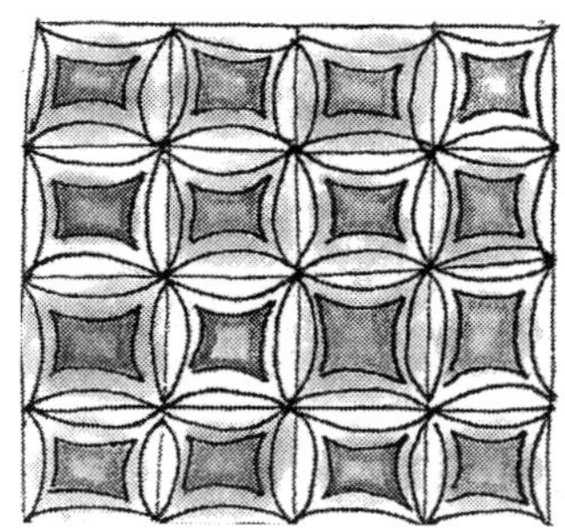

Alexa likes soft shading in the open space blended onto the petal auras.

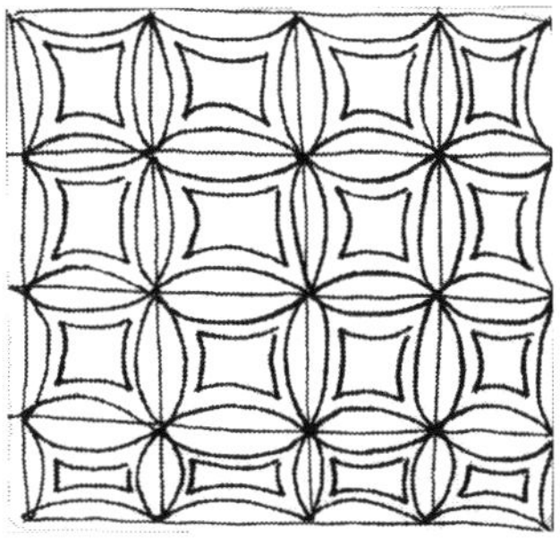
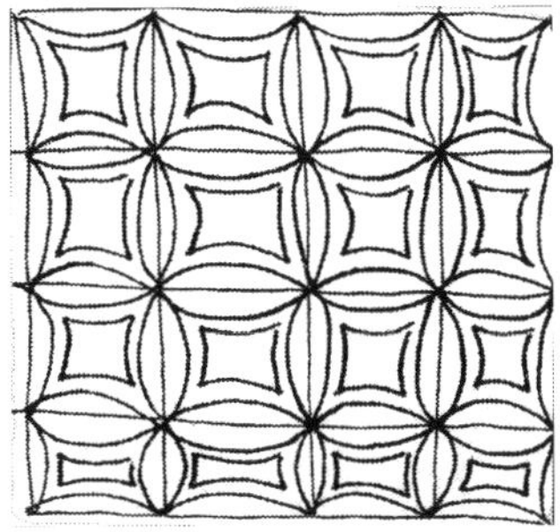
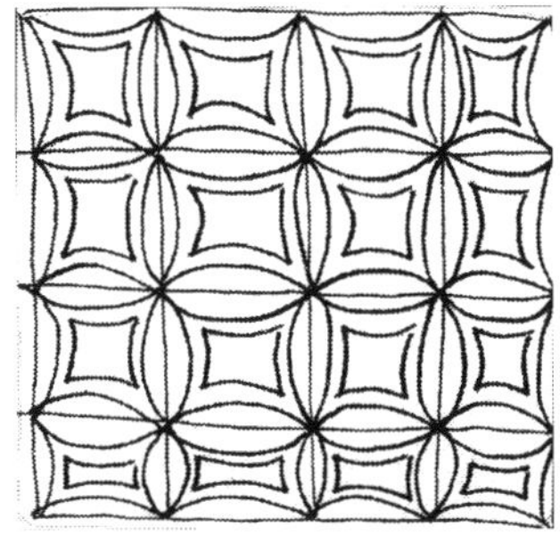

Exercise 45. ***Shade these*** **BALES*****, copying some of our ideas or making up some of your own.***

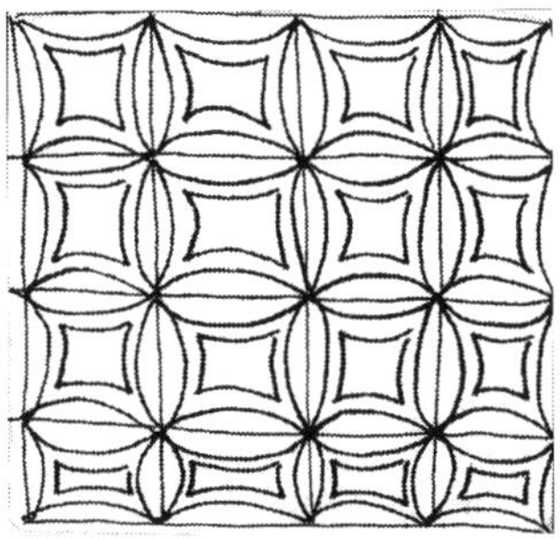
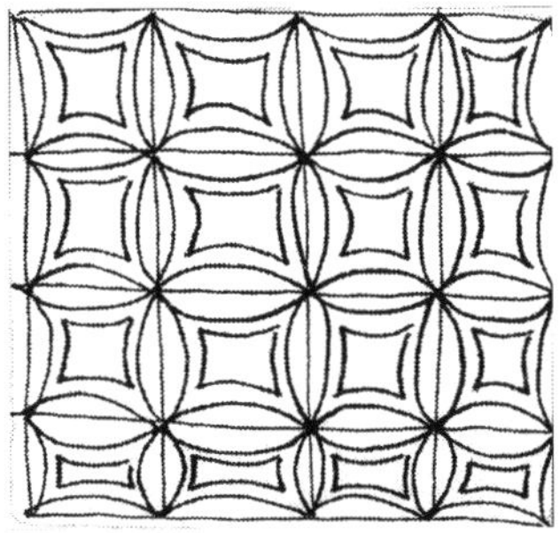
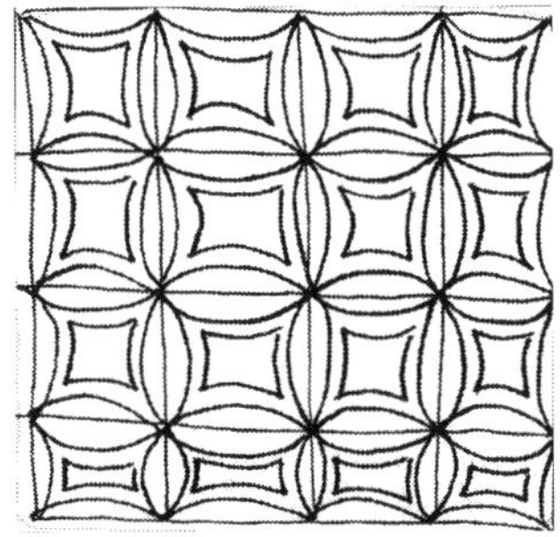
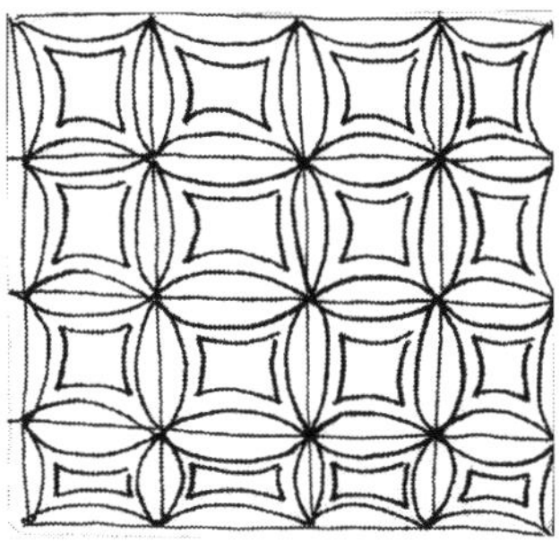
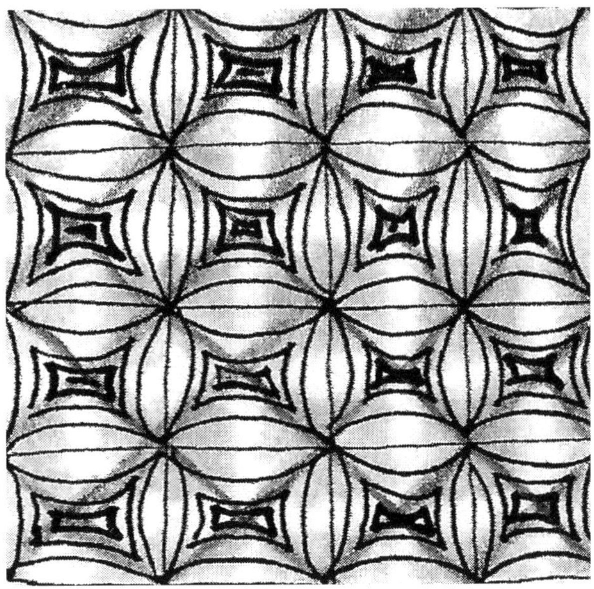

I hope you love this one as much as I do. It is Alexa's favorite way to shade **BALES***. You can get this look by filling the open space with auras, then drawing a soft X diagonally from corner to corner, and then blending outward. My tip is to make sure you leave a highlight in the center of each petal.*

New Tangles For You

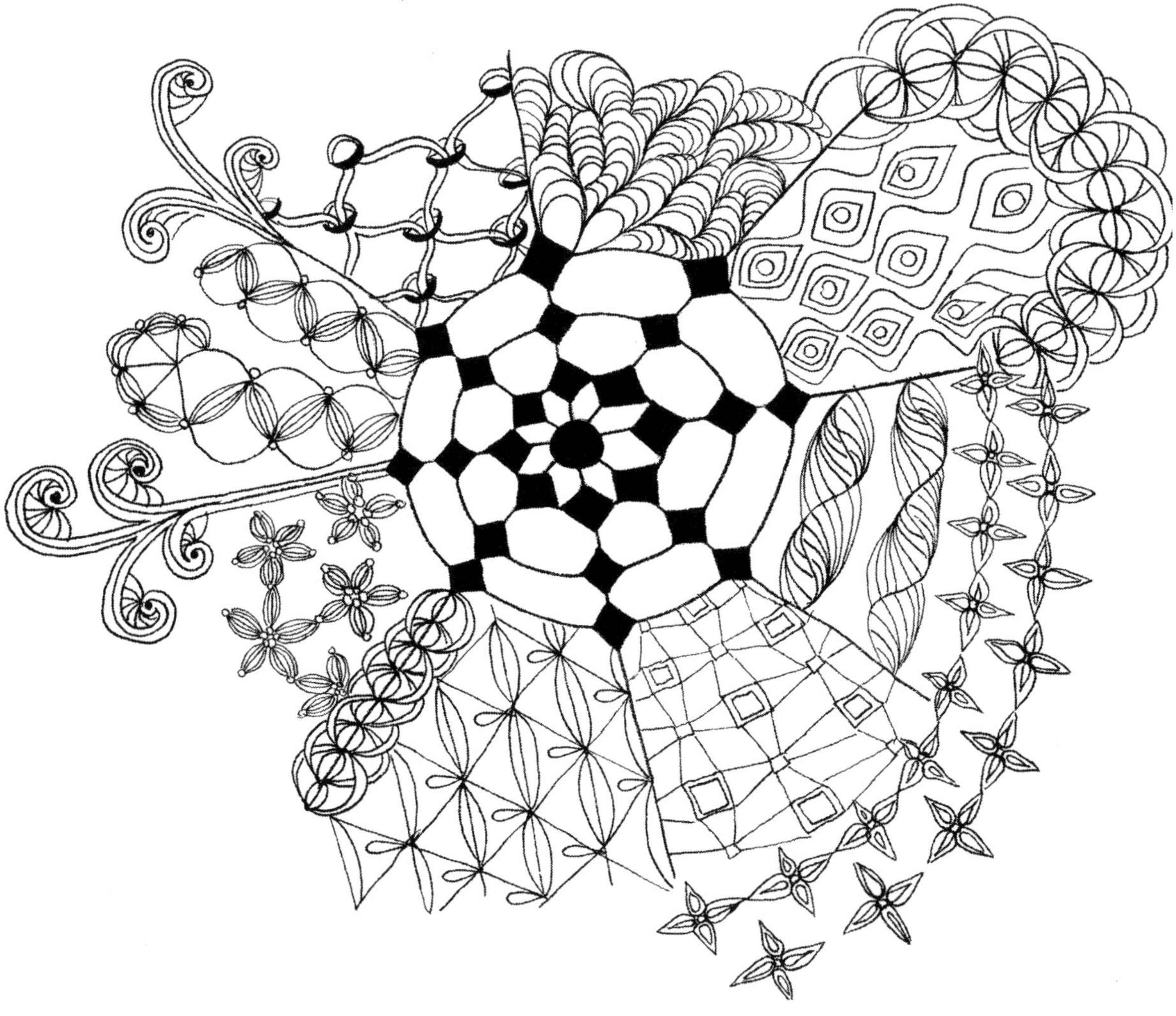

Tangles used (clockwise, starting in the center): MARCEL, SQUIRMY, PILLA, STEF-AH-NI, SINUOUS, MEES, CRUX, MYRTLE, CREWELERY, THANKSGIVING, ZA, KNOPEN.

CHAPTER 4 NEW TANGLES TO SHADE

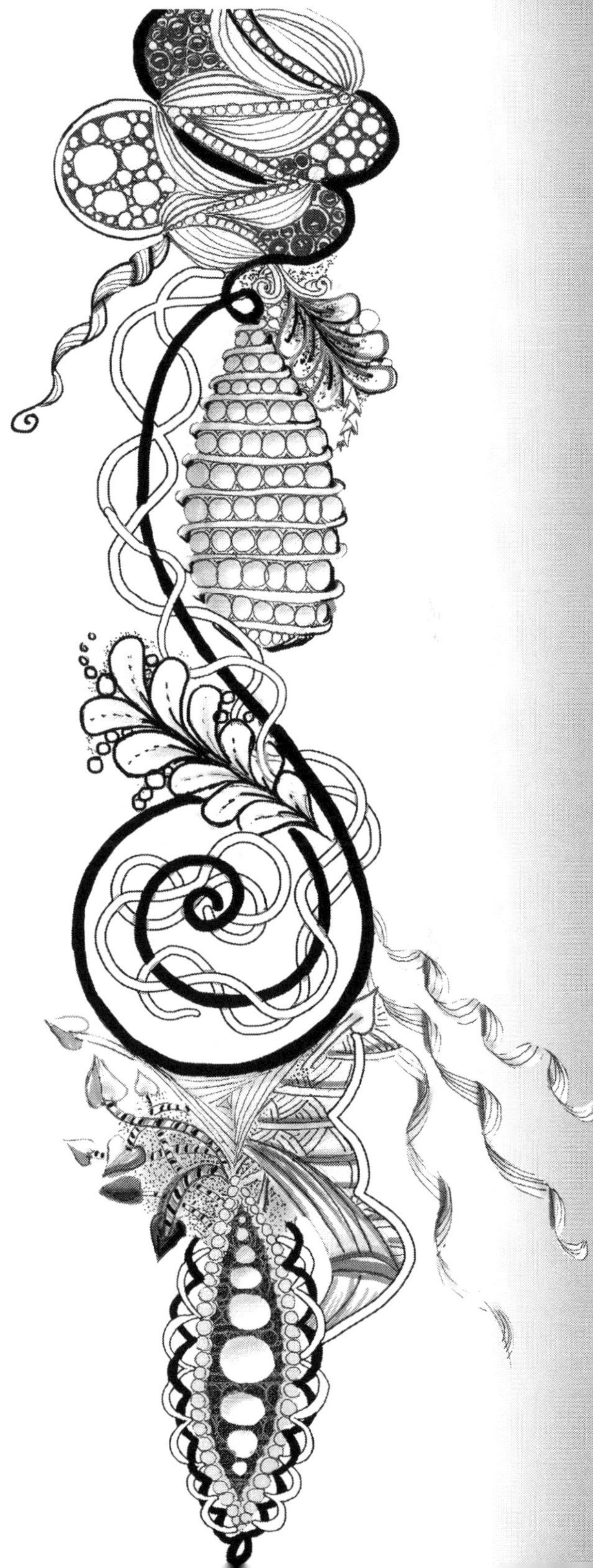

The previous chapter contained 20 official tangles with almost fifty ideas for shading them. You probably have seen them, and you may have even shaded them before. In this chapter, the tangles are new, so you will not be influenced by seeing what someone else has done with them. I created nine of them just for this book and there are three from guest artists.

In this chapter, instead of showing you how I would shade these tangles, I give the steps to draw them. Thinking about how they are drawn may help you decide how to shade them. You can also look back at page 44 for ideas, but use these new tangles to exercise your imagination.

If you get "stuck," look for a shaded version of the art on the facing page at the end of the chapter. It contains all of the new tangles in this chapter.

CREWELERY

This is for my friends who do crewel embroidery or for those who like the looks of it.

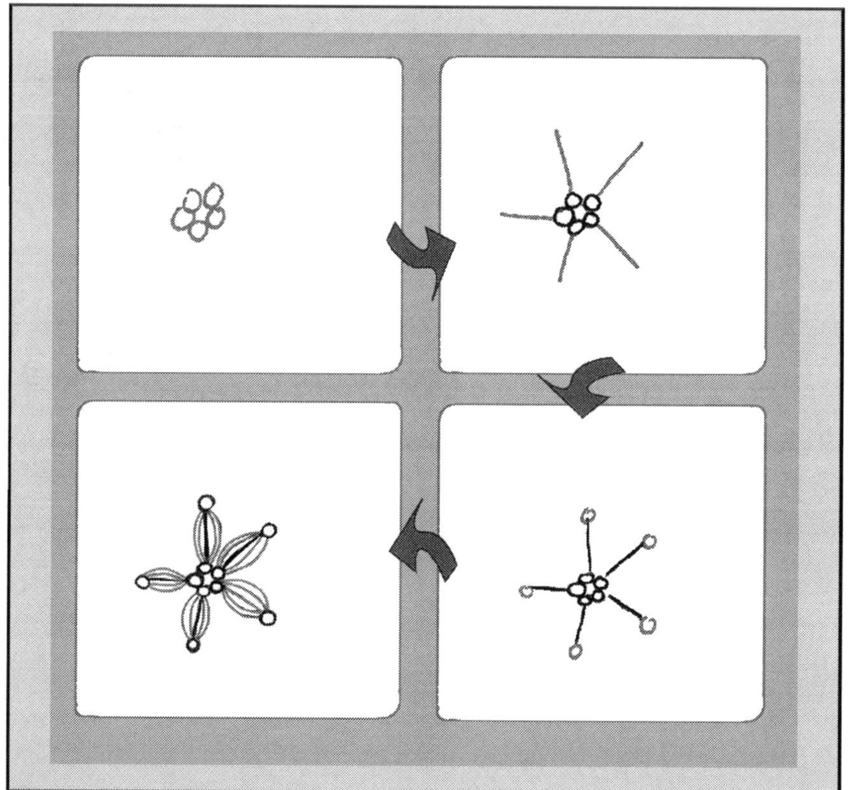

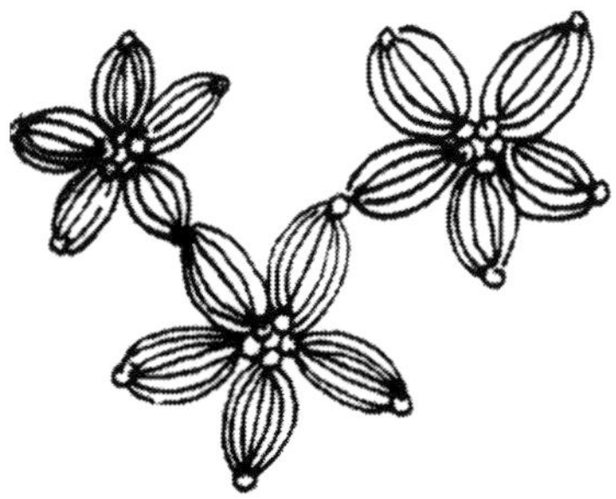

Exercise 46. ***Shade the three above and the row below.***

Exercise 47. ***Finish this tangle.***

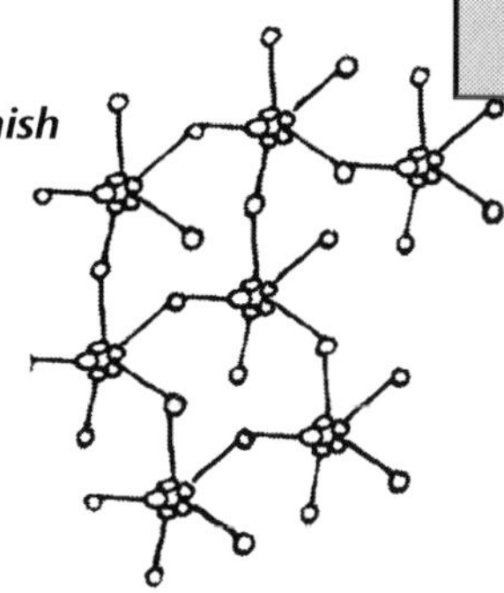

SINUOUS

SINUOUS means "winding, twisting, and having many curves." There are no straight lines on this tangle. It is a doubly apt name because you start out by drawing a sine wave.

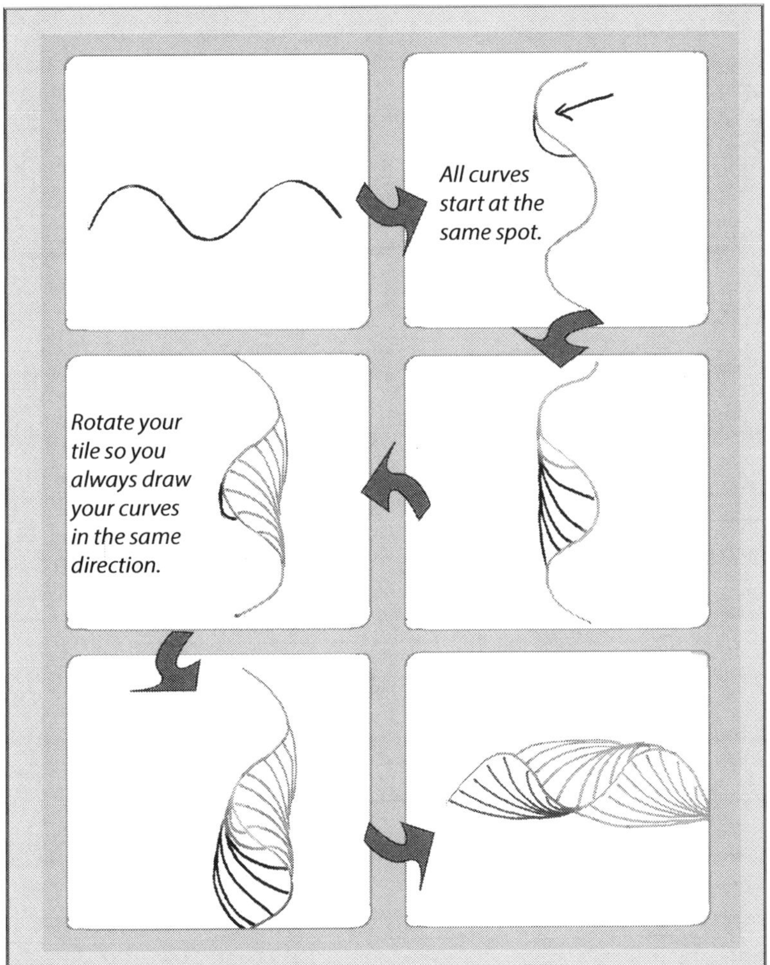

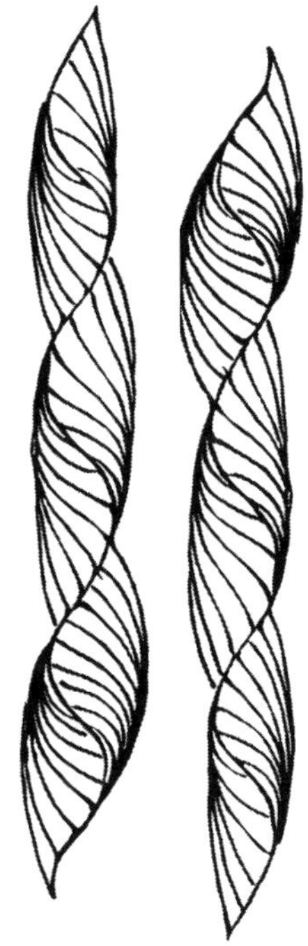

EXERCISE 48. ***Shade these three curvy tangles to emphasize their design.***

I even like this one half-done.

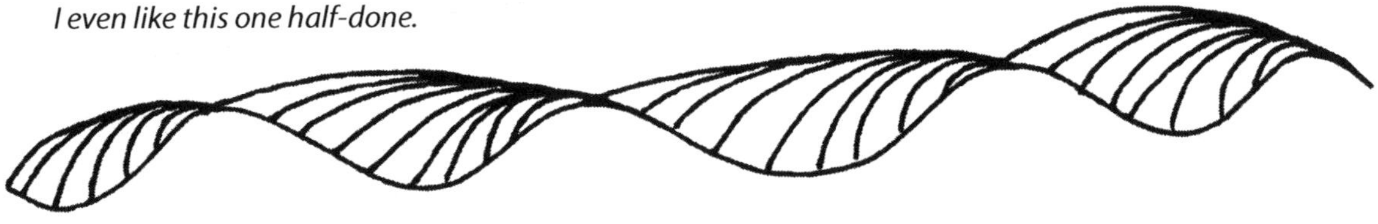

MARCEL

Birdie developed this tangleation of the tangle **FLORZ** and named it after her uncle. She made it especially to shade, so have fun with it.

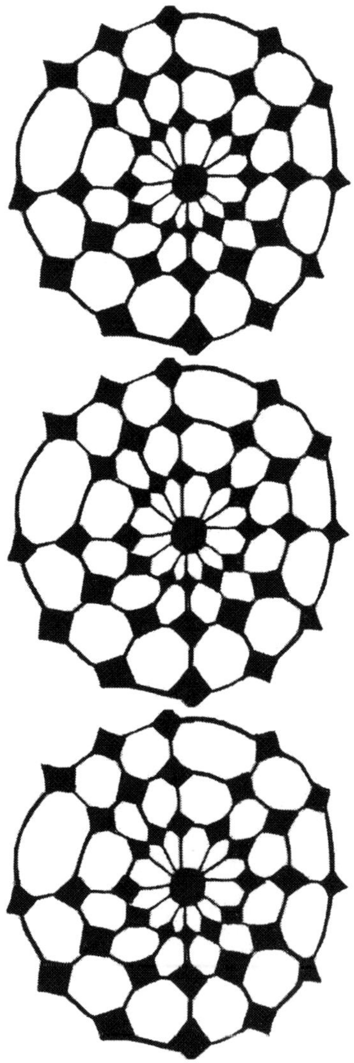

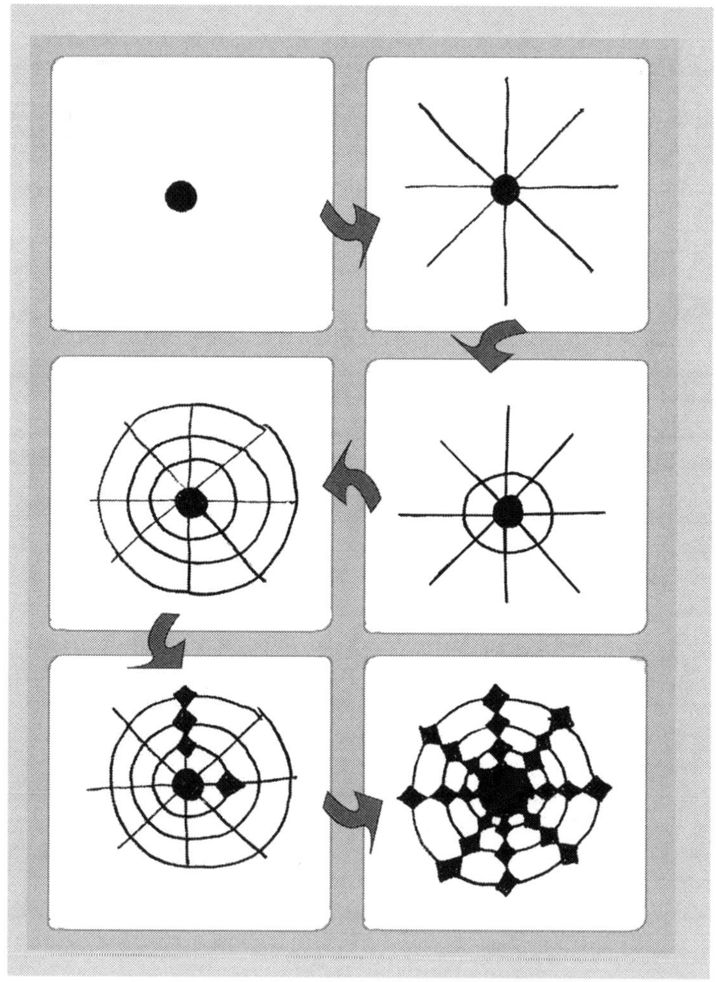

EXERCISE 49. ***See how you can jazz these up with some dimensional shading.***

KNOPEN

I got the idea for **KNOPEN** looking at a macramé handbag, naming it **KNOPEN**, the Dutch word for knots. When you are drawing this tangle, leave plenty of space between the rows of arcs. Also, it may help to rotate your tile a quarter when drawing the "S" shapes between the arcs.

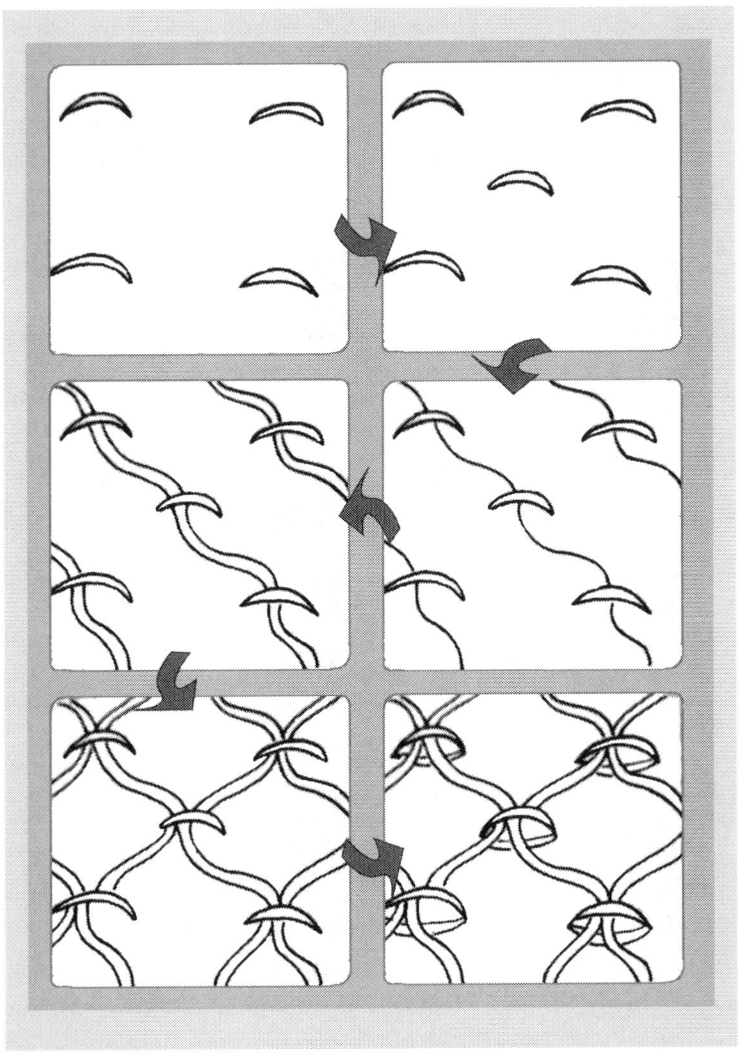

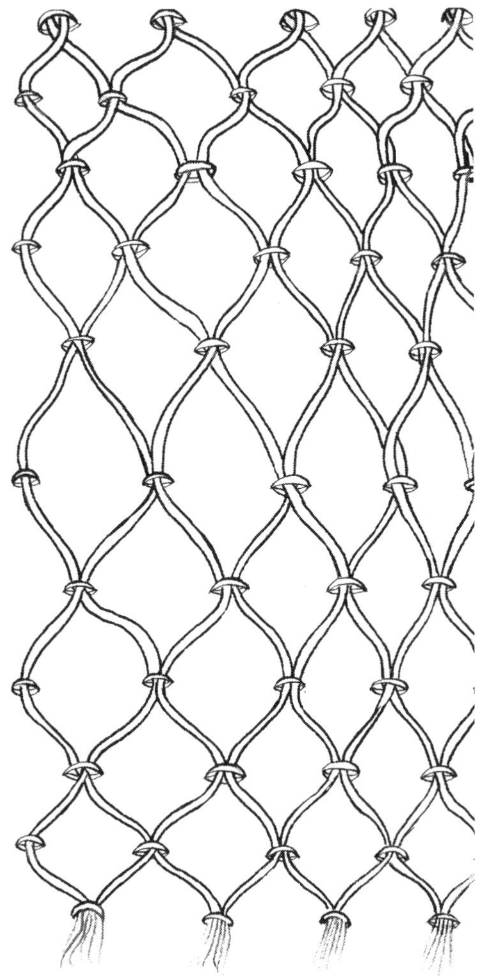

EXERCISE 50. ***Try your hand at shading KNOPEN. Don't be afraid to change your technique as you move from top to bottom.***

SQUIRMY

I love drawing the flowing shapes of FLUX, but I use it in almost every one of my tiles. To add a little variety while still keeping that flowing feel, I made this tangleation called SQUIRMY. Like the official tangle BUNZO, it has a single shape, but it has a different feel.

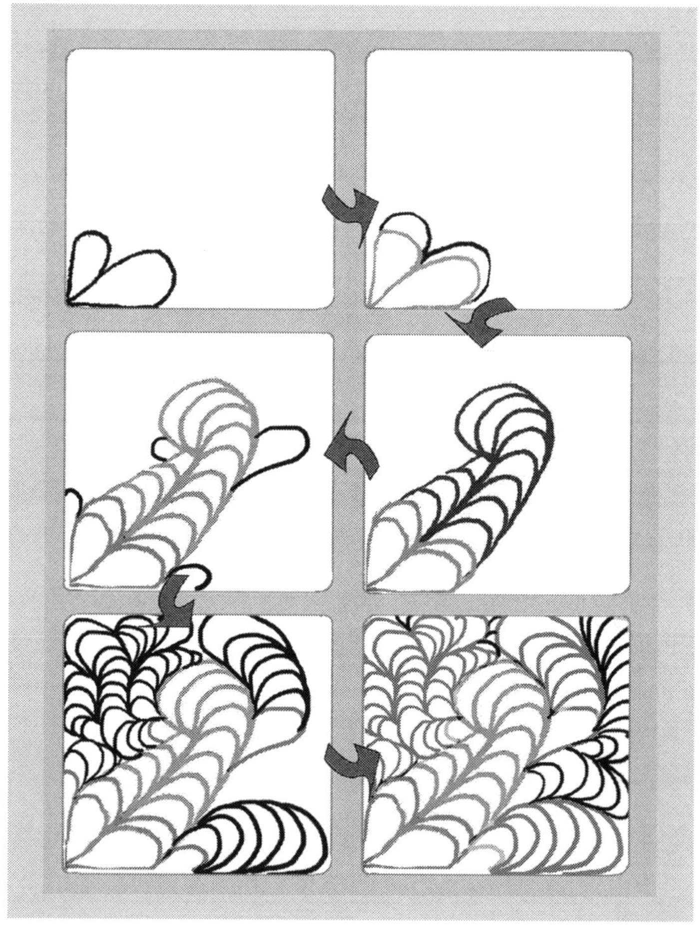

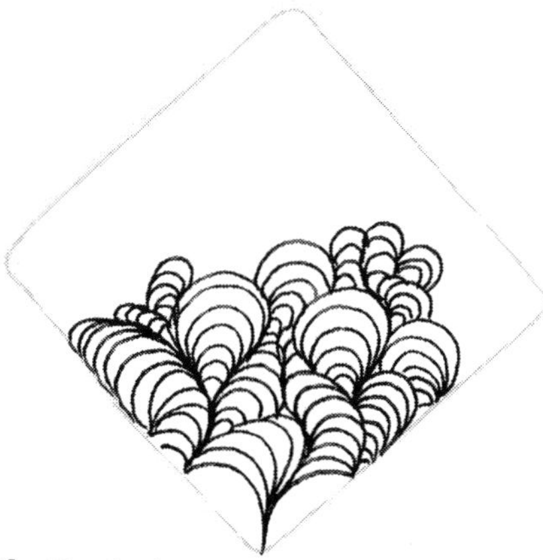

EXERCISE 51. ***Shade these two differently.***

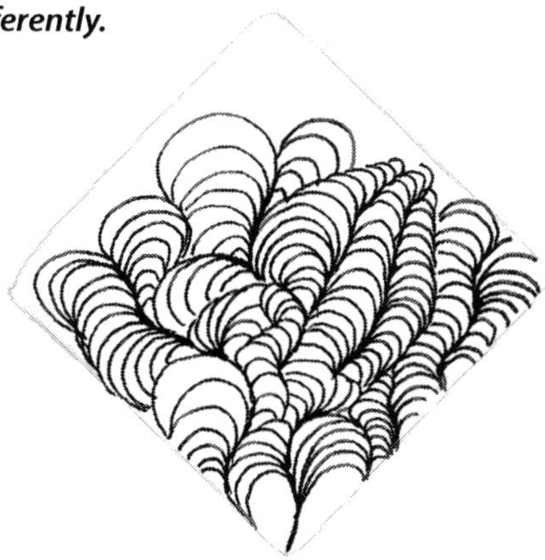

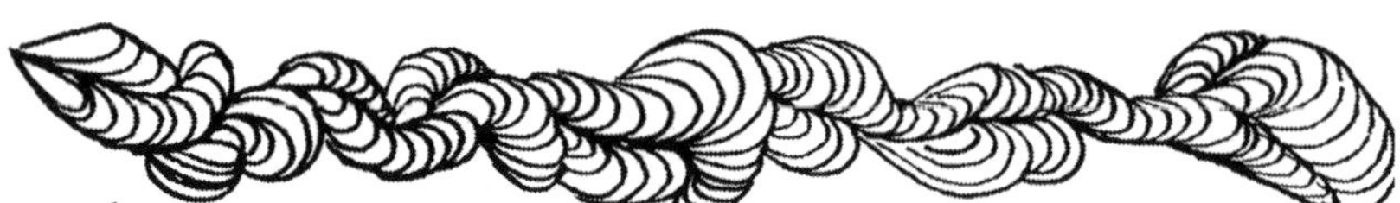

EXERCISE 52. ***Try using a cast shadow on this longer one.***

PILLA

PILLA was inspired by the design on a throw pillow. Make this one bold by leaving a lot of space between the auras or more refined by making a lot of auras. If you have trouble drawing the wavy lines, you can start with the circles.

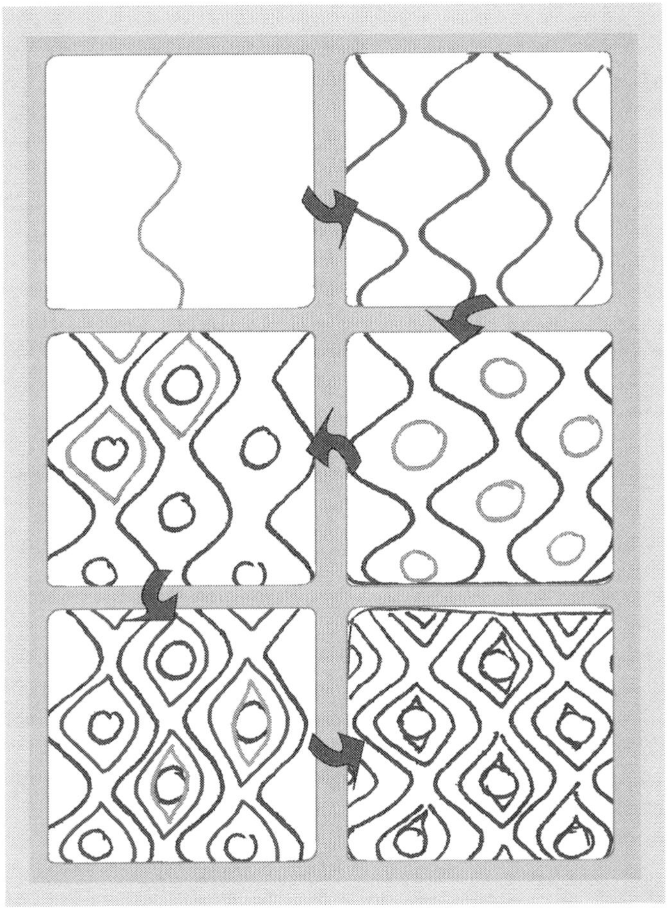

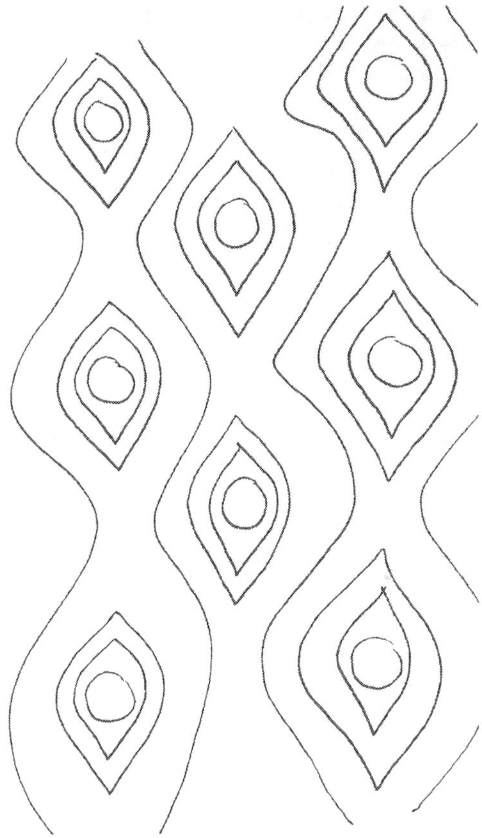

EXERCISE 53. ***Have fun shading PILLA. It has so many possibilities.***

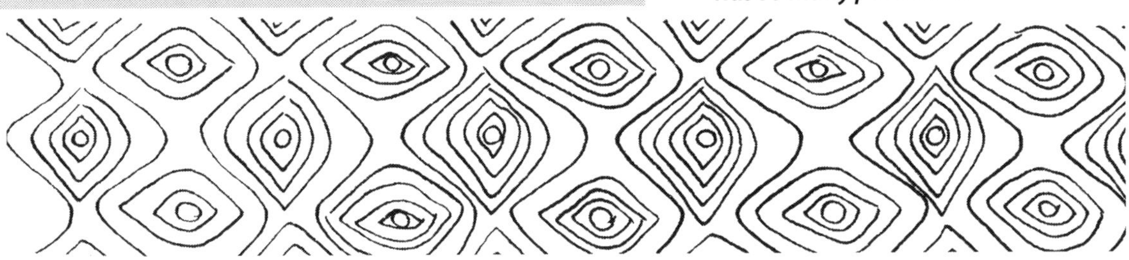

MYRTLE

Can you believe this beautiful tangle started out as a mistake? Remember that next time you are tempted to pick up an eraser. Sonya Yencer named this MYRTLE since she created it in MYRTLE Beach.

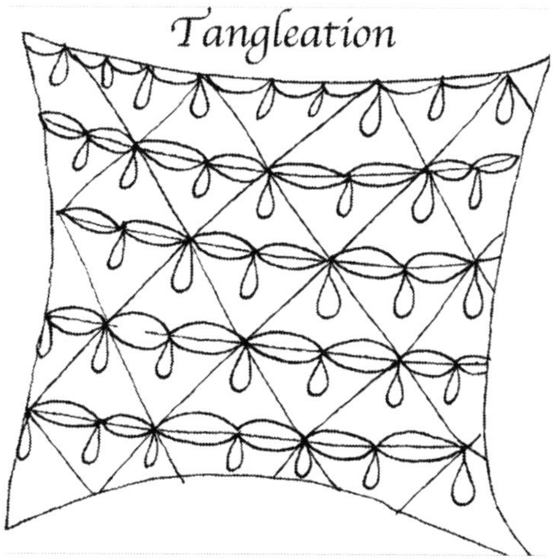

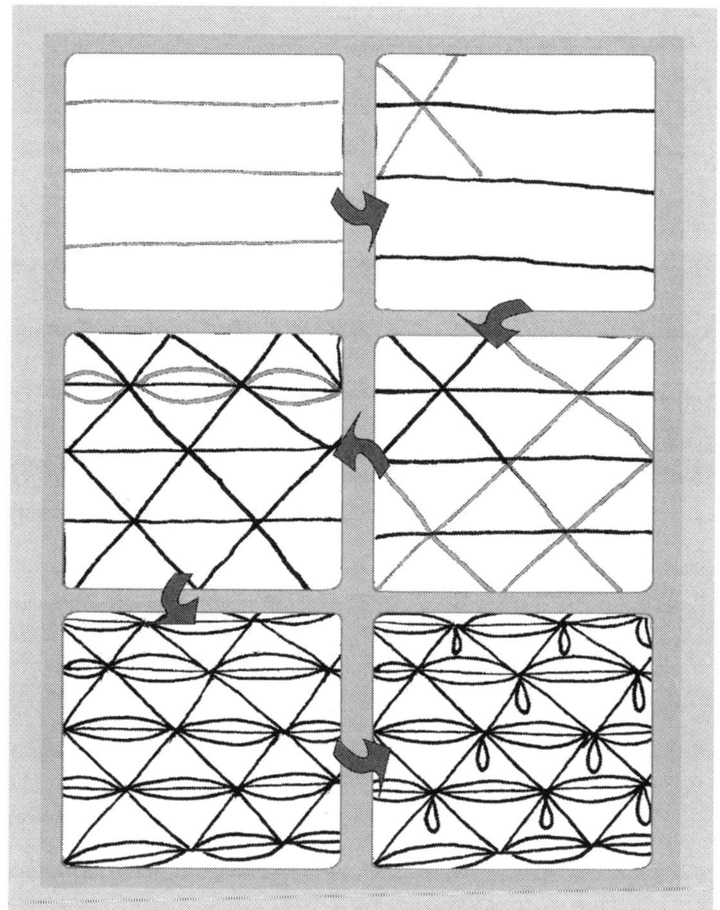

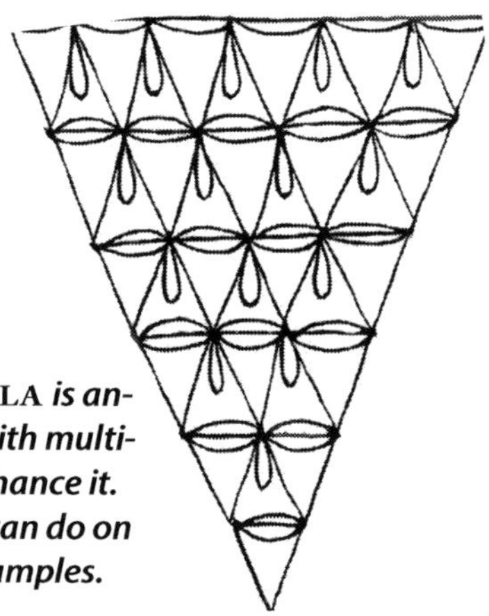

EXERCISE 54. PILLA ***is another tangle with multiple ways to enhance it. See what you can do on these three examples.***

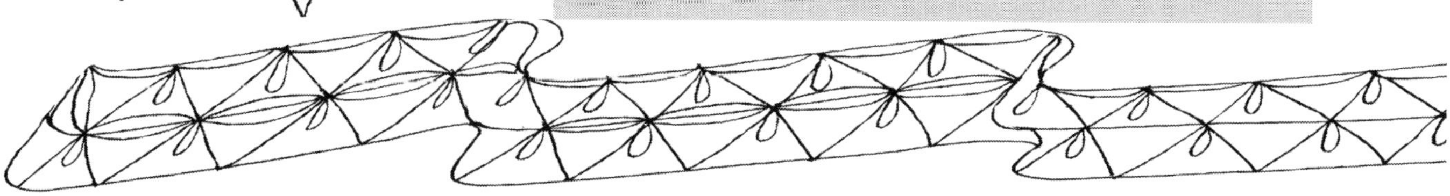

STEF-AH-NI

Stephania are Greek Orthodox wedding crowns. Traditionally, they have ribbons woven around them. The tangle **STEF-AH-NI** also has ribbons woven around and through it. It isn't hard, but it does require a bit of focus.

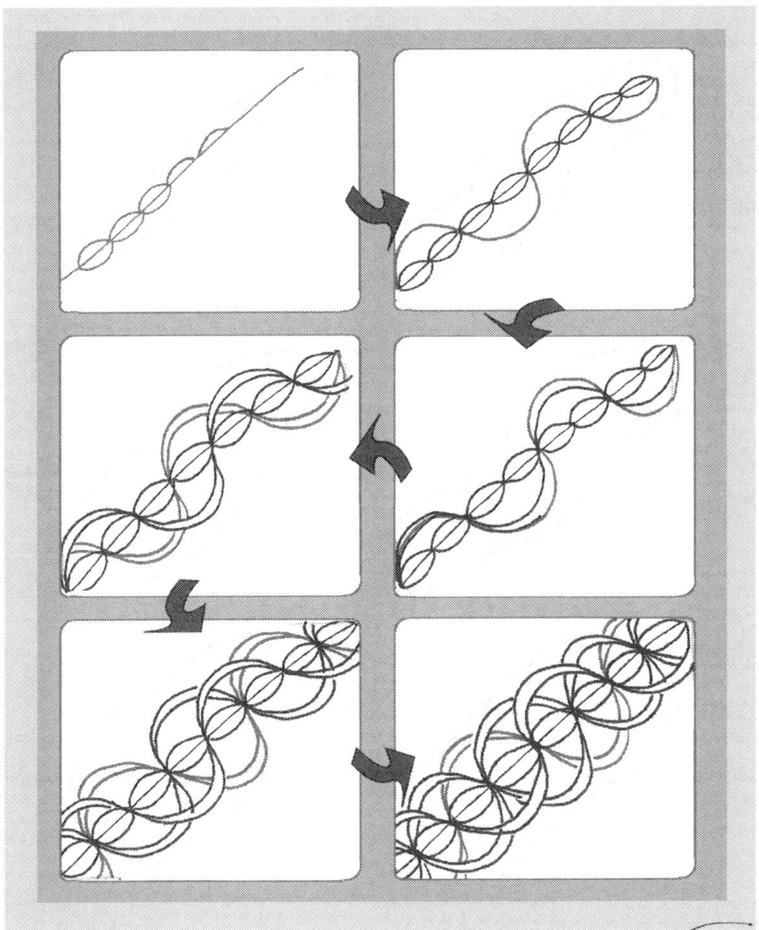

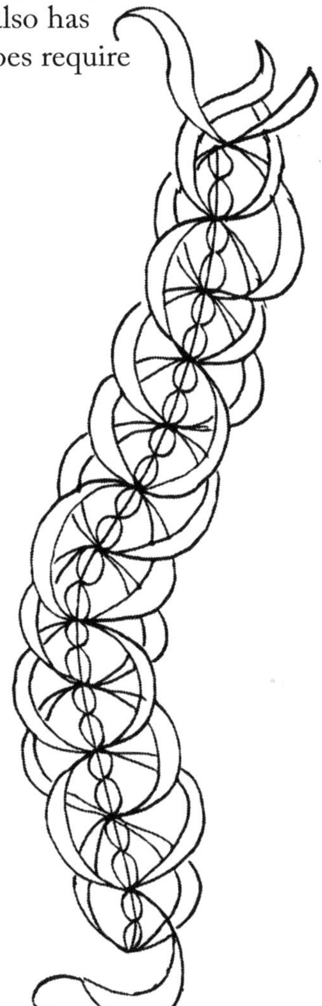

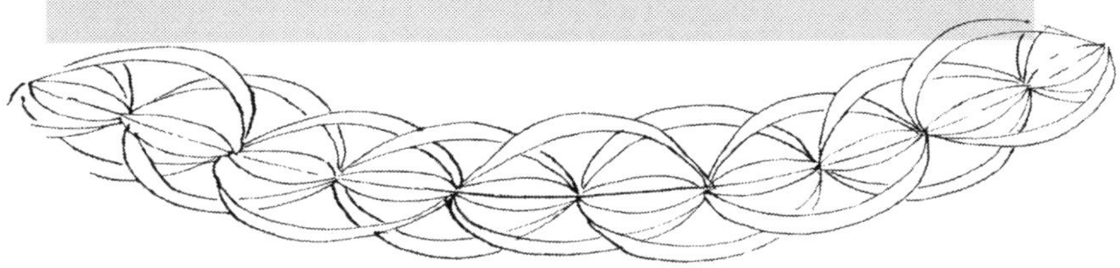

EXERCISE 55. ***Add some dimension to these tangles with shading.***

ZA

Scrabble players and teenagers know that ZA is slang for pizza. When ZA is "half-baked," it looks like a slice of pizza. This tangle is fun to do because it starts out all straight lines and angles and transforms into a curvy, flowing beauty. How else can you change ZA with shading?

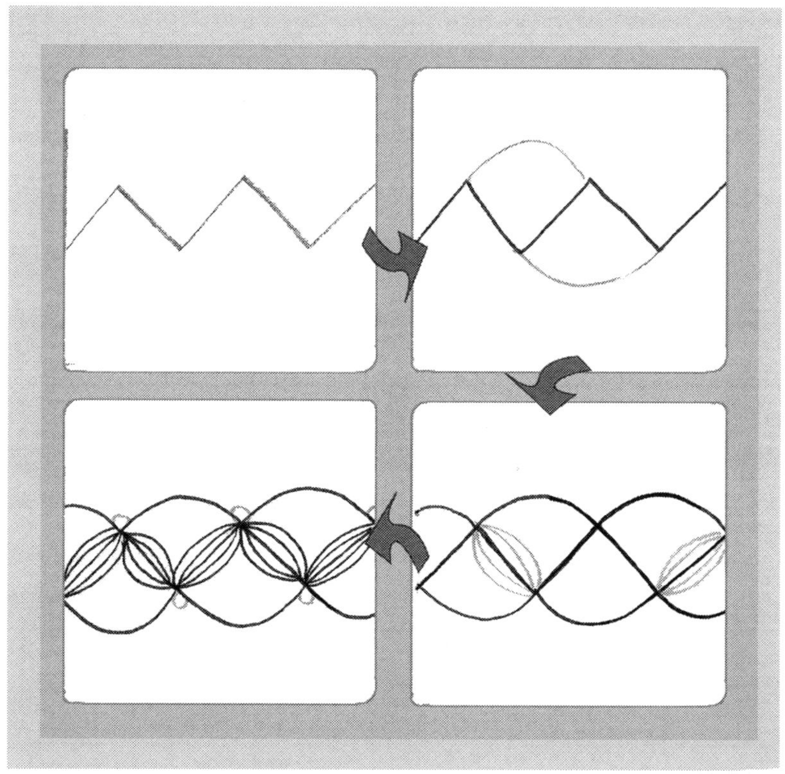

EXERCISE 56. ***See how else you can transform these with shading.***

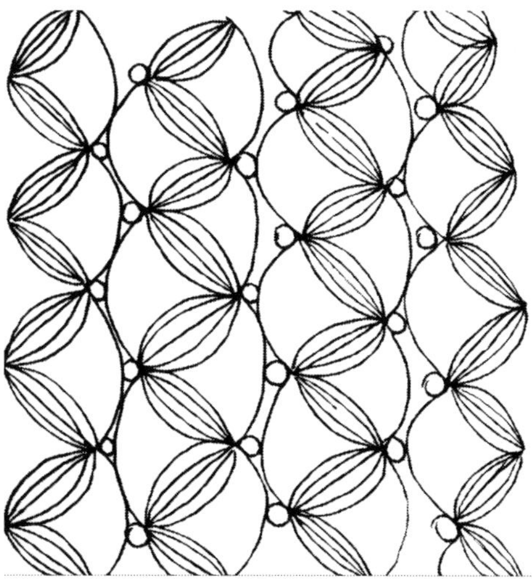

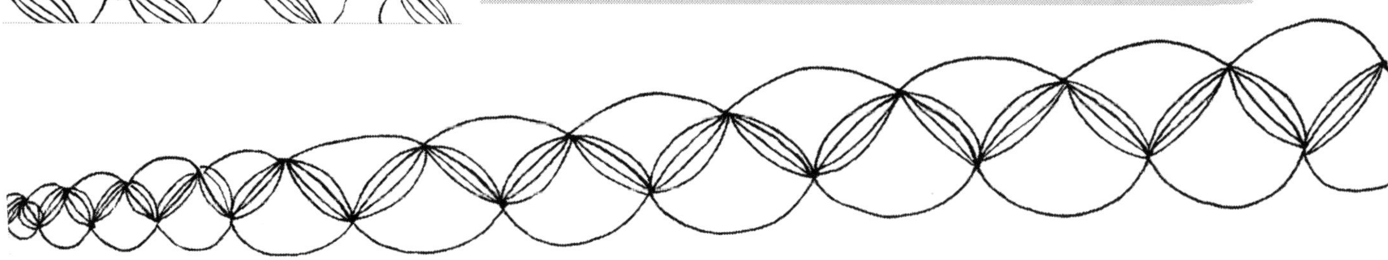

CRUX

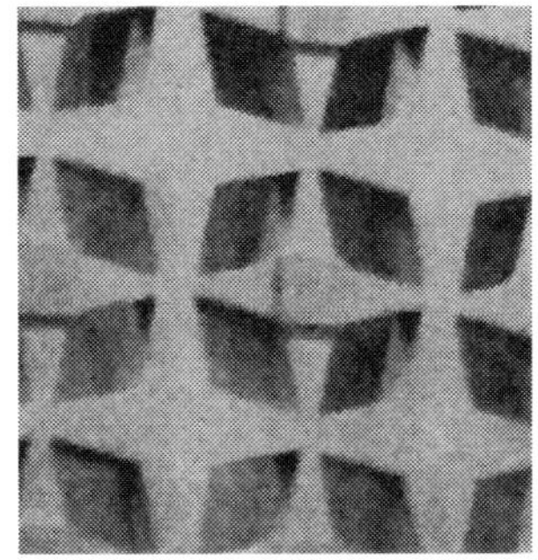

I got the idea for **CRUX** from looking at a wall of crosses in St. Catharine's church in Bexley, Ohio. The word "crux" is Latin for cross.

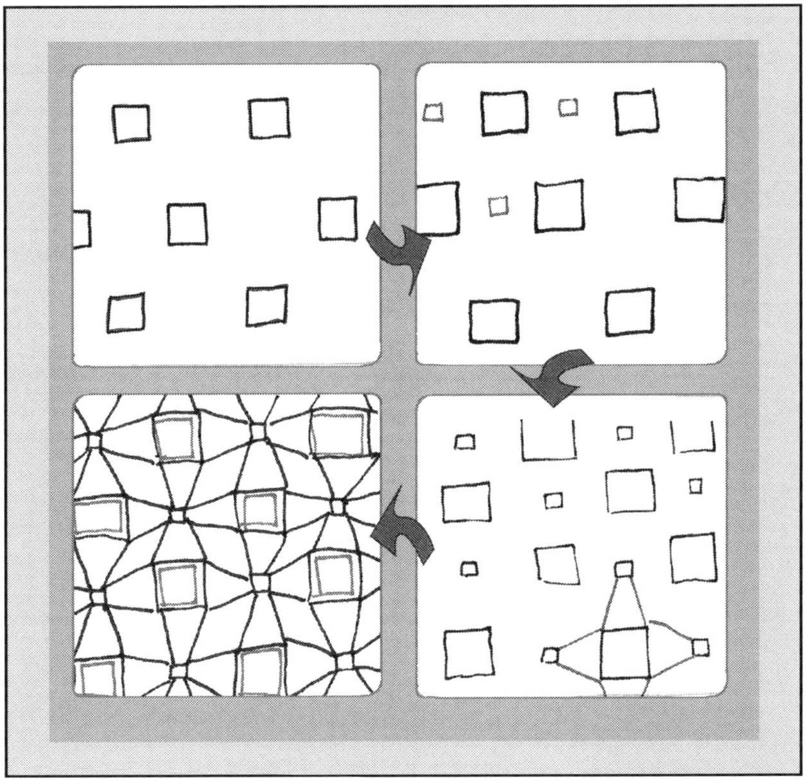

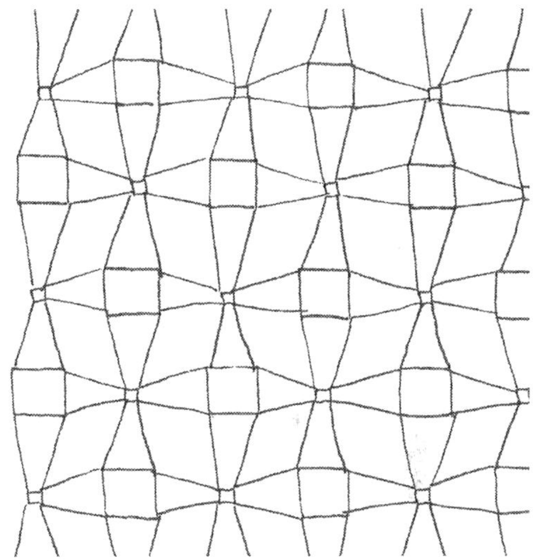

EXERCISE 57. ***See if you can mimic the dimensions of the wall in your shading. Or, just see how beautiful it can be.***

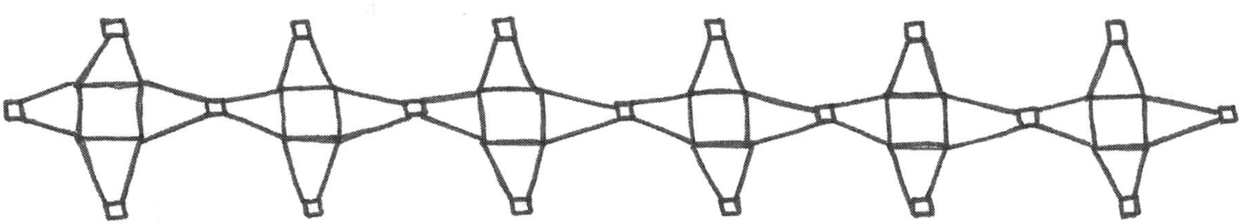

THANKSGIVING

THANKSGIVING is an original tangle by Kelley Kelly, CZT. This variation of OPUS looks like a cornucopia. See if you can fill it with the goodness of shading.

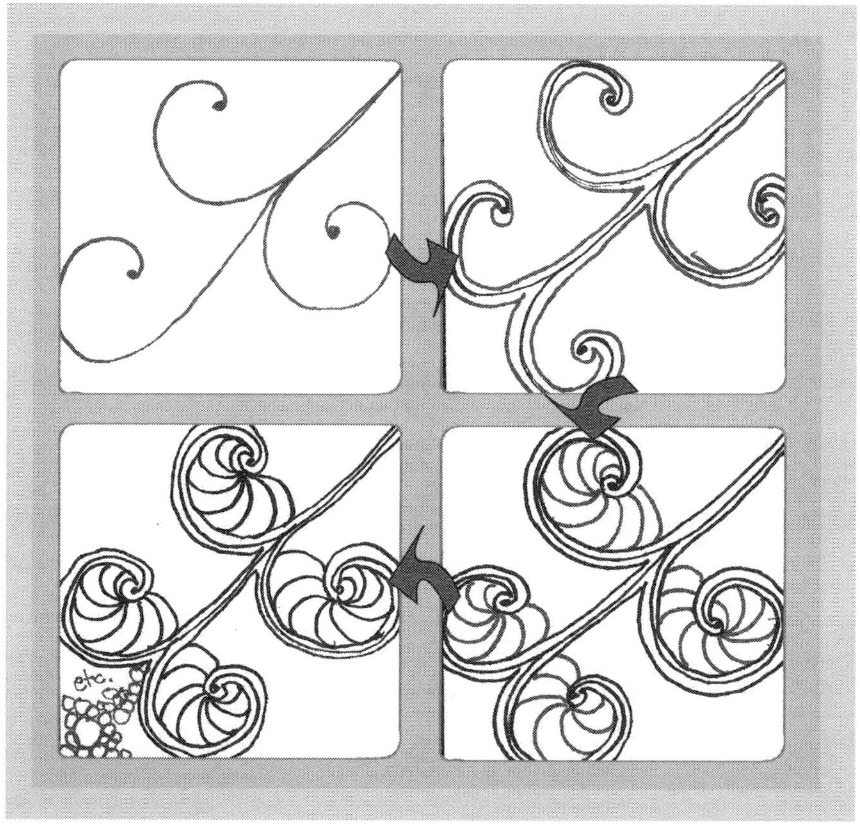

Exercise 58. ***Here is one for you to shade and a spot for you to draw your own.***

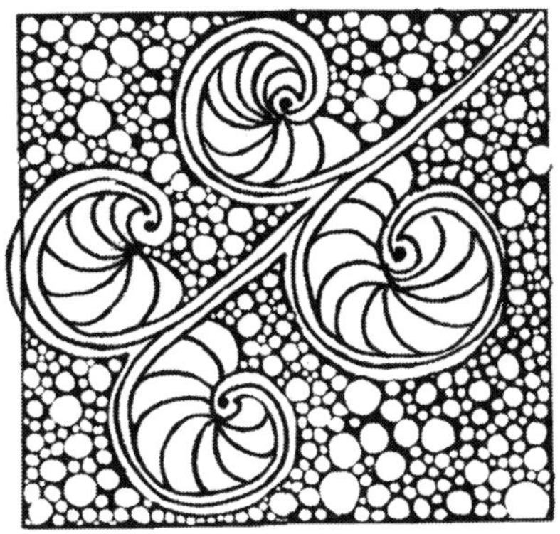

MEES

MEES is another tangle based on architecture. The Mees auditorium at Capital University in Bexley, Ohio has amazing wall decoration that makes a cute tangle.

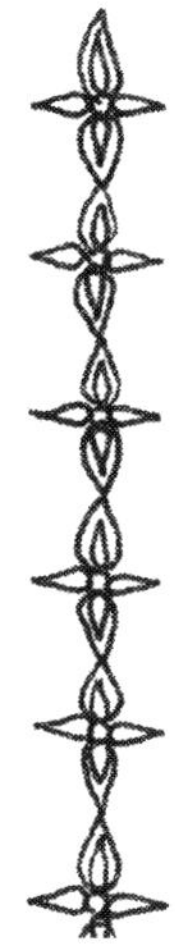

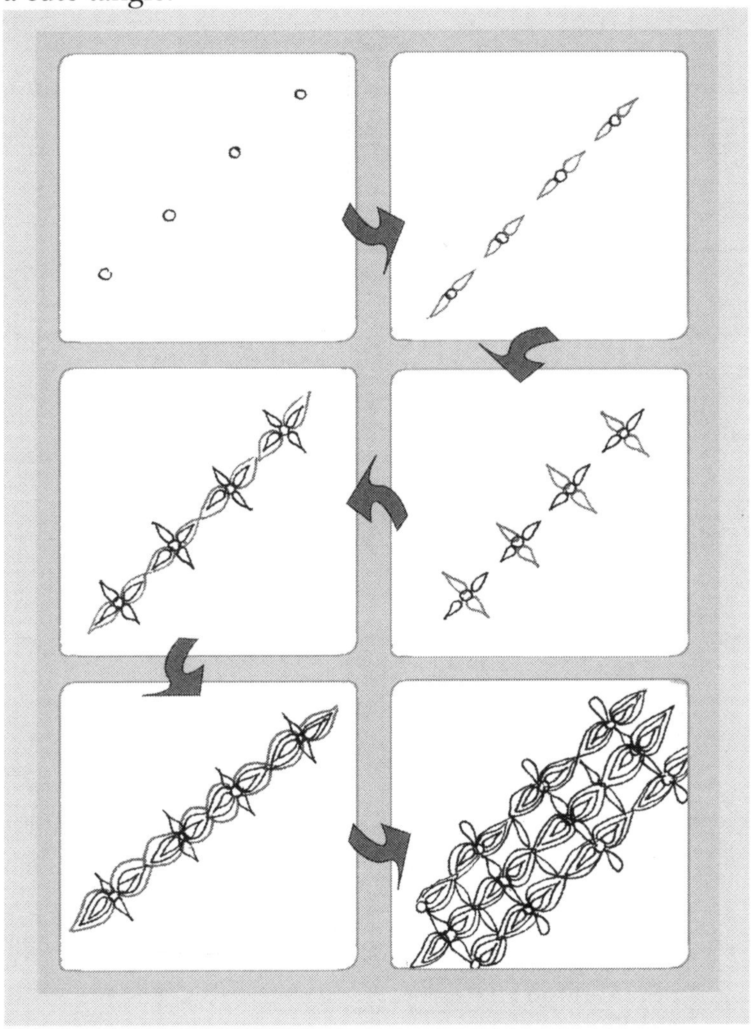

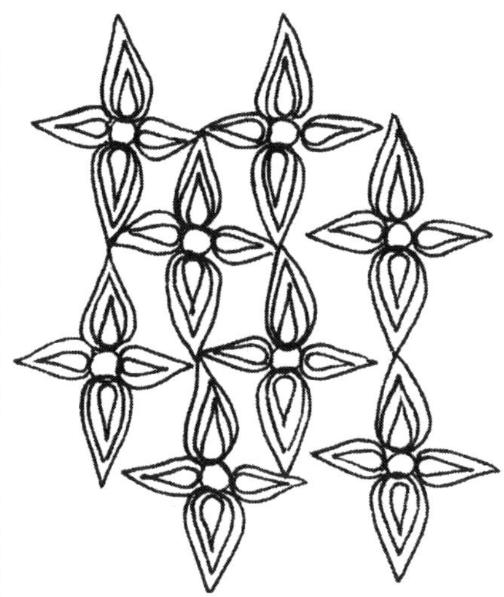

EXERCISE 59. ***Shade*** **MEES.**

New Tangles For You, Shaded

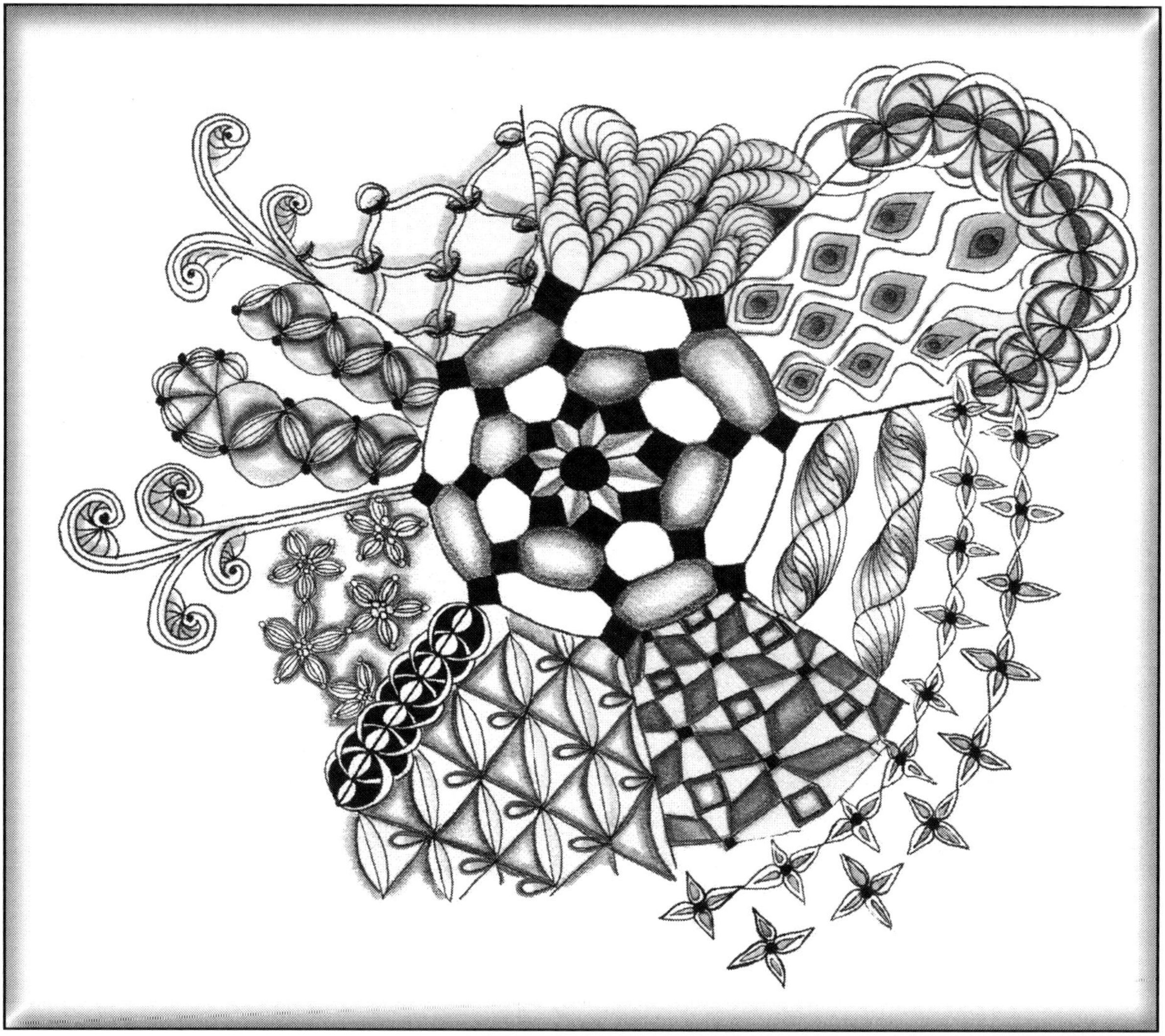

Tangles used (clockwise, starting in the center): **MARCEL, SQUIRMY, PILLA, STEF-AH-NI, SINUOUS, MEES, CRUX, MYRTLE, CREWELERY, THANKSGIVING, ZA, KNOPEN.**

CHAPTER 5 PUTTING IT ALL TOGETHER: SHADING YOUR ART

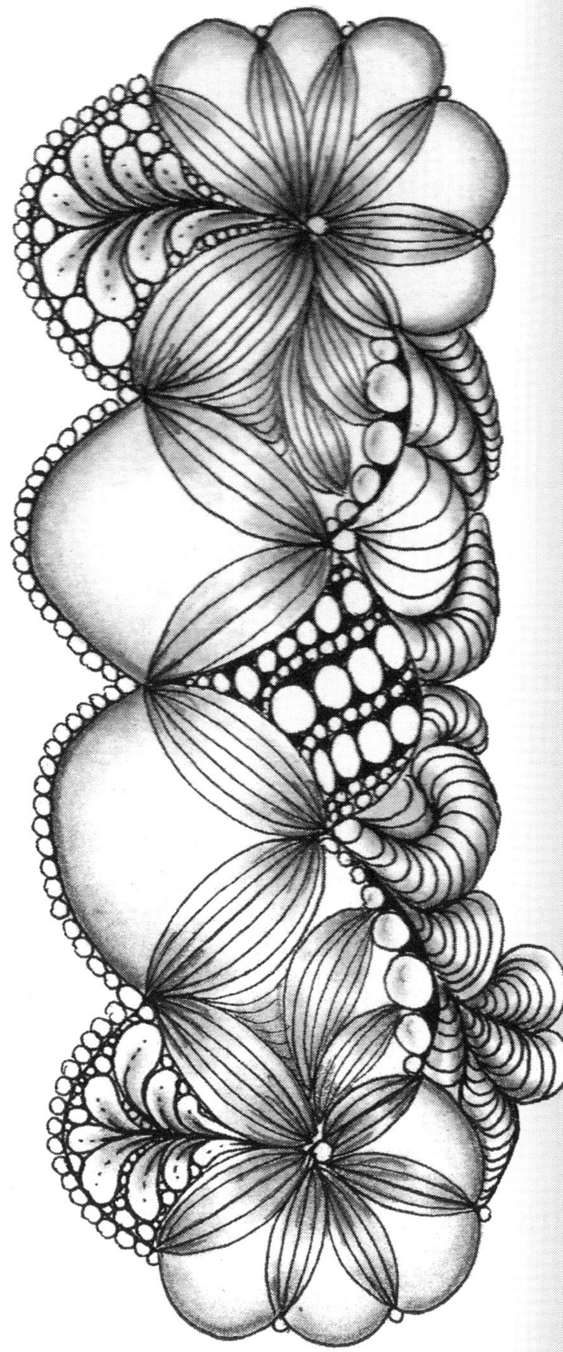

If you have been working through the exercises, you have had plenty of practice getting to know your tools and shading individual shapes and tangles, so now it is time to do a few studies on how to tackle a whole tile or ZIA. The projects in this chapter will show you in great detail how I would shade several different tiles and also give you tips on creating different effects with shading. Remember, though, that Zentangle is about developing your own creativity. If you feel as if you have to follow anyone else's rules, you can't let your own creativity free.

My Approach to Shading:

Sometimes when you finish tangling, you absolutely love the result. In that case, shading is easy. Add a bit of shading to bring out your favorite tangles, maybe shade around the border, and you're done.

TIP: *Sometimes it helps to get a different perspective on your tangle before starting to shade it. I often find it helpful to take a short break before I begin shading.*

Unfortunately, this doesn't always happen to me. I often finish tangling, and I'm not ecstatic about the result. In that case, more analysis is required. Here is the list of things that I consider before I begin shading my "problem" tiles. You can use it as a sort of checklist before beginning to shade.

1. First, look at the big picture.

   You have been focusing on the details of the individual tangles. Now it is time to step back and get a feel for the overall composition. Do this by holding the tile at arms length, turning it, and even squinting at it. Put it down and step away from it. What catches your eye? Is it something you want to enhance or something you want to camouflage. You can use shading to both attract or divert attention.

2. Consider the contrast.

   Is it easy to distinguish the tangles or sections of the tile? Sometimes you want one section to flow into the next, and it is a design choice. Sometimes there isn't enough difference in value or texture to distinguish between one area and the next, and you didn't mean for it to happen. In Project 2, I will show you how shading can add more contrast to a tile to make it more interesting.

TIP: *The most appealing designs have a good proportion of lights, mediums, and darks. In home decorating terms, the rule is "a gallon, a quart, and a pint."*

3. Check the balance of values in your tile.

   Is there enough variety? Are interesting bits of light and dark? Is there a good balance between light, medium, and dark values? As long as the tile is not too dark, you can correct many value issues with shading.

4. Is there a focal point?

   A focal point is simply an area that draws the viewer's attention. If there is no clear focal point, you can use shading to emphasize an area you like to make it a focal point. I show you how to do this in Project 3.

5. Is there something you don't like?

   Oftentimes if you shade this first, you may change your opinion about it. If not, then you can use shading to camouflage it.

Sometimes, you can ask yourself all of these questions and still not know where to begin shading. In that case, shade a tangle or two that you know how to shade and then reevaluate it to see what else would make it look better. Often, just getting started is all it takes for the answer to come to you.

Some Final Advice

Don't forget that it is always easier to add more than to take away.

As you work through these projects, read through the steps to see how and why I shaded the way I did, but don't feel obliged to shade yours the same way. Remember that there is no right or wrong way to create or shade your Zentangle art.

Many students have told me that shading "stresses them out." Once you understand the basic concepts and spend a bit of time practicing, you will be able to shade with ease and you won't have to think about technique or process. Think of it like learning to ride a bike. The learning phase may be tedious, even frustrating, and you have to think about every little thing. But once it clicks, you can do it without a second thought. You will be able to just enjoy the process and create without pressure or expectation.

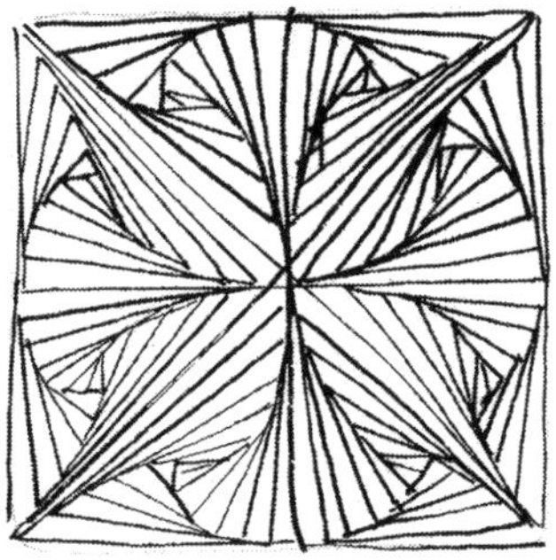

Project 1: Adding Depth

I made this spiral as a hostess gift, writing thank you in 5 languages along the ZANDER on the right side.

NOTE: *Shade this tile following the steps outlined. There is another copy at the end for you to do it however you want.*

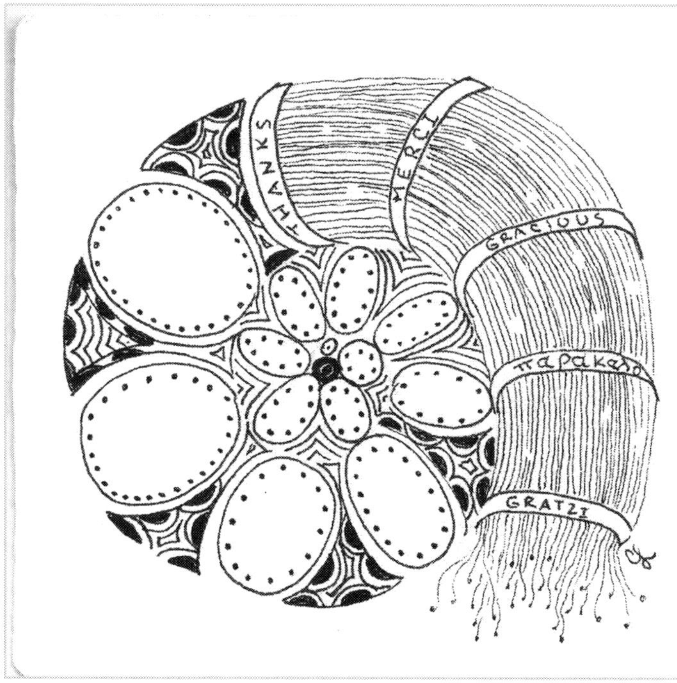

Evaluation:

I really like this tile as it is. There is a nice contrast between the black of the crescent moon next to the white ovals and a good balance between light, medium, and dark areas.

However, it looks kind of flat, and I feel some simple shading would make the spiral look more 3-dimensional.

The Process:

Follow steps 1-4 to shade the ZANDER, the tangle on the upper and right part of the coil. To save space, I've only illustrated each step on one part of the tangle. You will do each step on all of the ZANDER.

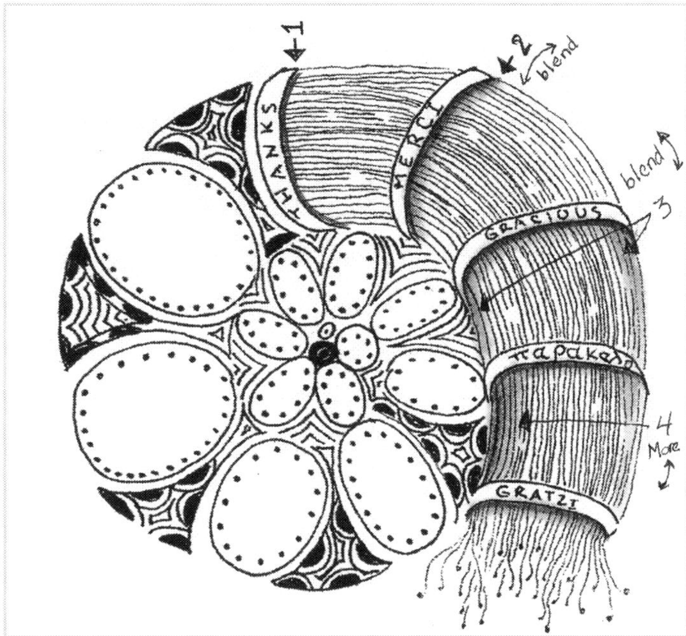

Steps 1-4 illustrated.

Step 1. Make a dark line with a soft pencil just below the bottom of each thank you band.

Step 2. Smudge it by moving your blender side to side in the same direction as the line as shown in the figure. Keep moving your blender back and forth while gradually pushing the graphite away from the band. This will make a nice gradation with the darkest part under the band, and it will look as if the bands are casting a shadow down onto the ZANDER. See how the bands now appear to be sitting on top?

Step 3. Now, to make the ZANDER look as it is cylindrical, you'll start shading it by drawing a line along the outermost edges. Begin with a line just inside the edge so they will look as they are curving towards the back.

Step 4. Now use your blender to push the graphite along the sides of the ZANDER. Follow the pencil lines you just drew, and gradually move towards the center. We're just shading the edges here, so don't push too hard and get any shadows in the center.

Step 5. On the inside of the coil (left side), you may want to shade a bit darker so it will look as the coil is wound up and the inside would be naturally more in the shadows.

Step 6. Starting on the ovals to make them look three dimensional also, lightly draw around the inside of the edges, just to the dots. The rest will be smudged.

Step 7. Smudge by going around and around the inside of each oval, but use less pressure as you get closer to the inside of the circle. Don't forget to leave white space for a highlight at the center of each oval. You only want to add shadows not turn the whole thing gray.

This is where I stopped, but you don't have to. Do you want to shade around the entire spiral to anchor it to the background? Maybe you could emphasize the spiral curve even more by continuing the inner shadow you started on the ZANDER all the way to the dark circle in the center. There is another copy of the tile for you to play with.

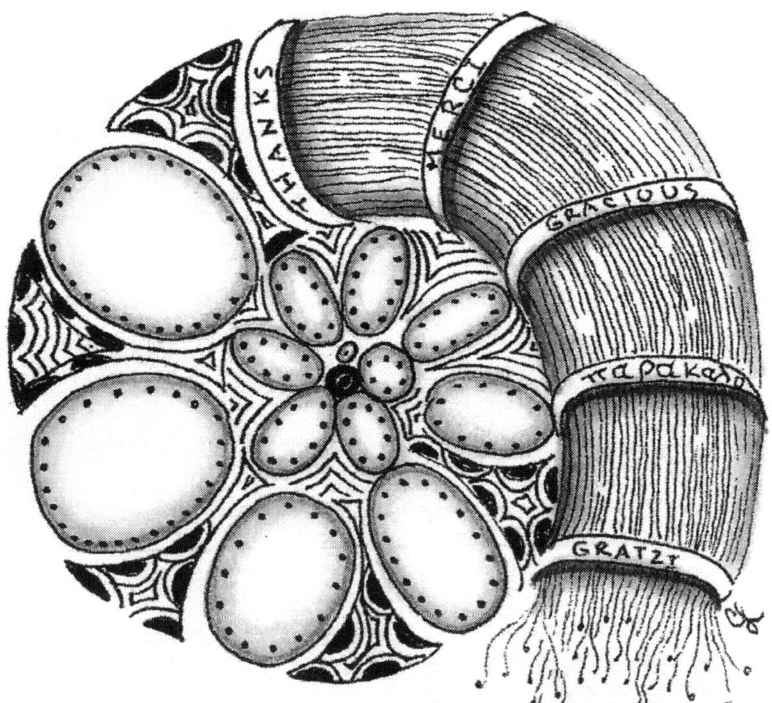

Project 2: Adding Dimension and Contrast

This is a duo-tangle using MSST and SQUIRMY.

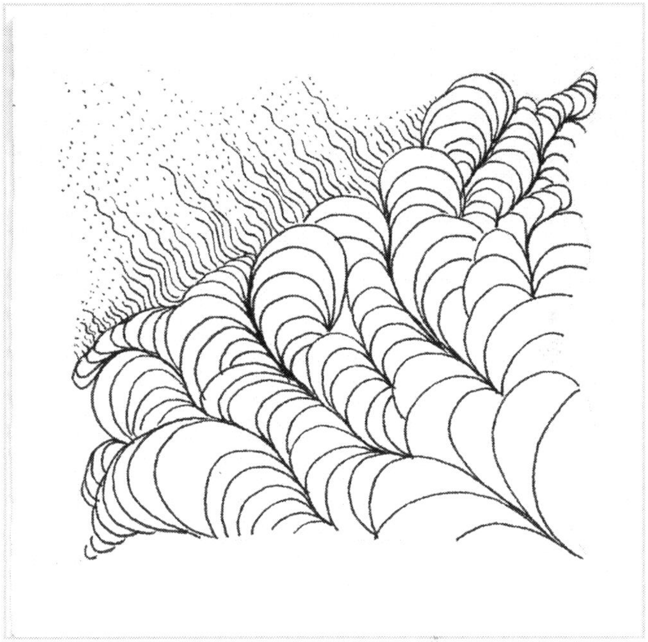

Evaluation:

This tile is a fairly light tile overall, lots of white and medium values. The only dark areas are the places where the arcs converge and touch the arcs of its neighbor.

To me, this looks a bit like built-in pen shading. MSST also has this phenomena because the squiggly lines are inherently darker than the dots. This makes it natural to emphasize both of these areas with some shading. Adding some dark values will spice up the contrast in this monotone piece.

The Process:

Step 1. Take a soft pencil and lightly trace each of the arcs. You don't have to be perfect here because you'll be smudging the lines in the next step. You just want to deposit a bit of graphite that you can move around.

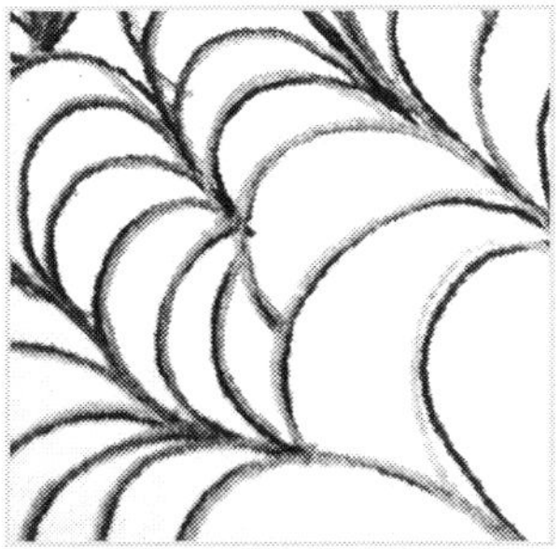

PERFECTION NOT REQUIRED.

Step 2. Gently smudge the pencil lines you just put down, moving in the same direction you drew your lines. Think of it as tracing your pencil lines, but again, you don't have to be too careful here, just make sure that the shadows stay close to the pen lines. It is easy to put down too much here and ruin the effect by turning the whole area gray.

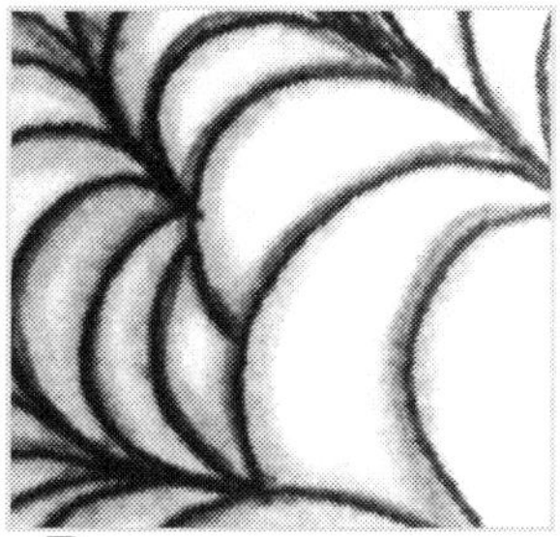

BLENDING SMOOTHS AND SOFTEN.

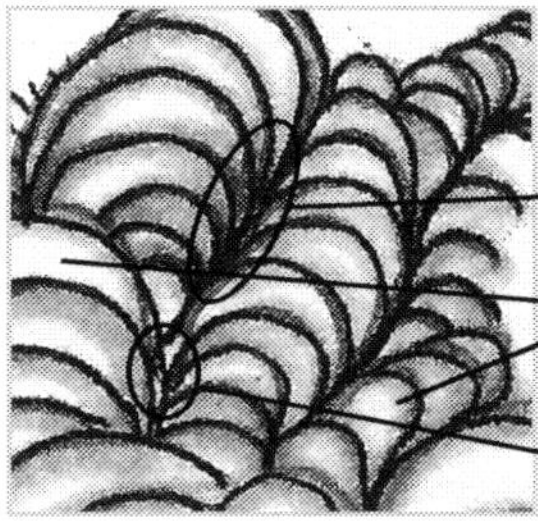

Step 3. Now add extra shading along the edges of each arc, where they intersect. You can press harder in this area and smudge from the edges towards the middle. Make sure that you leave the middle of each arc unshaded. This will cause the center to appear raised and give your piece a beautiful 3-dimensional look. There are a few spots where the SQUIRMY doesn't seem to fill completely. Locate those and color them with your pen. This will add an area of high contrast which adds interest.

Step 4. Finally, shade your MSST. If you shade darkly, just where it runs into the SQUIRMY, it will look as the MSST is coming from behind the SQUIRMY. Blend the dark out towards the dots and aim for a nice smooth shadow. I always leave the dots unshaded.

Here is my final version. I also shaded a bit, just with my tortillion, around the outside, since the string disappeared, and I didn't like how it was just floating there.

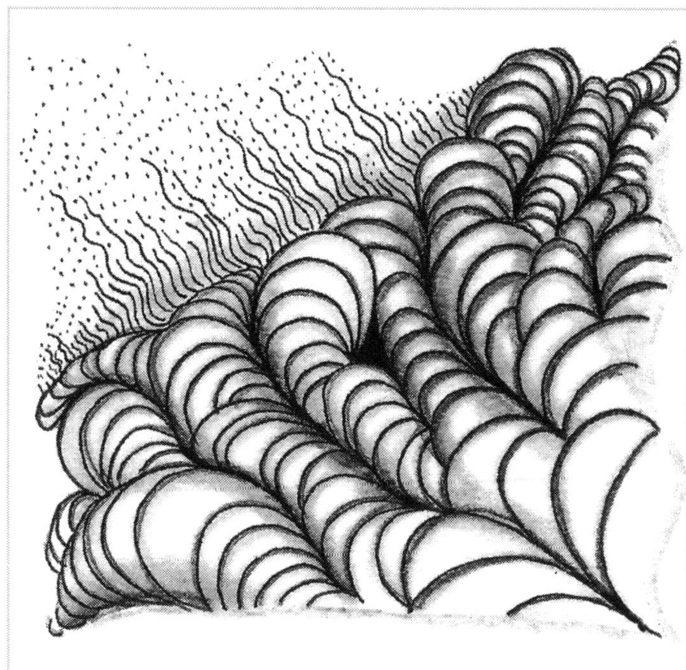

Project 3: Enhancing a Focal Point

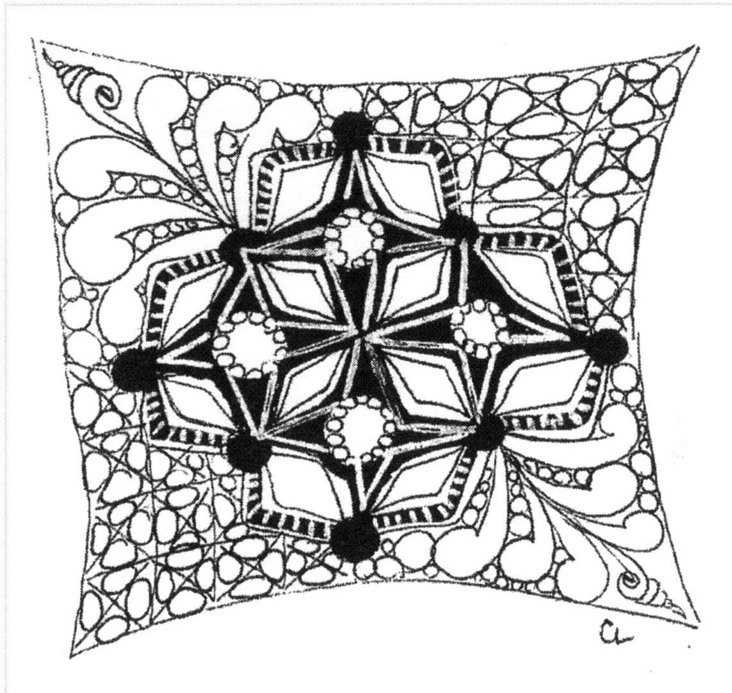

It can be challenging when nothing immediately jumps out as a starting place to tangle. That happened on this one. When it does, I don't do my shading immediately. I put my tile on the fridge or my desk where I can see it often and wait until the inspiration strikes. Turning it around for a different perspective can help.

Evaluation:

All of the 'NZEPPEL and the TIPPLE around the FLUX look very busy and blend into one another as a medium value. There are nicely defined dark areas, but the light areas are getting lost in all of that pen work. I'll use shading to enhance the light areas and also give the eye a place to rest. That will help with the overall busy feel of the piece.

The Process:

This tile does have some nice white areas; the FLUX in the corners is completely white, but it doesn't stand out against the busy background. To make the FLUX appear lighter, and thus more attention-getting, shade around the outside of them. A heavy contrast will make them pop, so shade darkly here.

TIP: *It is easy enough to darken sections of your tile, but lightening areas can't be done without resorting to white-out or paint. Keep this in mind when you are tangling.*

Step 1. Take your favorite soft pencil and draw just around the outside of the FLUX, going right over the TIPPLE surrounding it. You can make a nice thick line here, so take your time and use a very soft pencil. Then take your blender and soften the edges on the outside only. Since the goal is to increase the contrast between the

FLUX and its surroundings, don't smudge into the FLUX. You want to keep that line sharp. Not only does this increase the contrast, making the FLUX pop, but it also makes it seem to cast a shadow which tricks your mind into believing that the FLUX are on top of the TIPPLE below them.

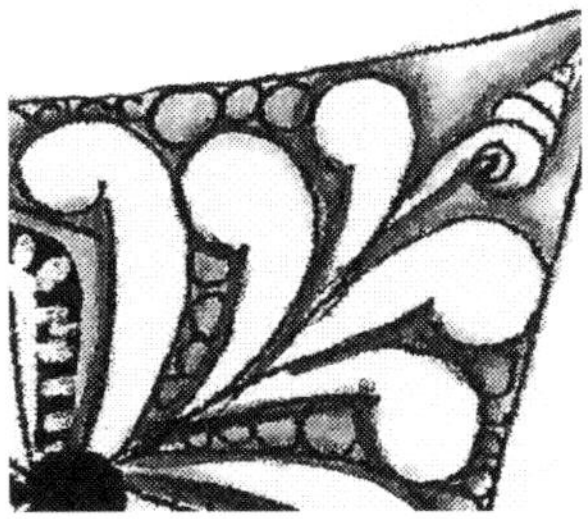

With its new darker background, the white FLUX *really stands out.*

Step 2. Even more FLUX shading. To make this effect even more pronounced, go back over the original shading line with a softer pencil. If you don't have a softer pencil, just go back and press harder to get a darker line. It doesn't matter if you completely hide the part of the TIPPLE that is right next to the FLUX. It will just help to increase the contrast.

Step 3. Tame the background. I love 'NZEPPEL, but in this tile, there is still a lot going on and it is one of many things competing for attention. To tame the 'NZEPPEL, shade around the center shapes and around the inside of the frame, right over the 'NZEPPEL. This pushes it into the shadow, so it is still visible, but not screaming for attention. In this case, you don't want to completely hide the 'NZEPPEL, just let it hang out in the background. See how nice it looks with a little of the 'NZEPPEL unshaded? Take care to leave that area as a highlight, so it doesn't look as you just decided to give that area a coat of gray paint.

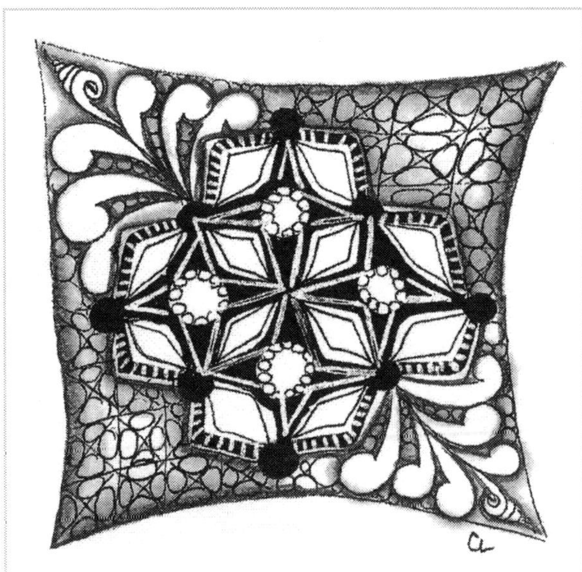

I've finished even though I feel there may be room for detail shading in the center. I stopped because I'm afraid of things getting that busy look back. But don't let that stop you. Give it a try and see what happens.

Project 4: Shading ZIA

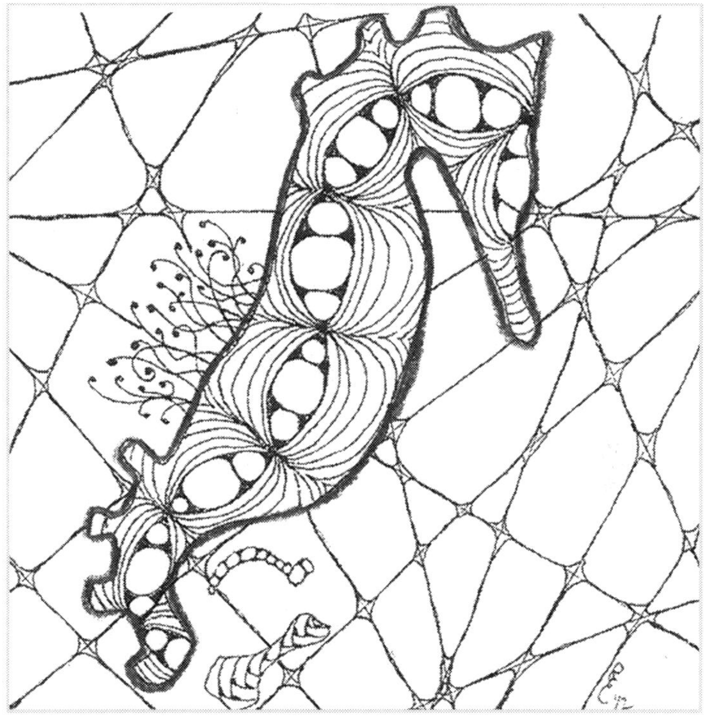

Sometimes instead of a Zentangle tile, which is abstract, you may have something that is intended to look like something else. That is called Zentangle-Inspired Art, or ZIA. While there is no doubt you can shade ZIAs the same way you can a tile, sometimes you want your shading to enhance the realism. This project is a ZIA seahorse by CZT Emily Classon. She created her "string" by tracing a seahorse stencil.

Evaluation:

This seahorse is so adorable that I want to make sure he stays the focal point. He is a bit darker than the background, but the contrast could be improved with shading. I'd like to have him look more 3-dimensional, so I will shade him to do that. I want to add interest to the background with shading, but I need to keep it light so there will be a good contrast between the water area and the seahorse. I feel using some scumbling or stippling might add an interesting texture and suggest waves. The 'NZEPPEL reminds me a bit of a net, and I'd like to minimize this. I don't want the little guy trapped!

The Process:

Since I wanted to experiment with this one, the first thing I did was to make a photocopy of the original so I could test some things out. It is a good thing I did. My first attempt was way too dark, so I made another copy and started over. If you are worried about trying something totally new or wild, making a photocopy is a good idea. That way you can let go totally and not have to stress about permanently "messing up" your original.

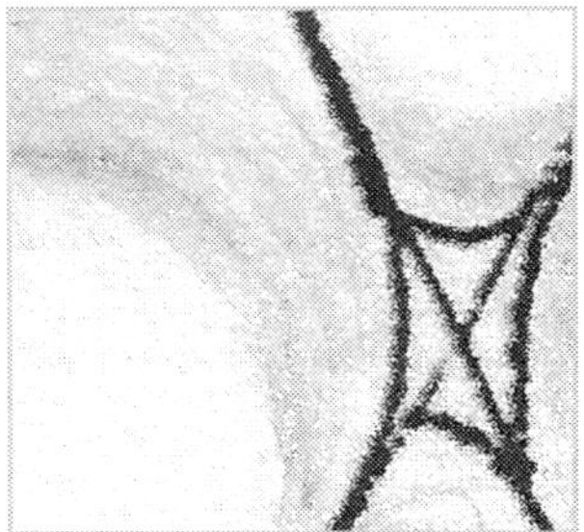

STEP 1: SHADING WITH CONTOUR HATCHING

Step 1. On my first attempt, I started with the seahorse and ended up tossing it because the background was unacceptably dark. So, this time, I started on the background instead. I used a 4H pencil and did extra light contour hatching to shade around the corners of the 'NZEPPEL to round them out. If you have a heavy hand, you may want to use an even harder pencil, or instead of contour hatching, you may want to shade with your blender. I want them to look more like bubbles than a fishing net.

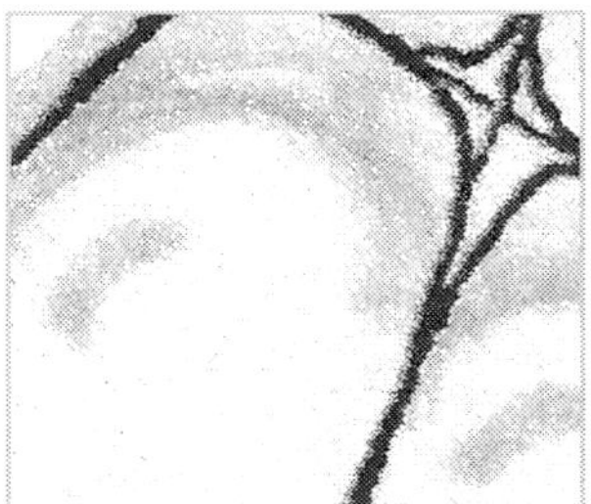

STEP 2: "SMILE" MARK TO SUGGEST FORM

Step 2. I took my dirty blender and put little "smiles" in each of the rounded 'NZEPPEL spaces to suggest a more rounded shape. This made the background too dark again, so I went back with a kneaded eraser and gently lifted out some of the graphite in the corners.

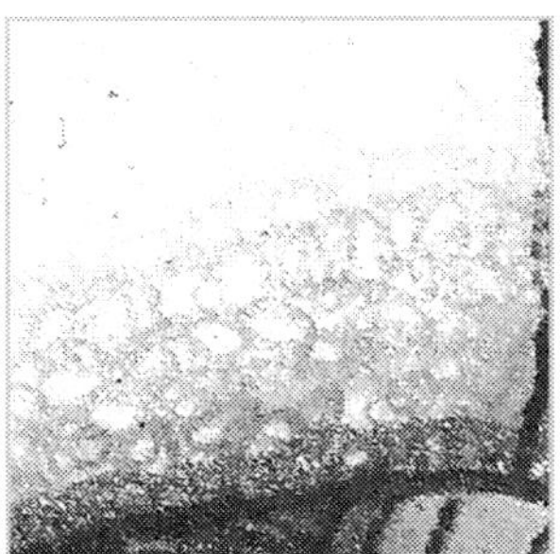

STEP 3: SCUMBLING DETAIL

Step 3. Now that I knew the background wasn't going to be too dark this time, I shaded around my seahorse so he would stand out. Since I wanted him to look as if he were in water, I decided to use scumbling. I first used a 4B pencil with medium pressure to make tiny circles right next to the outside of the seahorse. Then I went back in with a 4H pencil and went around again, half on and half off my original scumbling. I repeated going around with the 4H pencil 4 more times. After that, I went back with my 4B pencil and drew a fine line over the outline of the seahorse. (I had to sharpen my pencil twice on the way around to keep the tip sharp enough.)

Step 4. To make his dorsal fin look more realistic, instead of using a fine line inside the scumbling, I used hatching. I

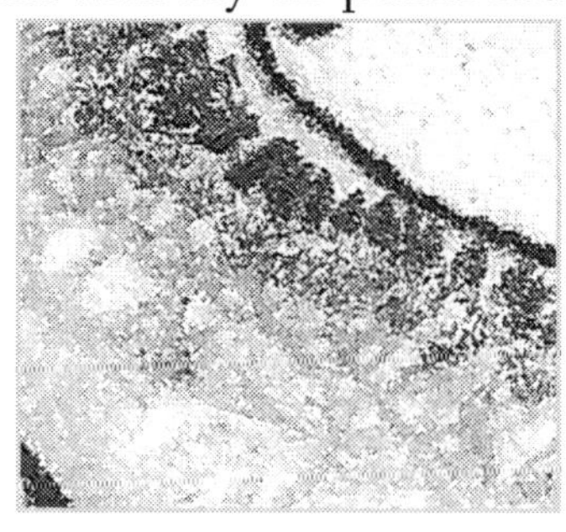

STEP 4: HATCHING ON THE DORSAL FIN.

like the texture of the lines next to the curves.

Step 5. Shade around the circles on the sea horse's back to make them pearls. A simple line with a 4B pencil blended round half the circle will do the trick.

Step 6. Shade the triangular areas on the outside of the sea horse's body, and then blend toward the center.

Step 7. Finally, give his nose some character by hatching in both pen and pencil. Make sure to leave a highlight.

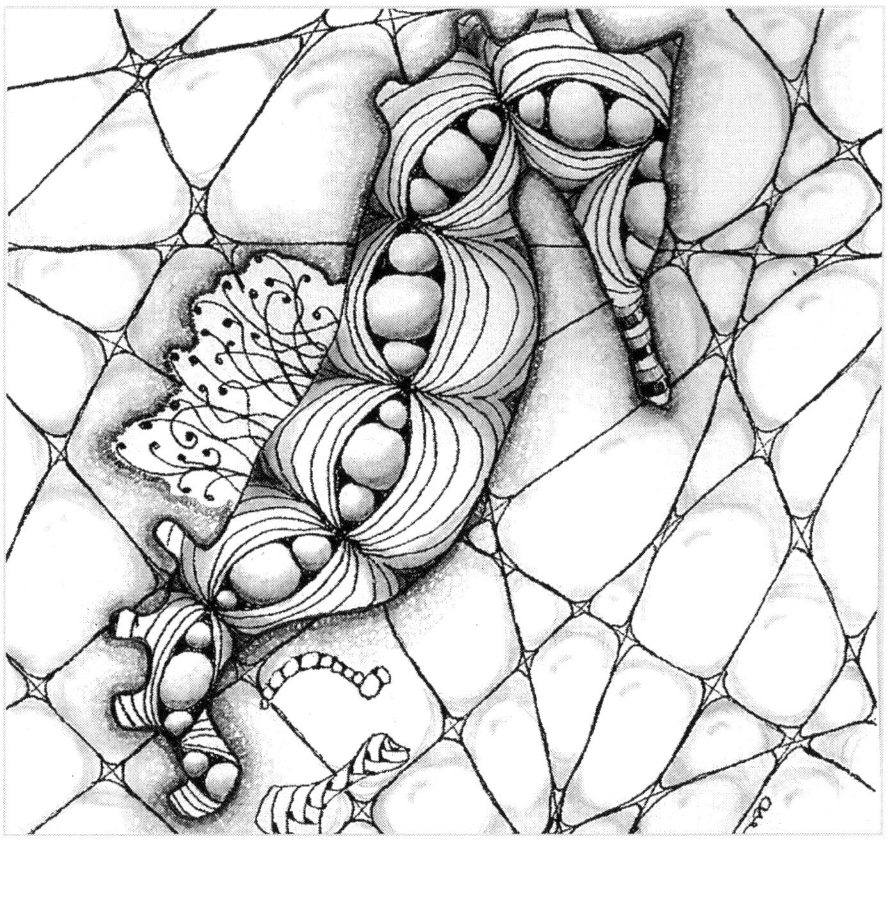

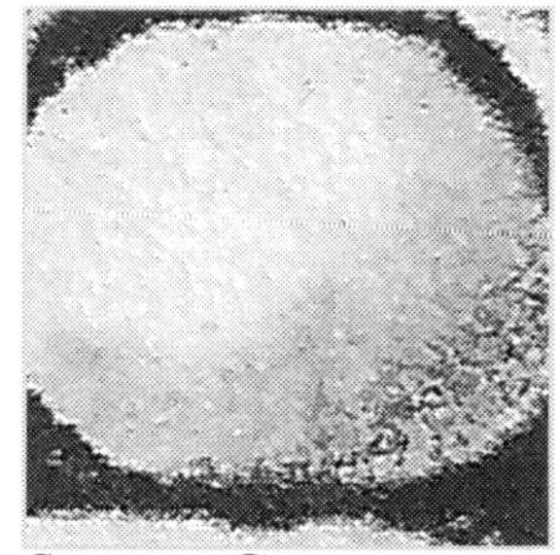

STEP 5: CIRCLE SHADING DETAIL.

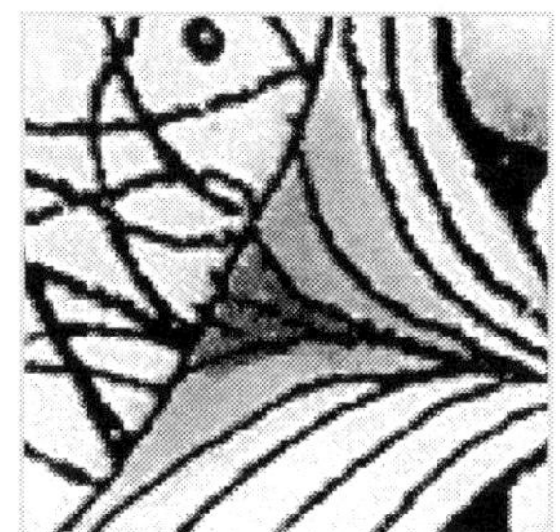

STEP 6: TRIANGLE SHADING DETAIL.

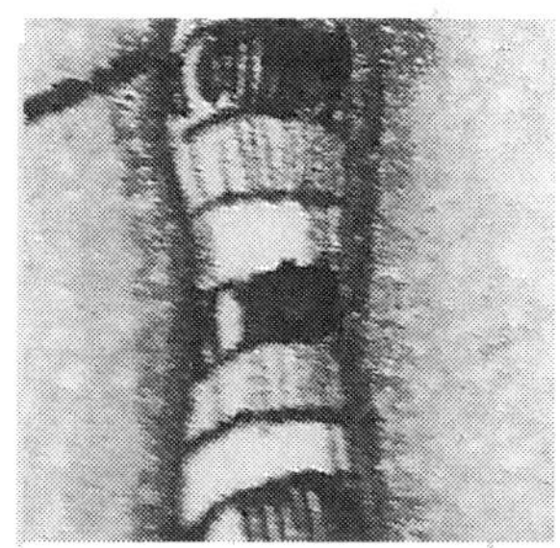

STEP 7: NOSE DETAIL.

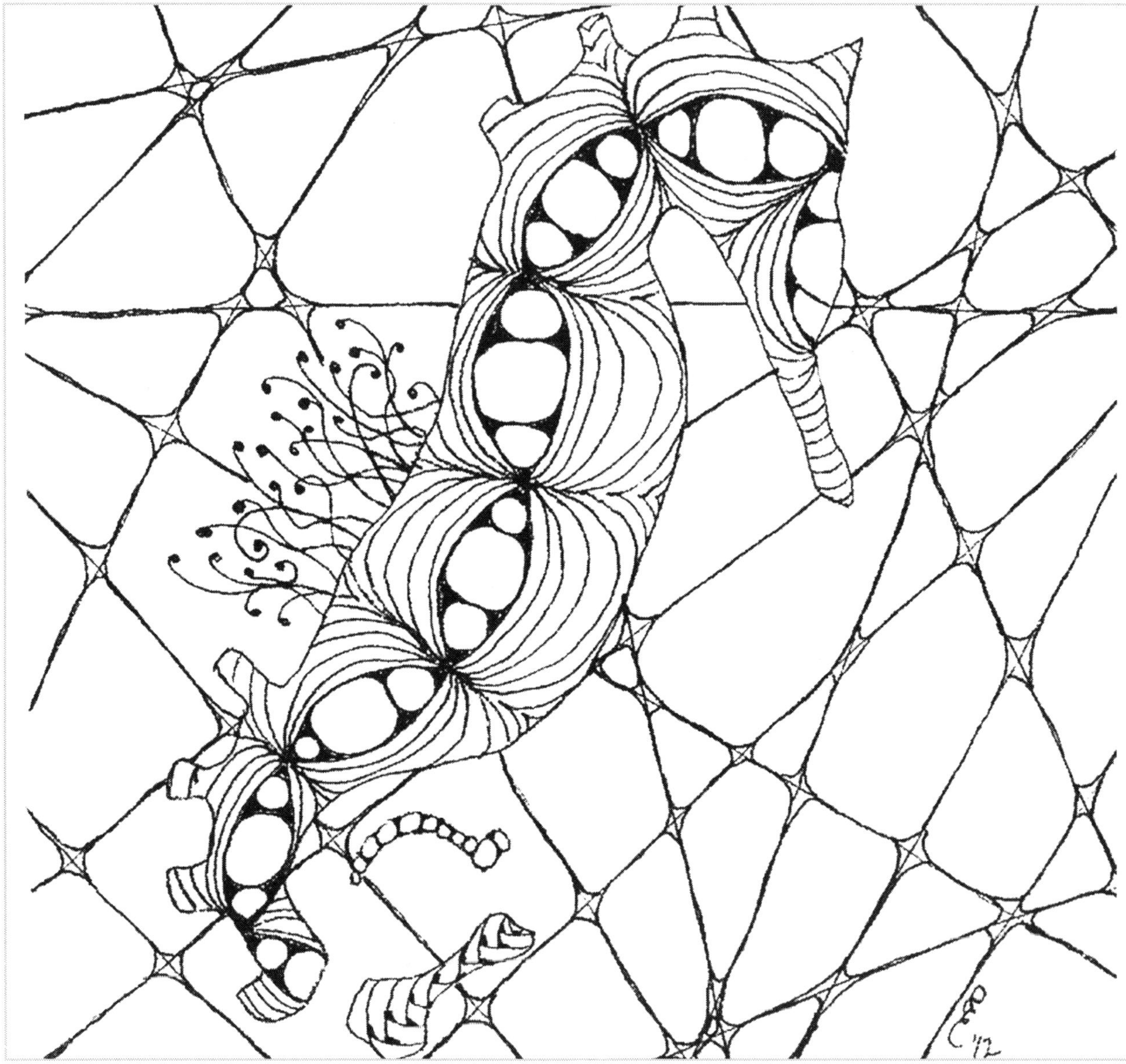

Exercise 60. *A Seahorse for you to go play with.*

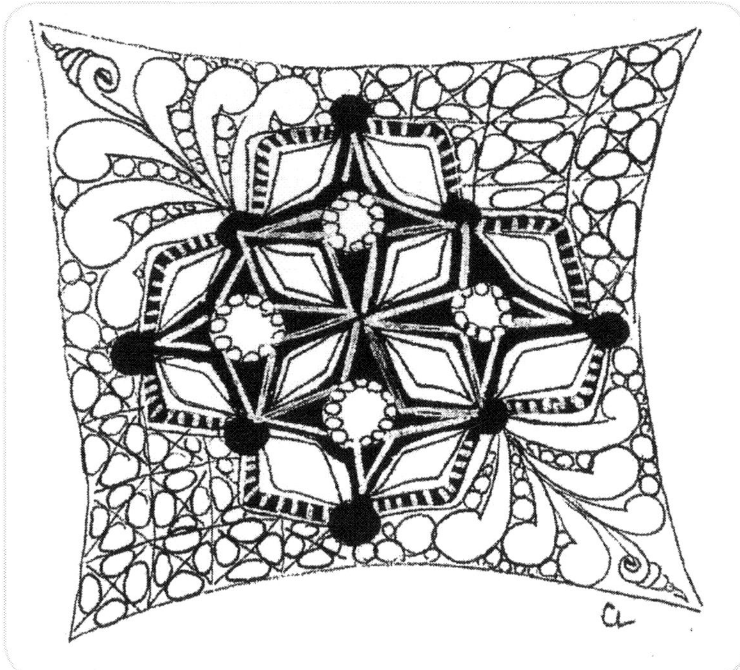

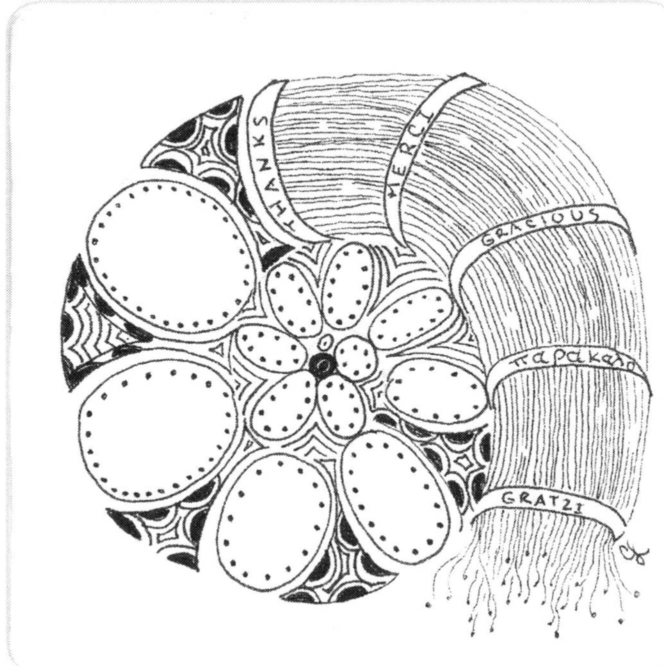

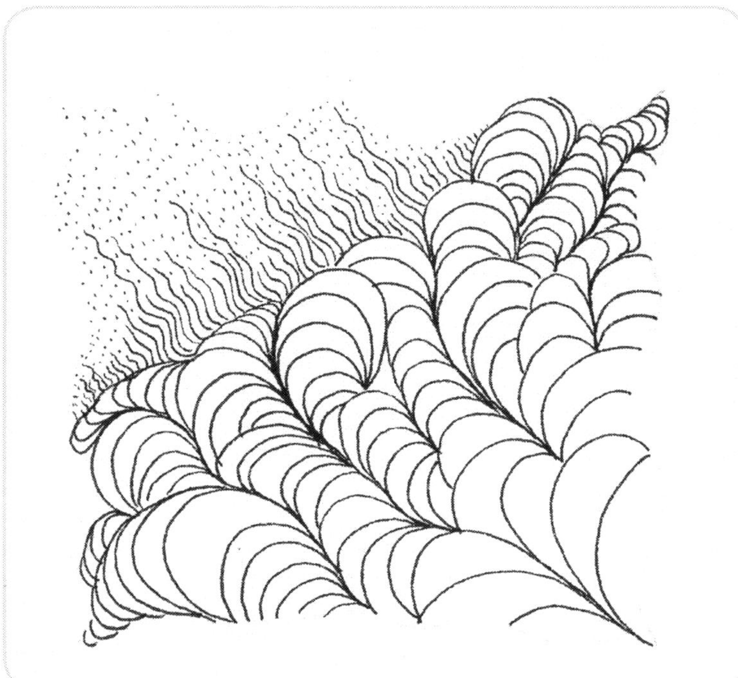

Exercise 61. ***As promised, here are the other three projects. Try your own ideas for shading them.***

Zonder Schadow

©Maria Vennekens 2012

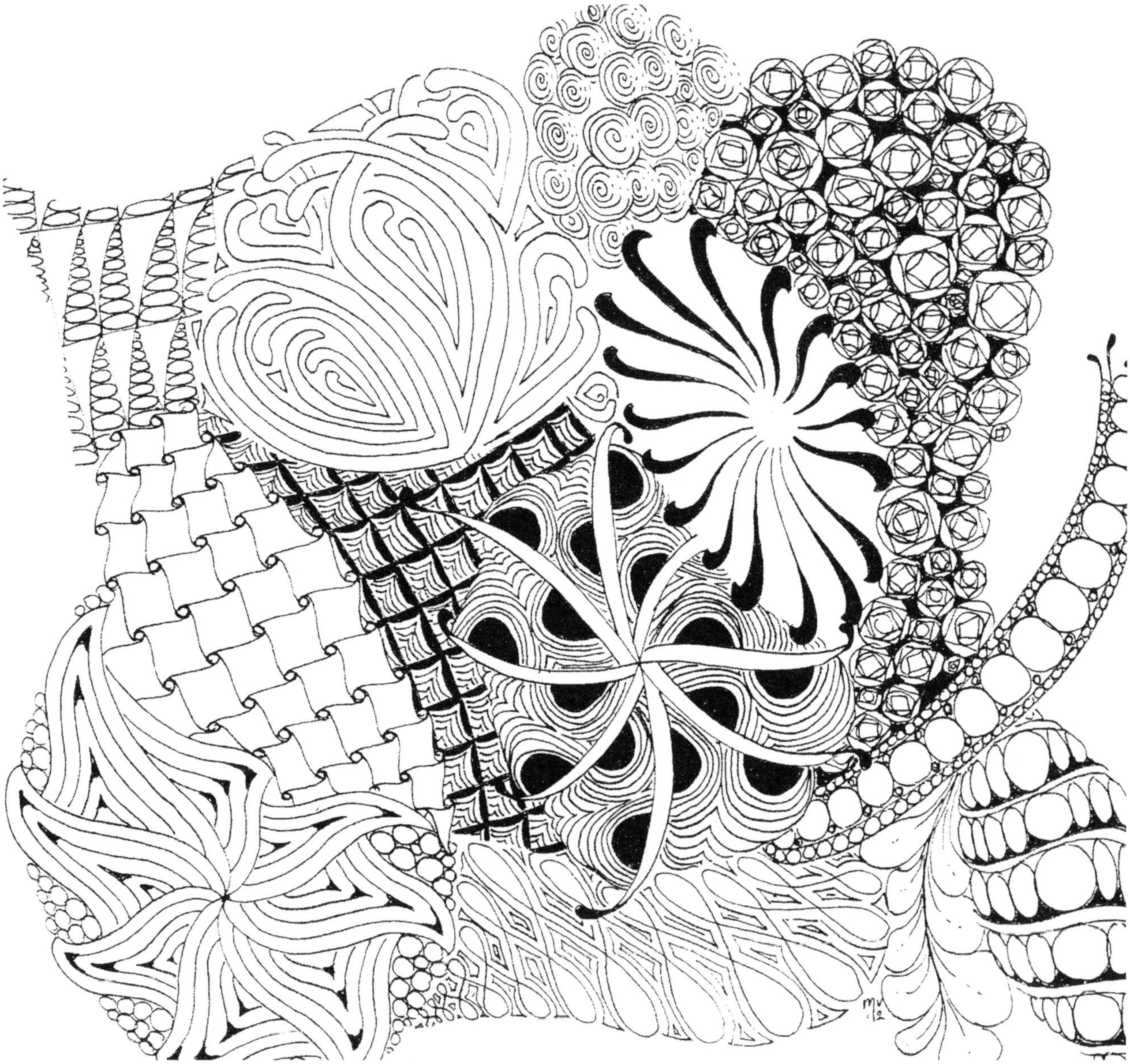

Tangles Used: MOOKA PRINTEMPS, CADENT, ONAMOTO, PURK, FLUX, IXORUS, VITRUVIUS, ECHOISM, WARBLE, FENGLE, *and* LOKOMOTIVE *by Stephanie Kukla*

CHAPTER 6 SHADING PLAYGROUND

The remainder of this book is your chance to use everything you have learned thus far. Consider it your playground full of completed Zentangle tiles, ZIAs, and artwork from talented artists around the world. It is fun to shade art that is different from your own style. Enjoy trying out your new skills and techniques.

You can start by shading Maria Vennekens's ZIA on the facing page.

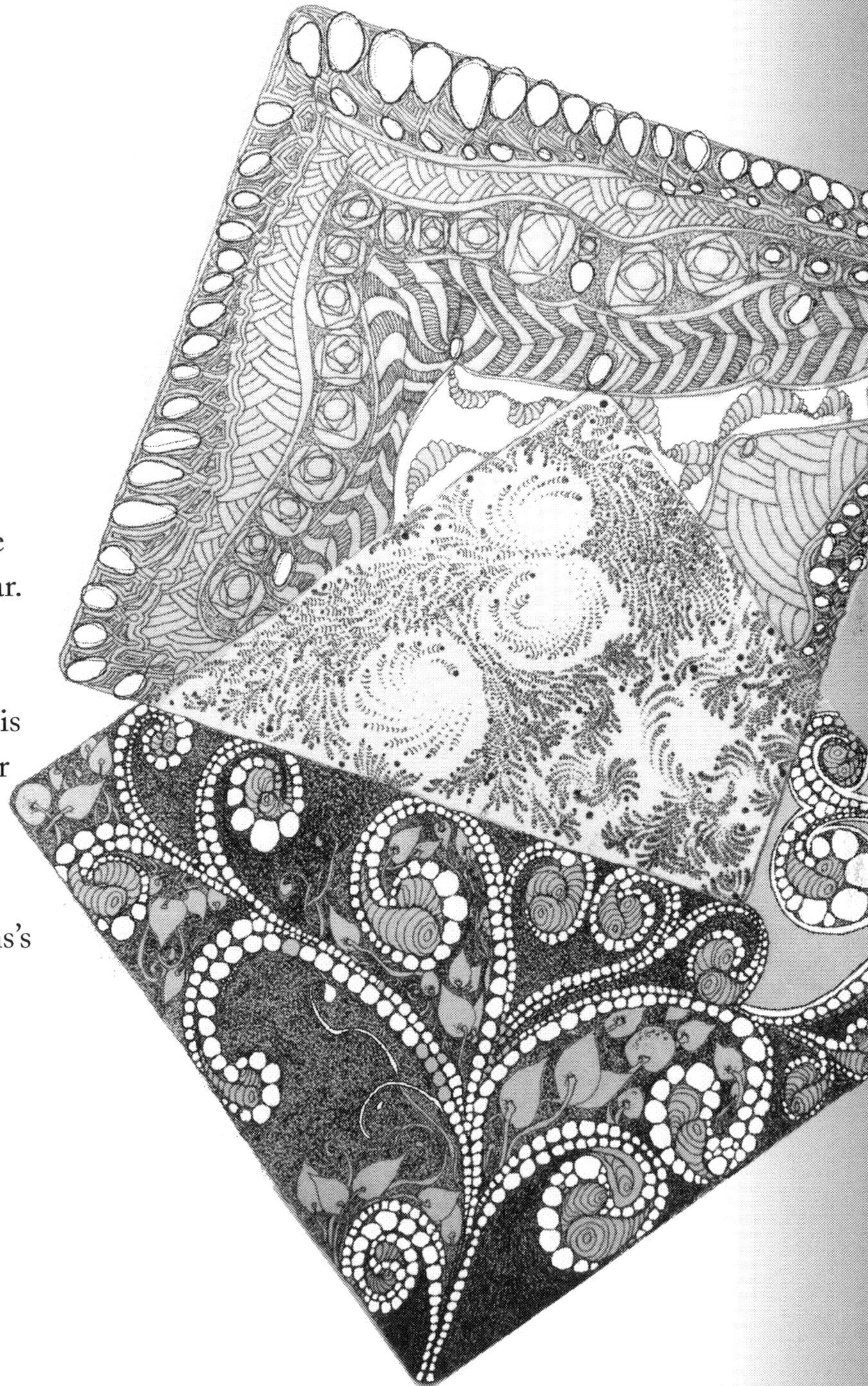

Original art ©Brinn McFetridge

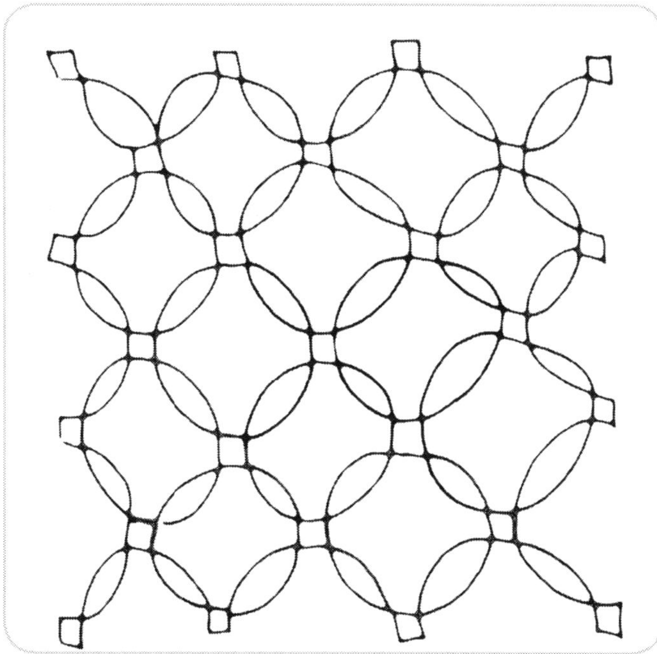

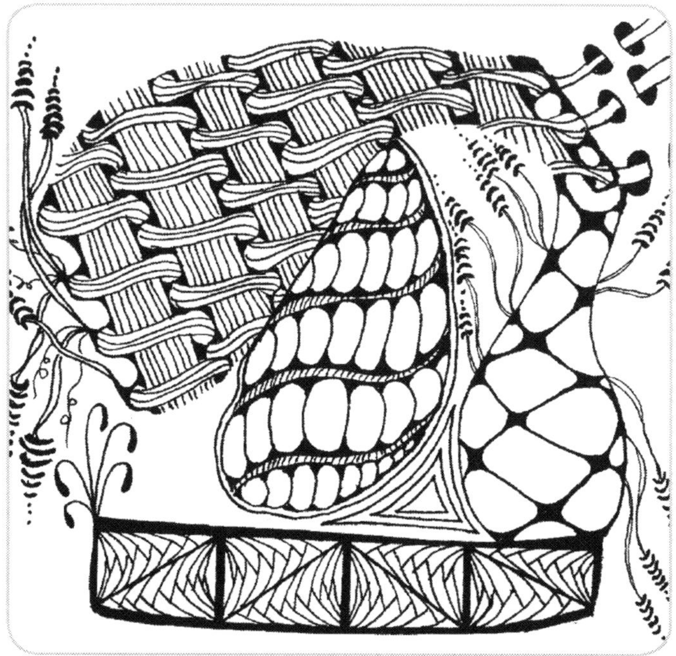

Original Tile by Alice Hendon

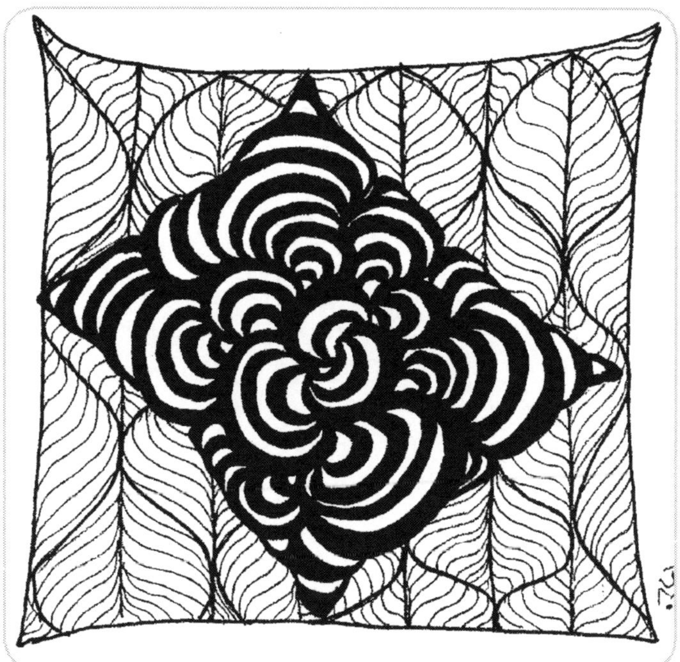

Original Tile by Jane MacKugler

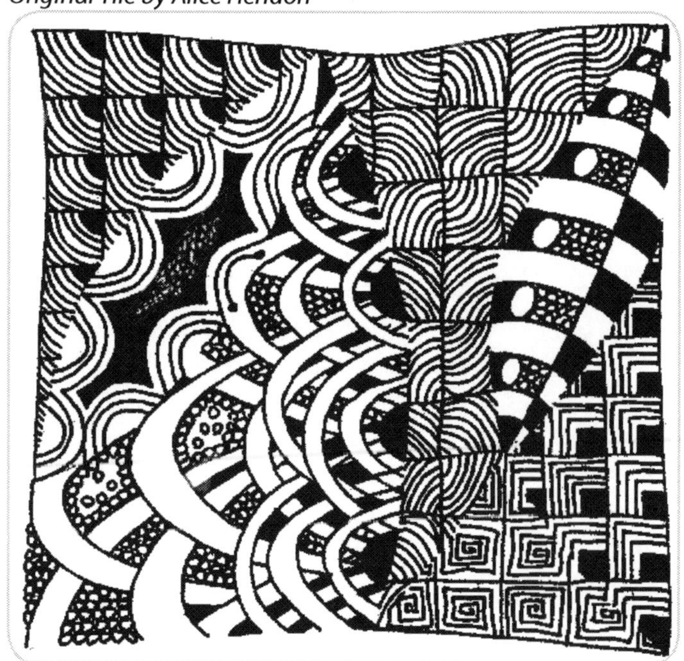

Original Tile by Margret Bremner

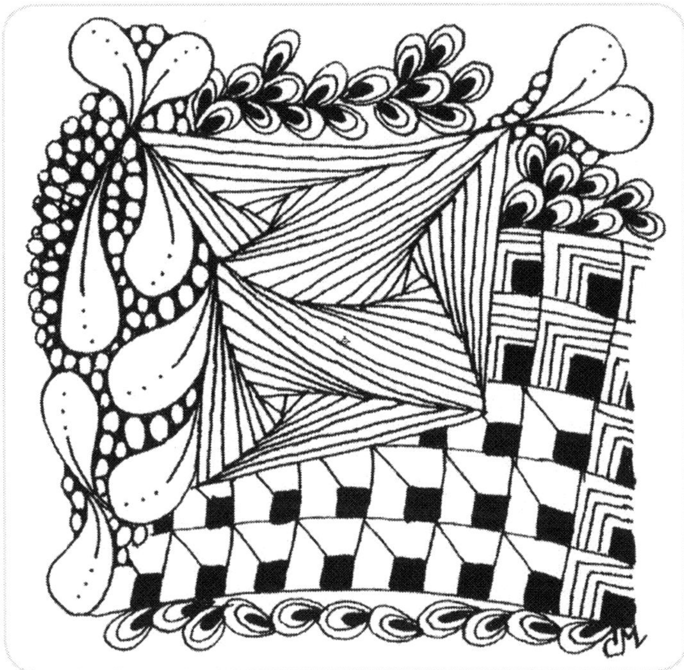

Original tile by Caren Mlot

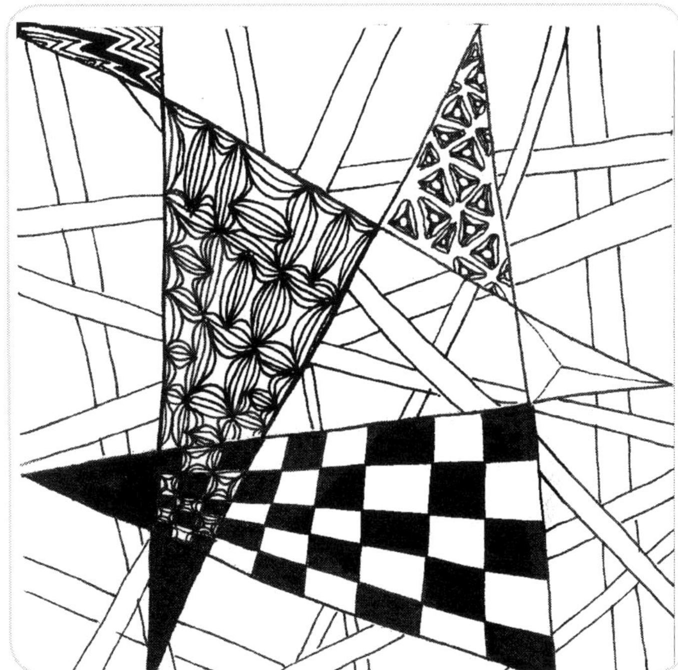

Original Tile by Sue Sharp

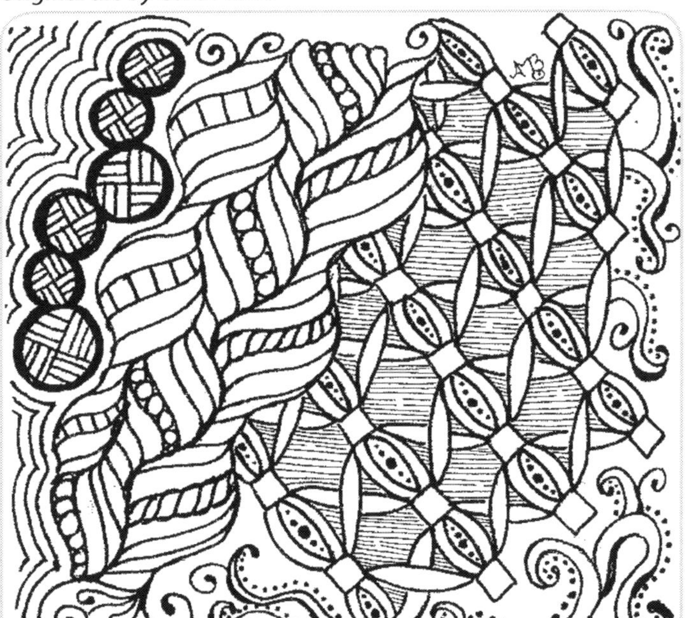

Original Tile by Amy Broady

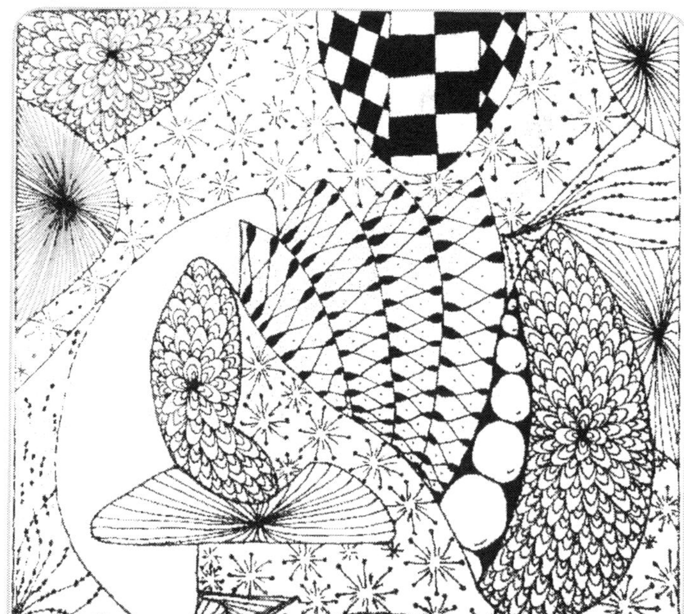

Original Tile by Ellen Gozeling

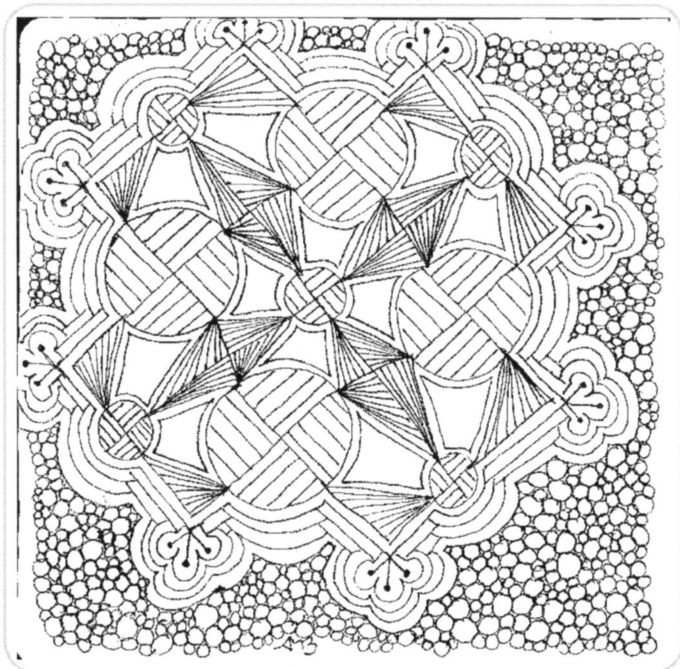

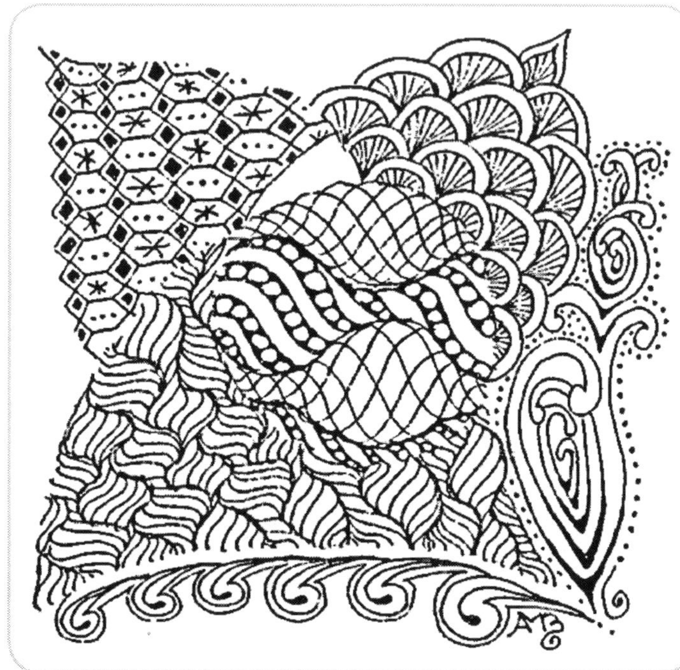

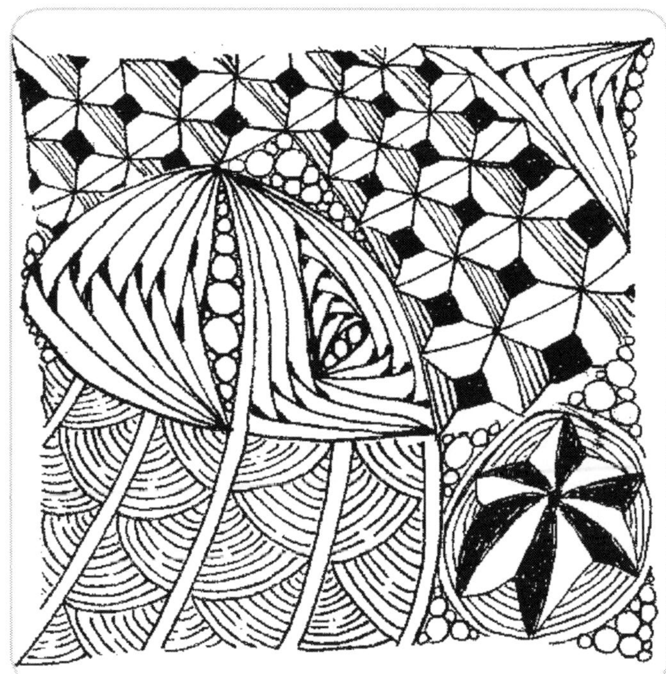

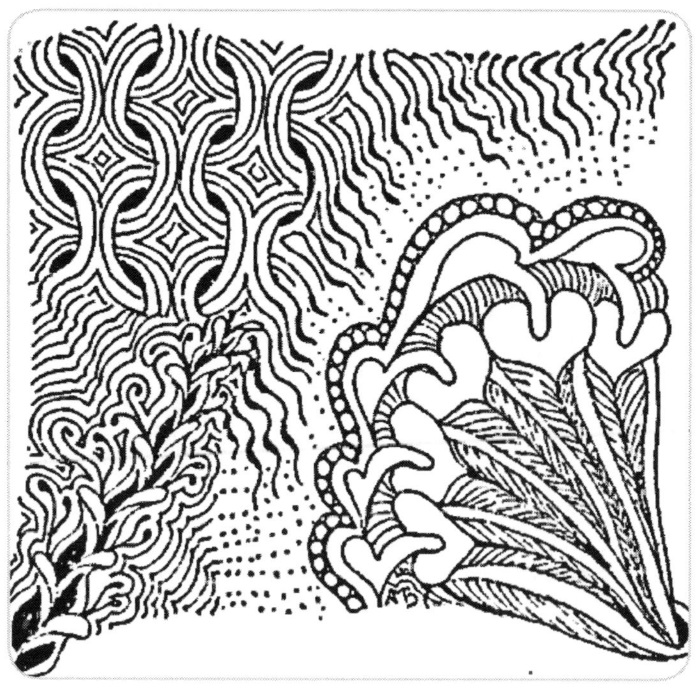

Original tiles on this page by Amy Broady

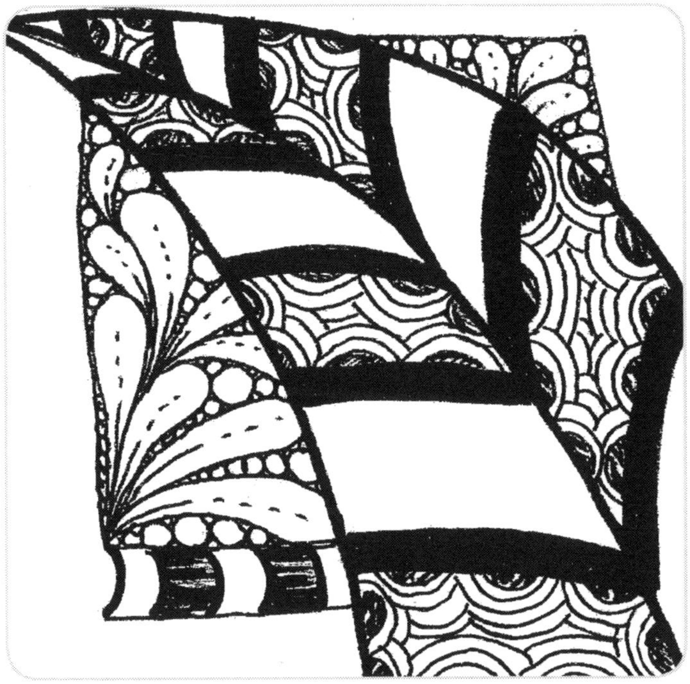

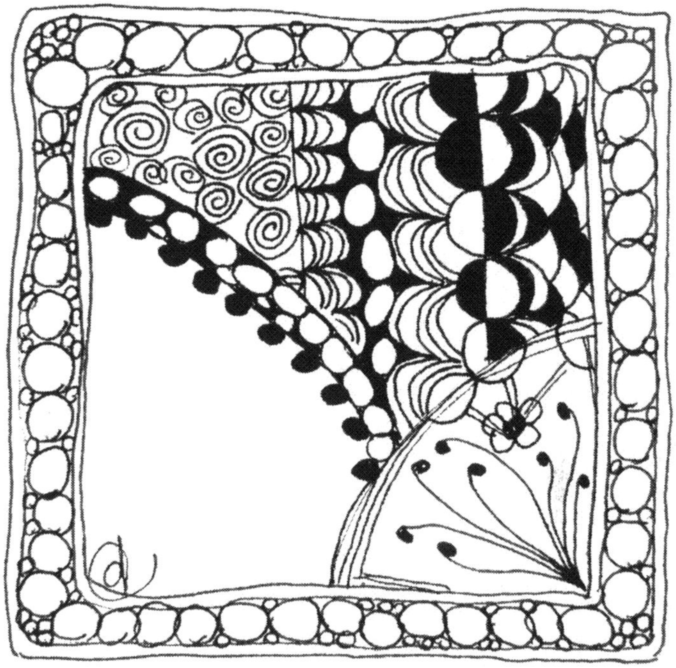

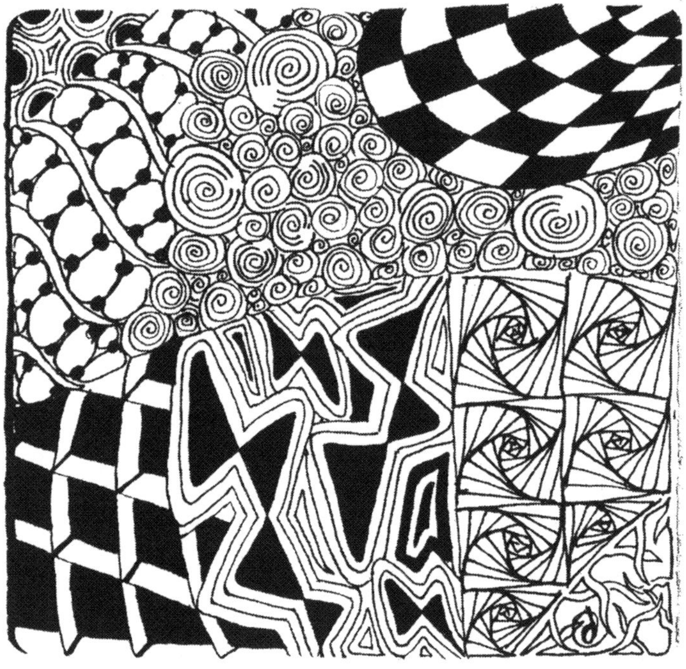

Original tiles on this page by Diana Hirsch

Notice how the tangles on this page by are darker than those on the facing page. Because they are somewhat dark to begin with, it is easy to over-shade them, so use a light touch with your shading. Maybe use a harder pencil than you usually do and make sure you leave some areas pure white.

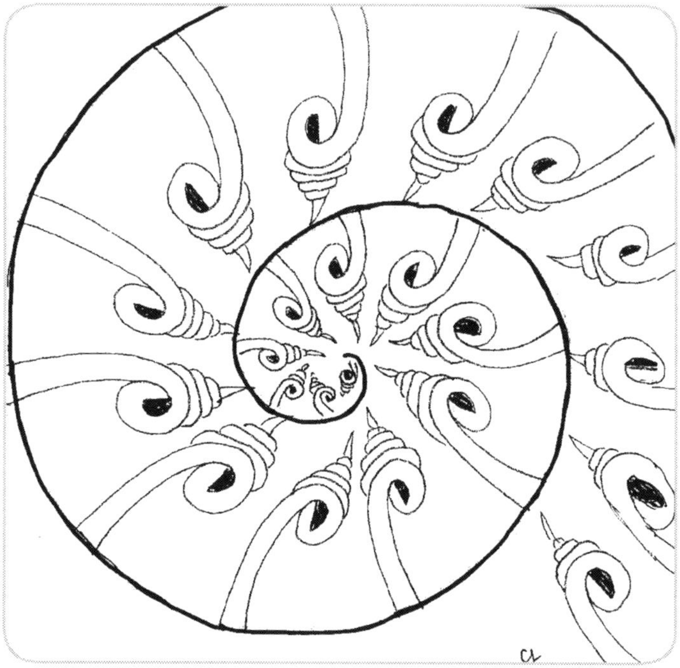

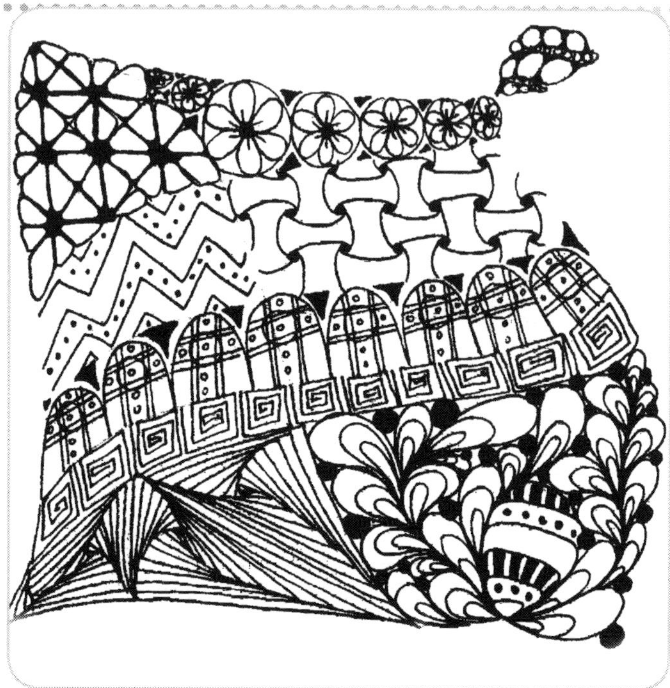

Original tile by Paula Dickerhoff

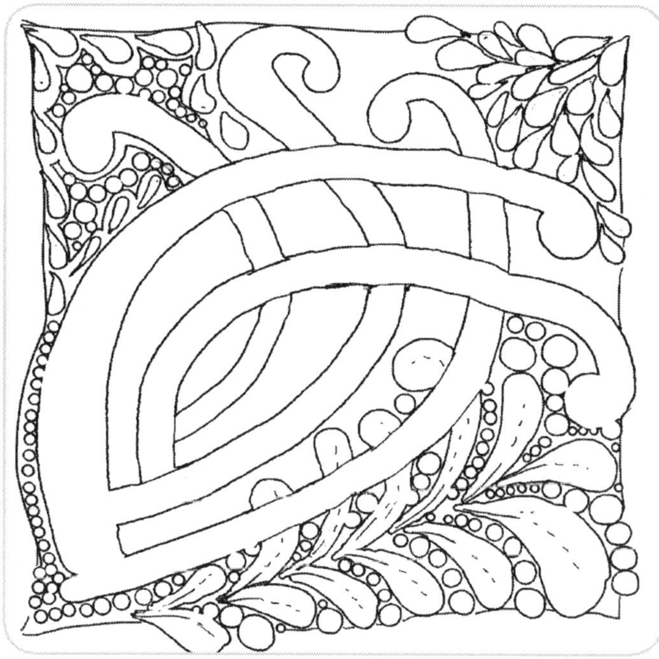

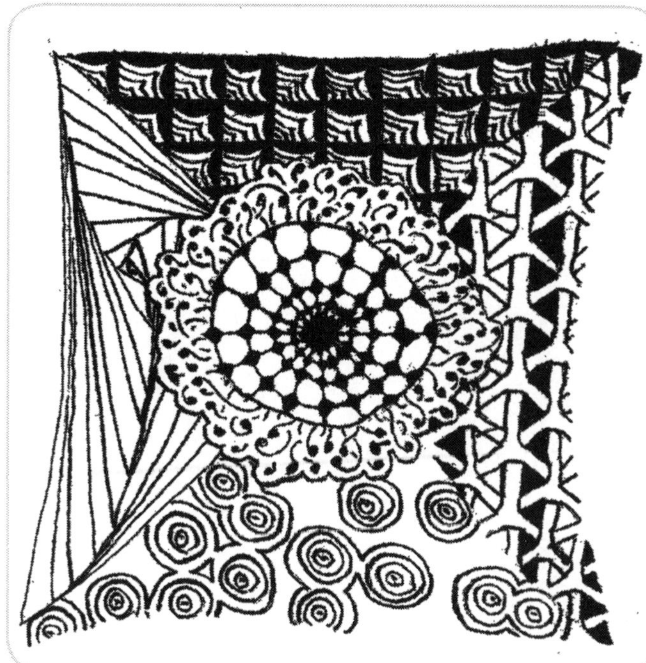

Original tile by Alexa Letourneau

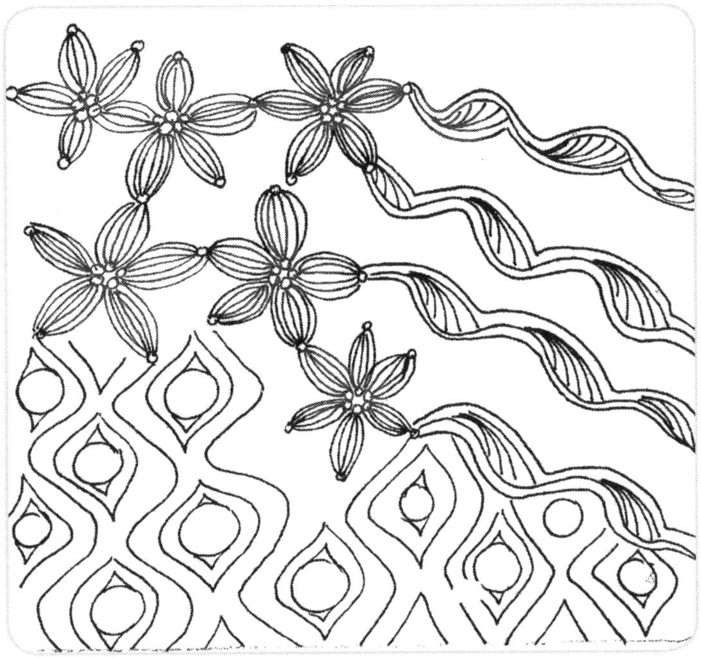

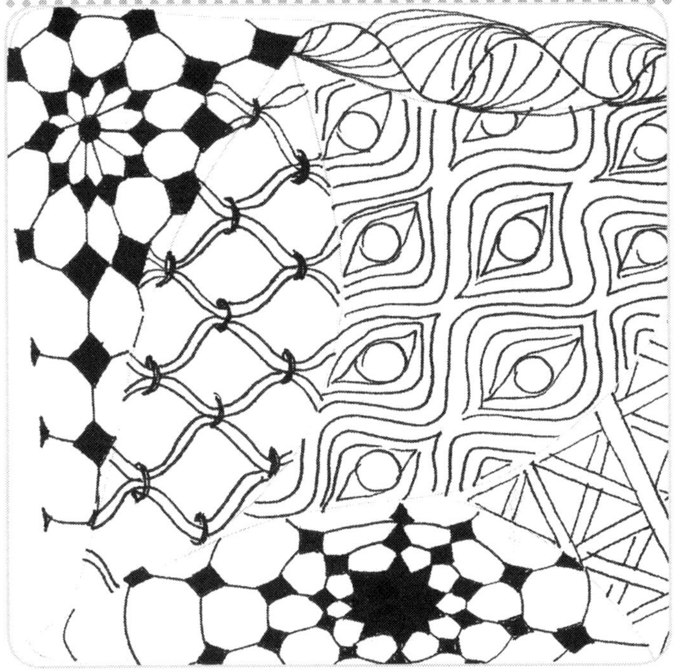

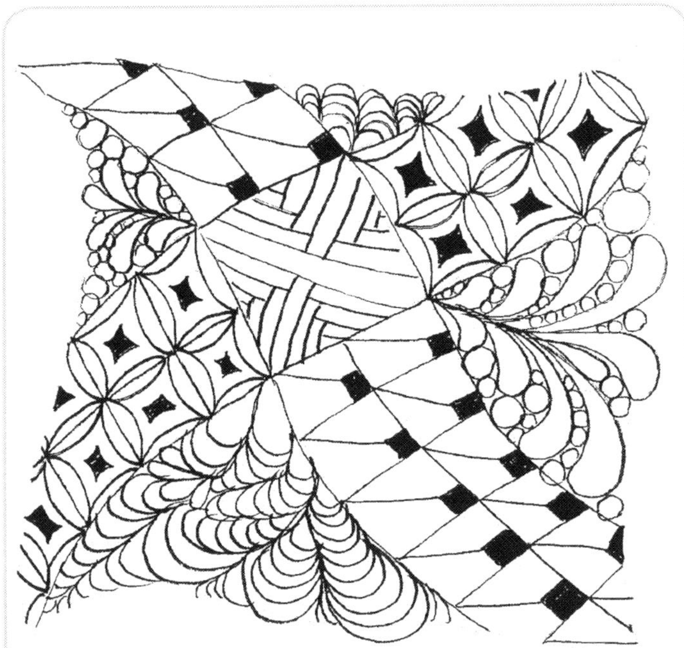

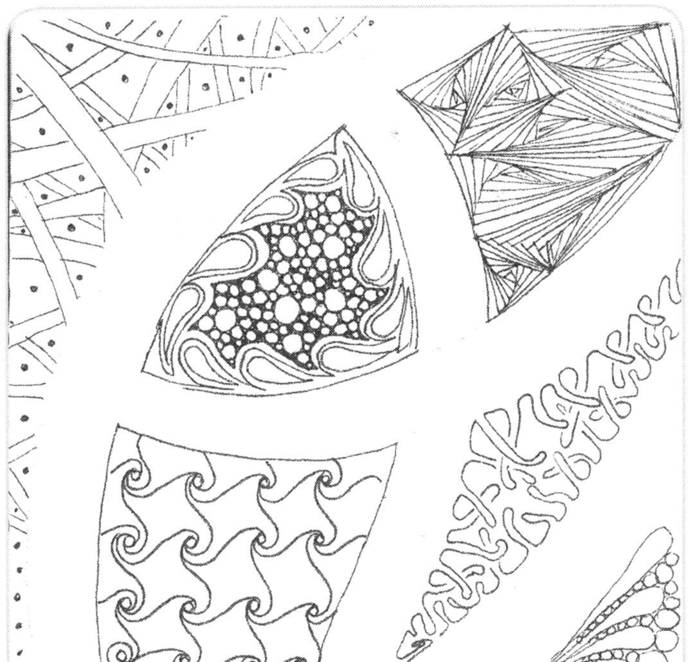

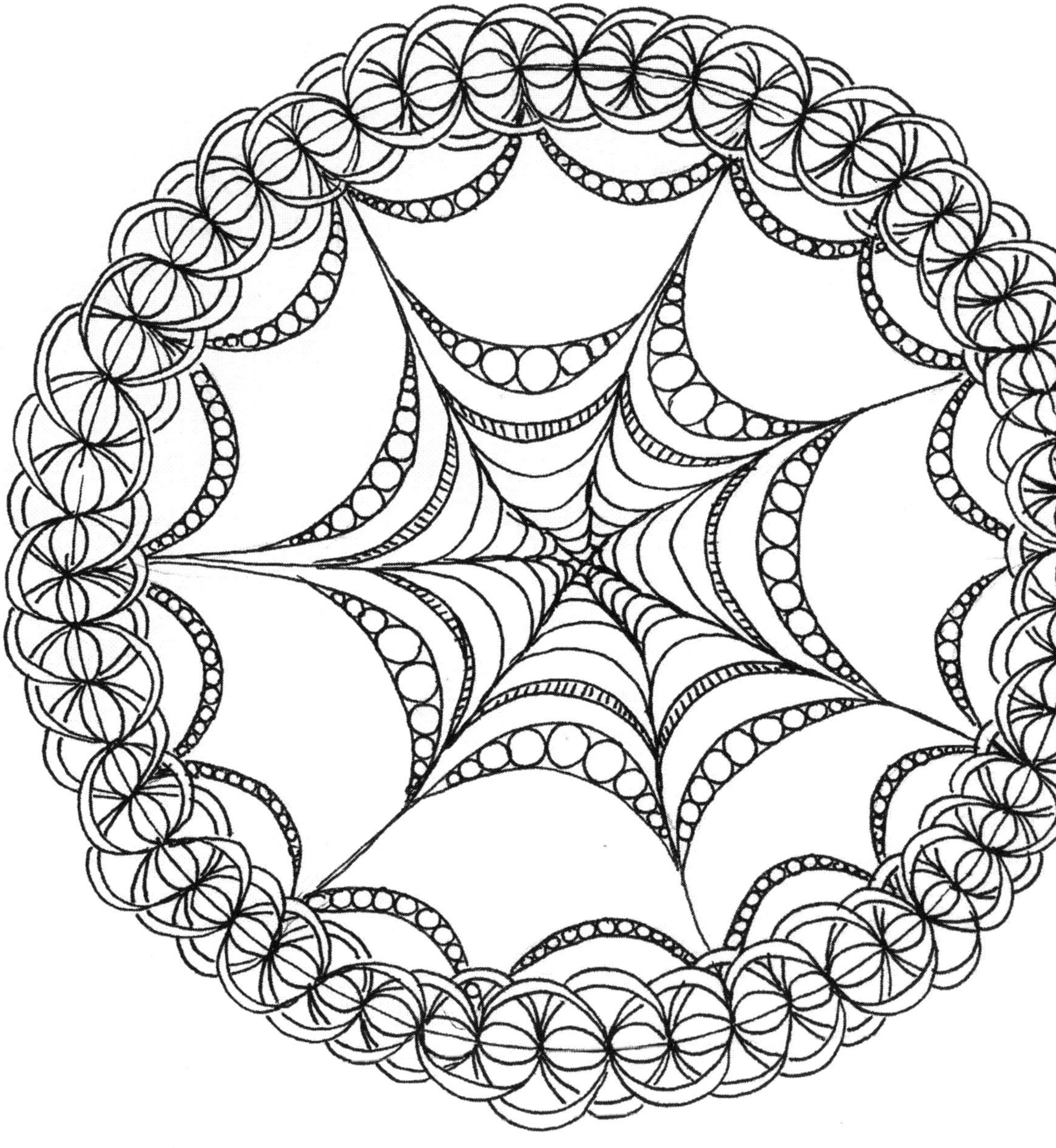

Zendala with STEF-AH-NI

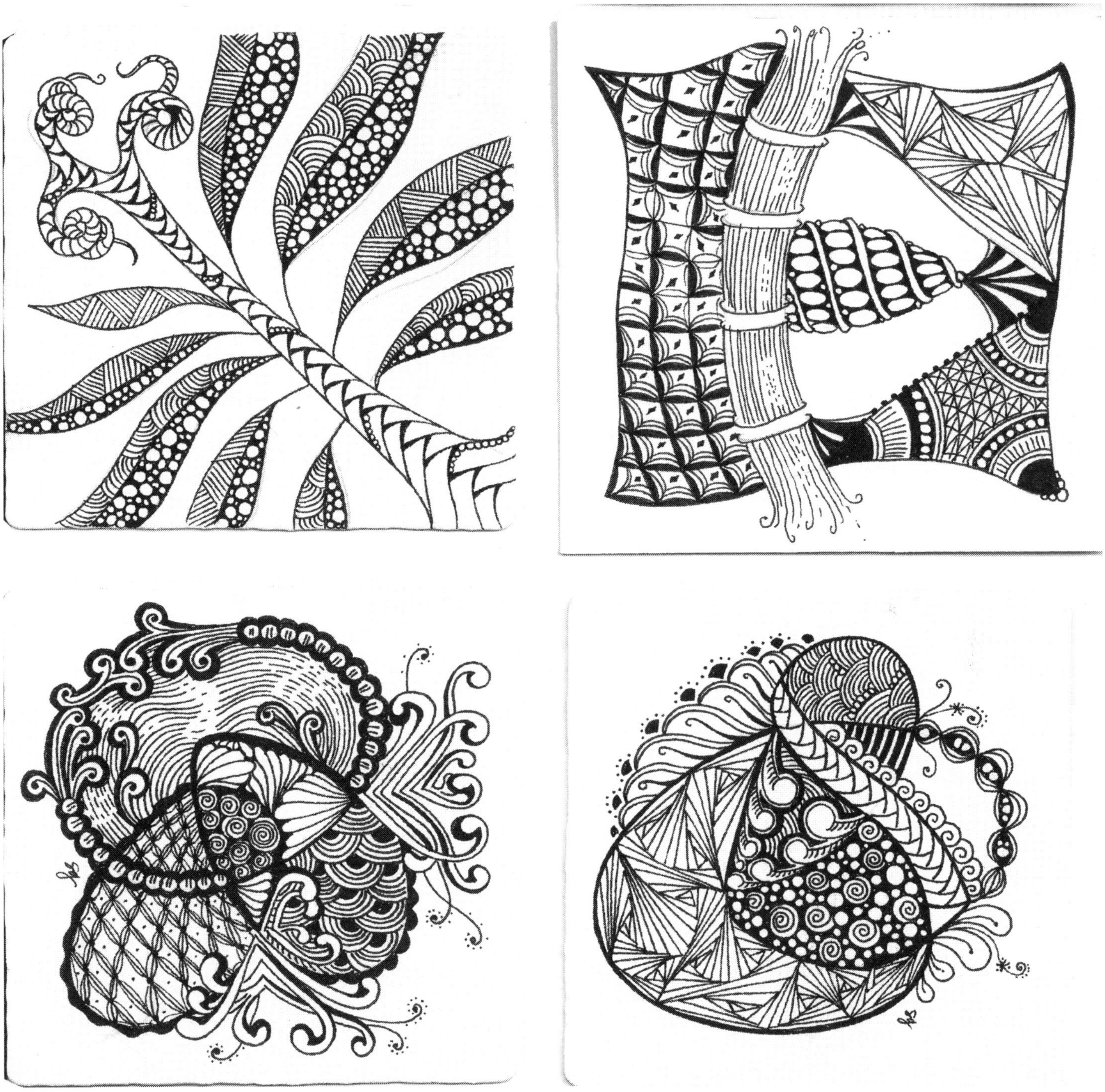

Four from Sonya Yencer

A

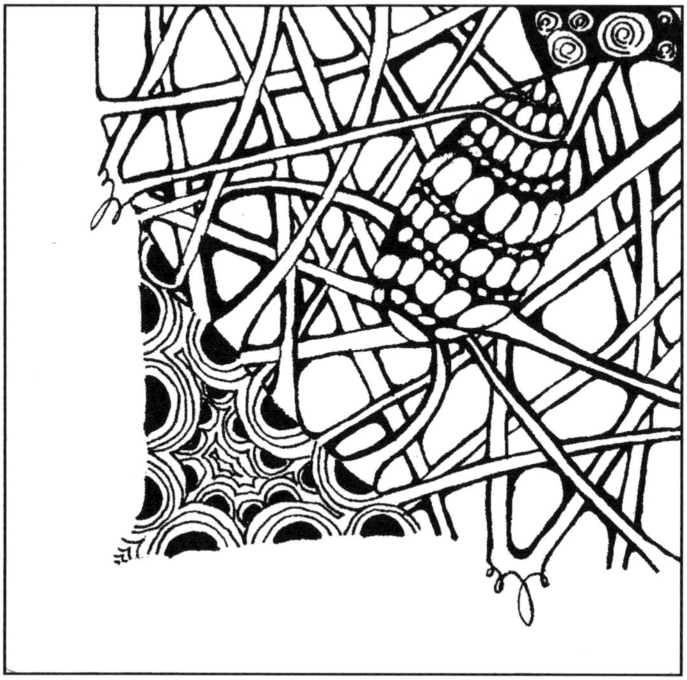

B

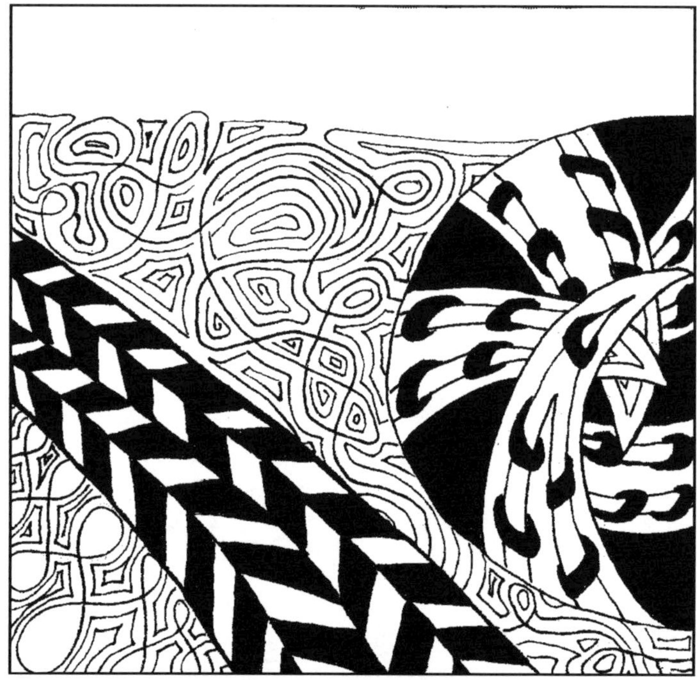

Ensemble: Sandy by Jane Menard

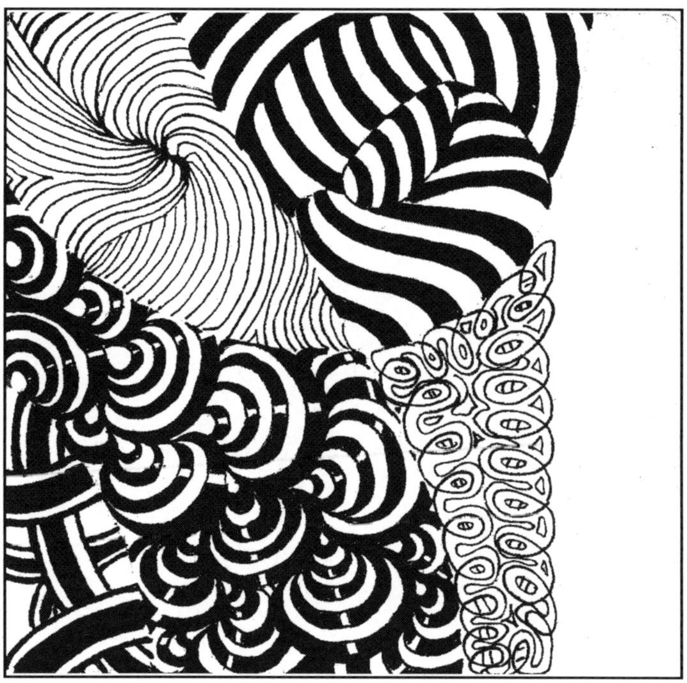

C

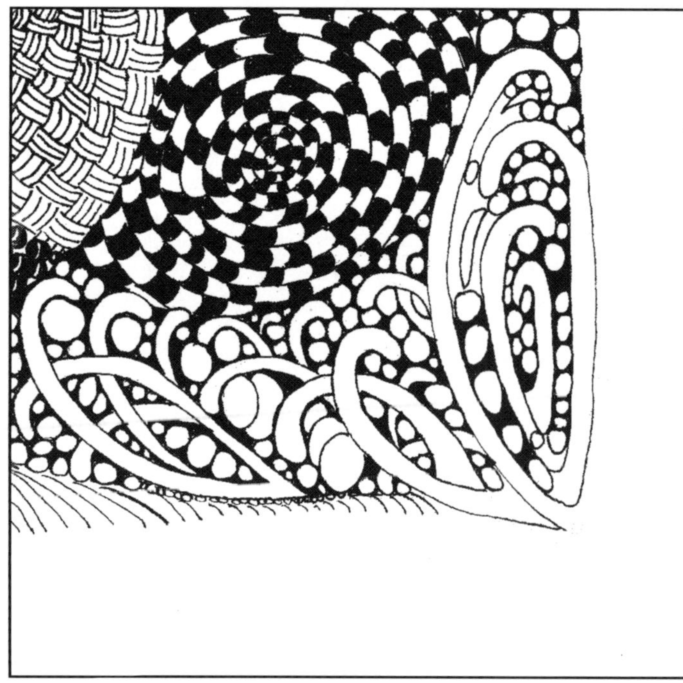

D

A

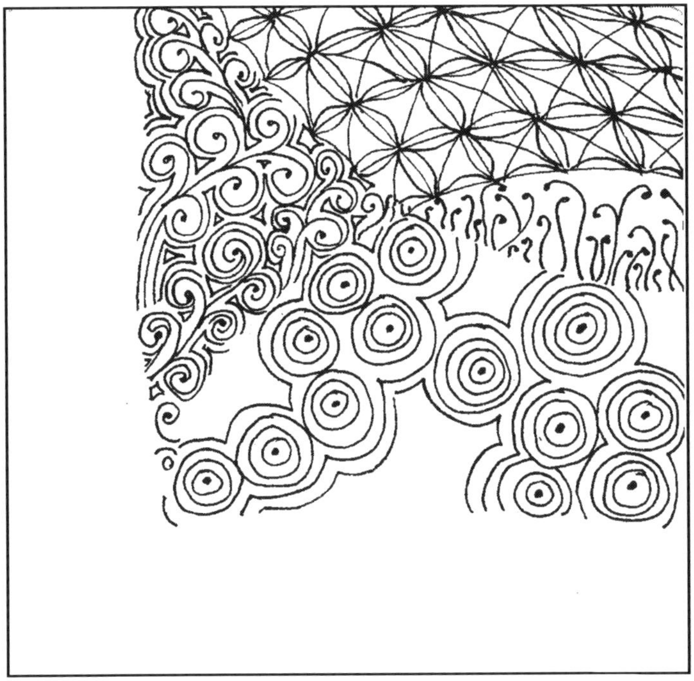

B

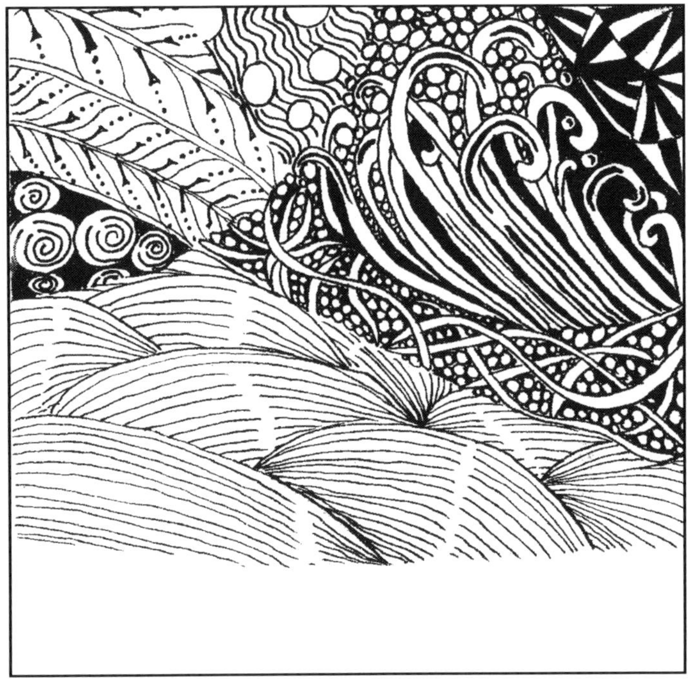

C

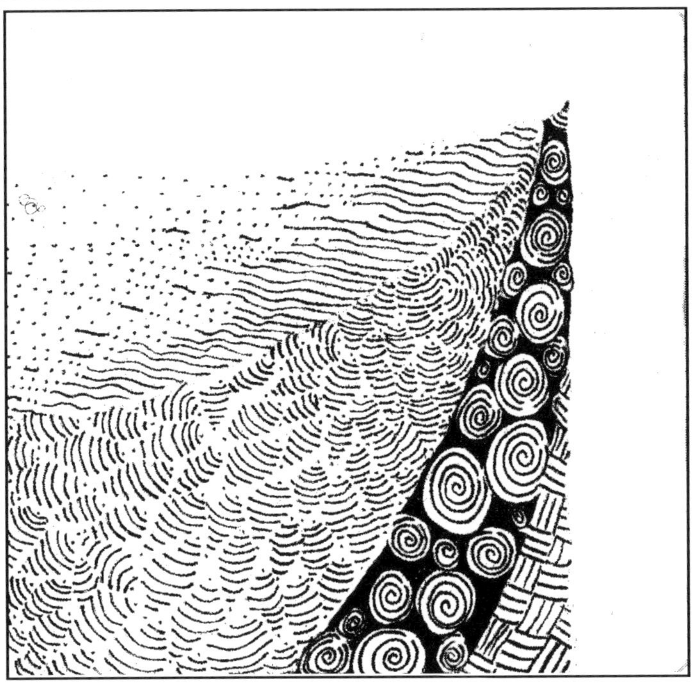

D

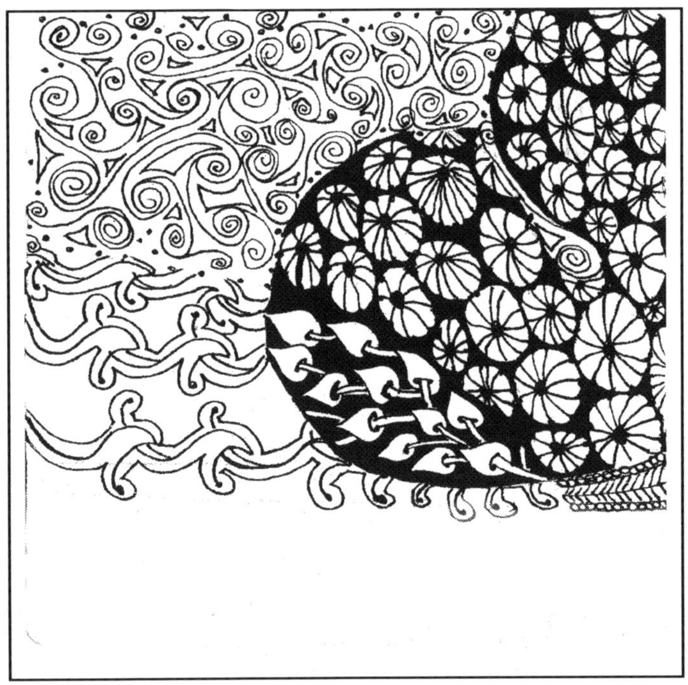

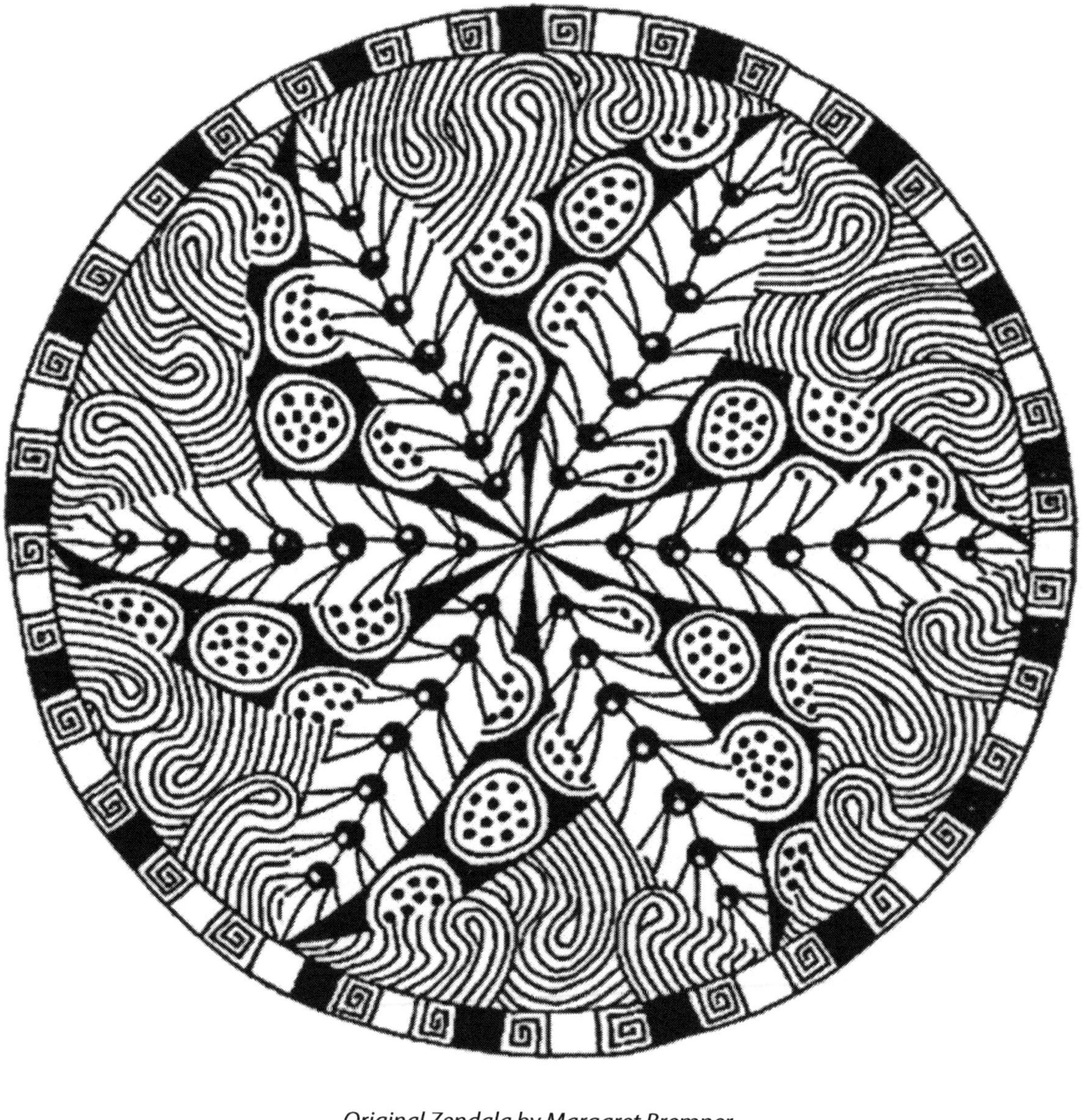

Original Zendala by Margaret Bremner

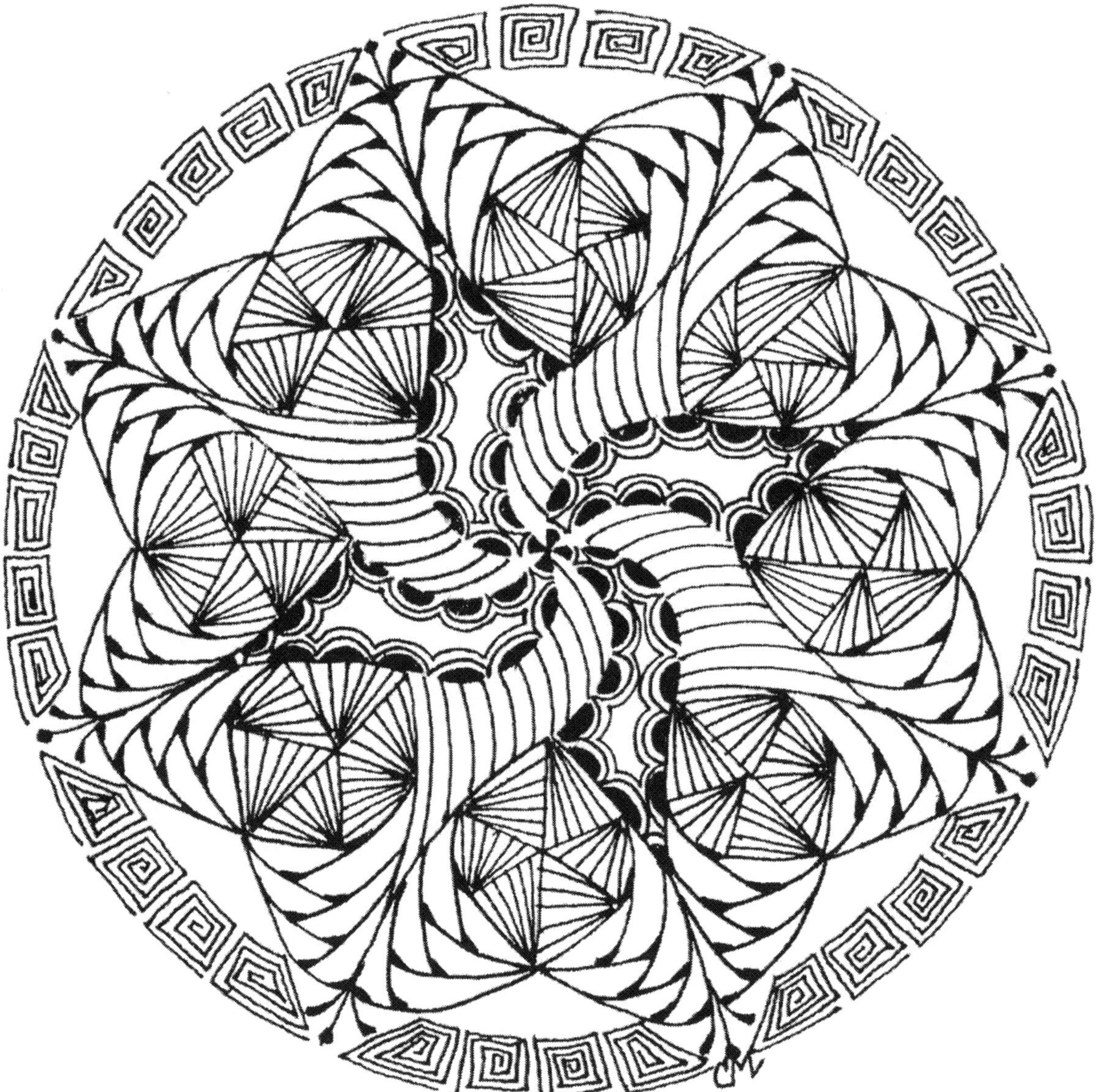

Original Zendala by Caren Mlot

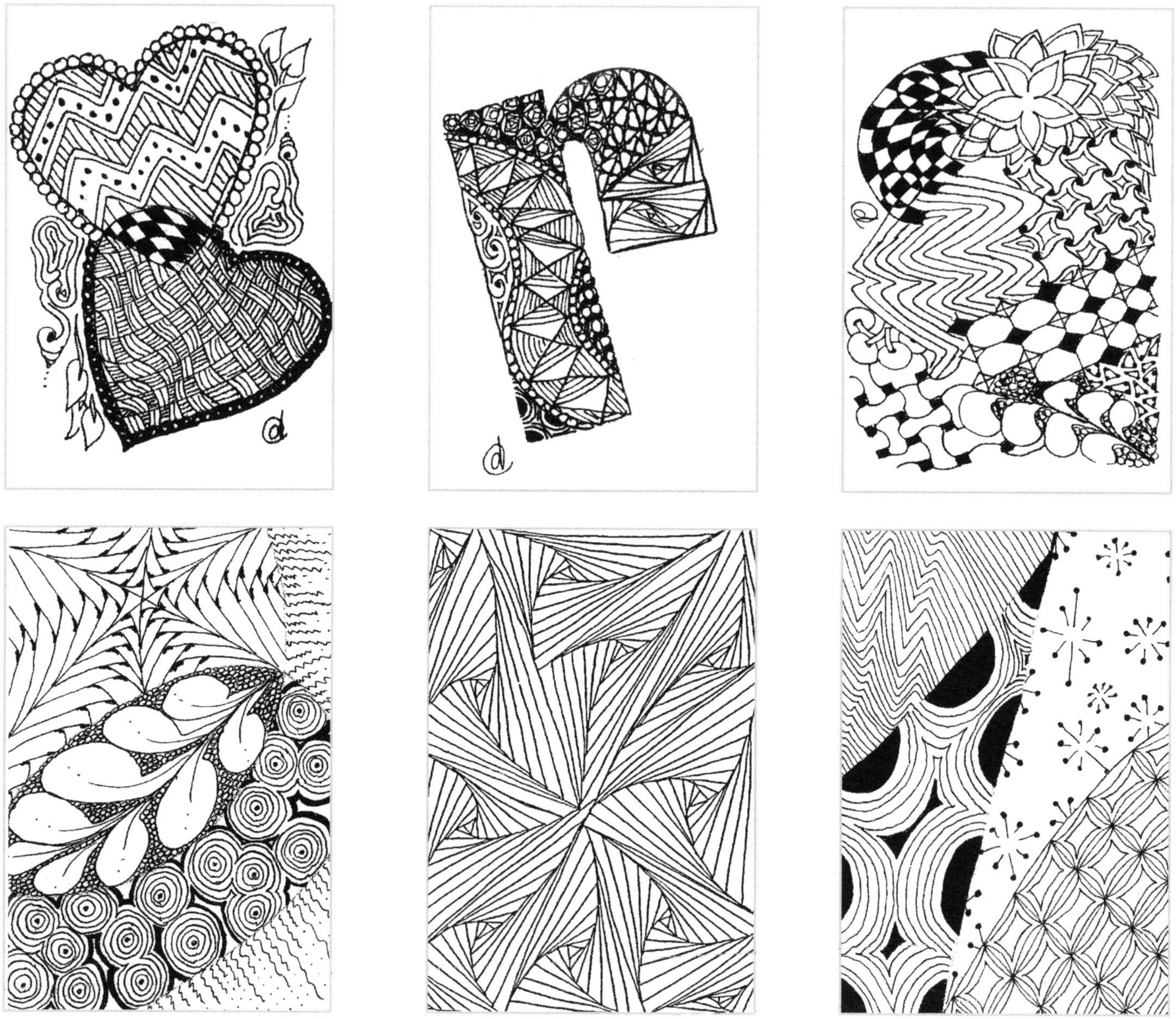

6 ATCs
Top 3 by Diana Hirsch
Bottom 3 by Emily Classon

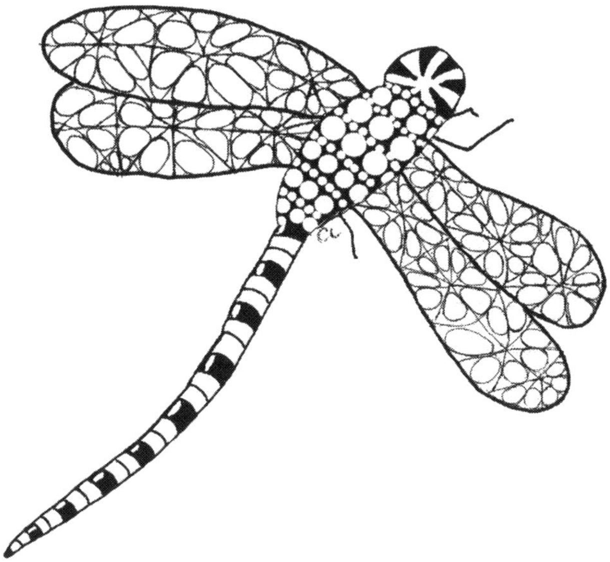

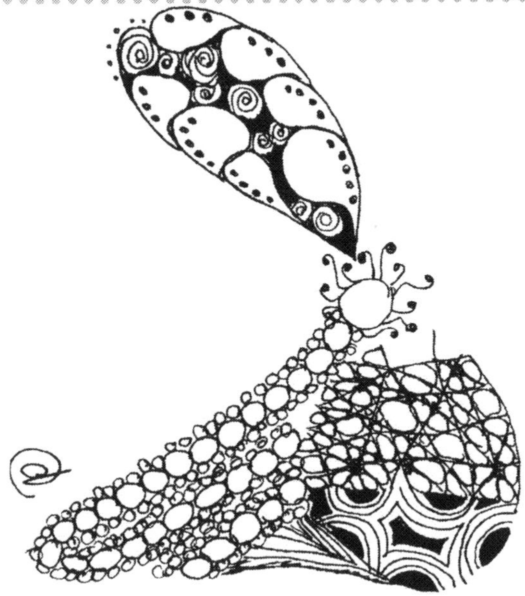

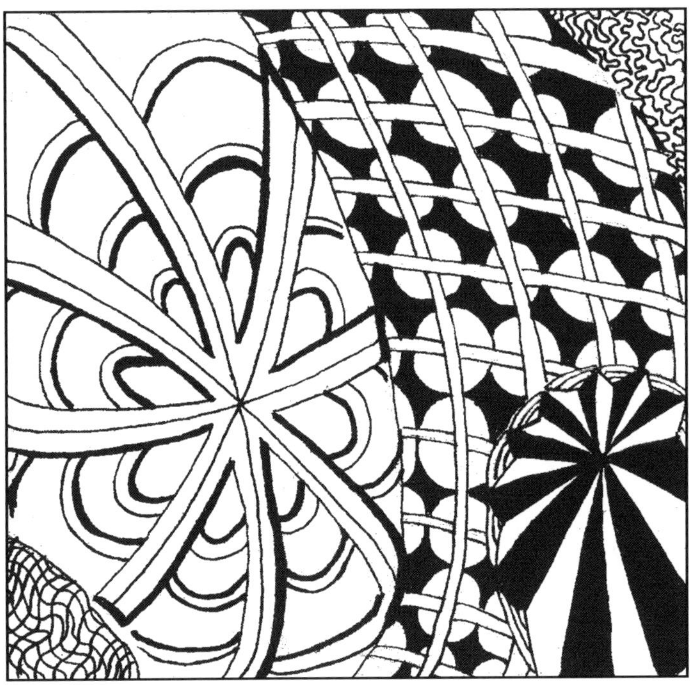

A pair of dragonflies by me(l)and Diana Hirsch(r) and the last piece of a puzzle. The tile to the left is the center of a 9-square ensemble tangled by Jane Menard. If you have never made an ensemble before, I encourage you to do so. It is almost magical when you put the finished tiles together. Here is how to do it:

Step 1. Shade all of the tiles on page 112-113 and the one to the left.

Step 2. Photocopy your completed art and cut out each square.

Step 3. Referring to the letters on pages 112-113, assemble your tiles in this order, fitting the pieces like a puzzle.

113C	112B	112A
113D	THIS ONE	112C
113A	113B	112D

Step 4. Rotate your tiles so the white border is towards the outside of the square and the string matches.

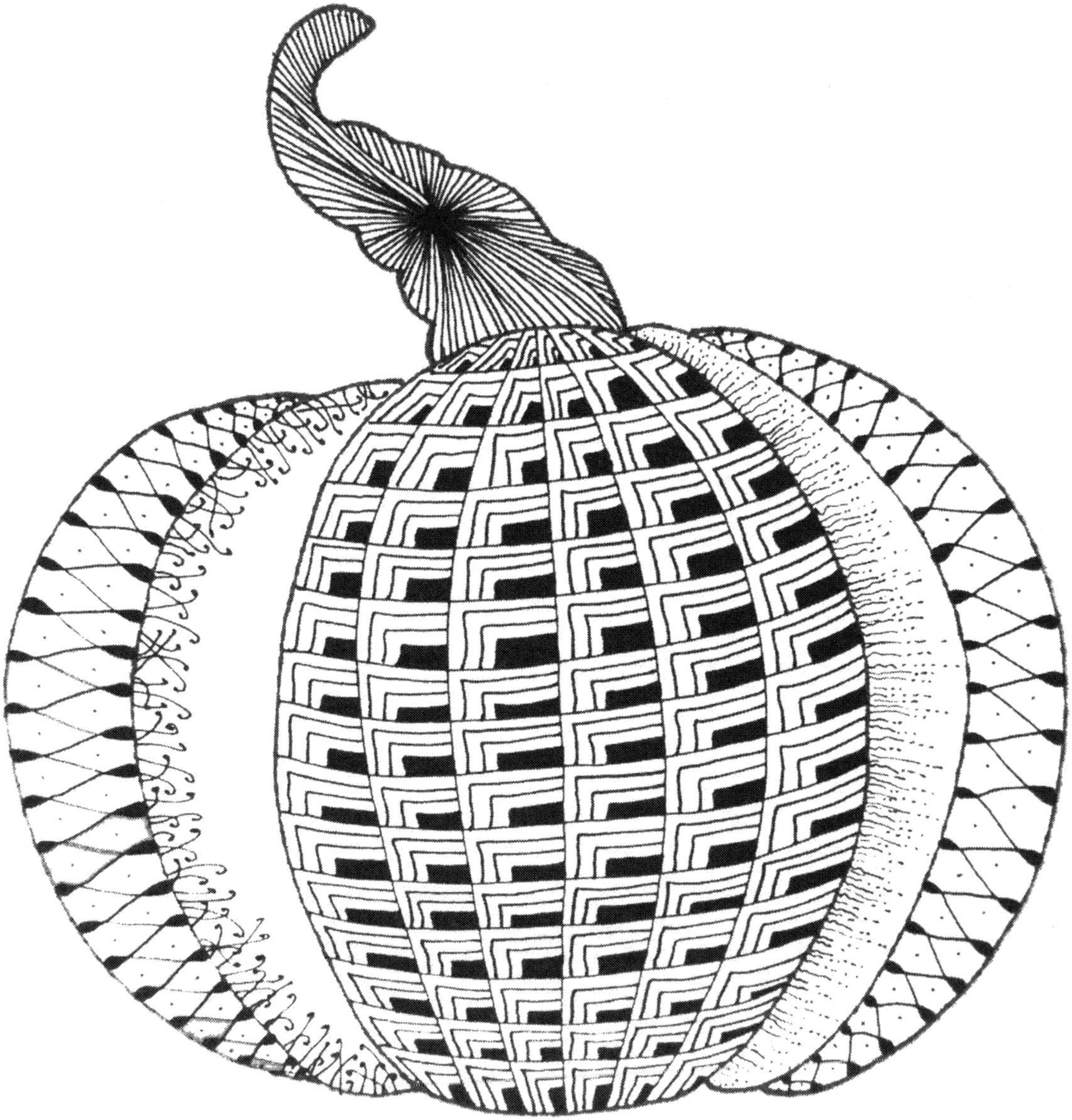

Original Art by Ellen Gozeling

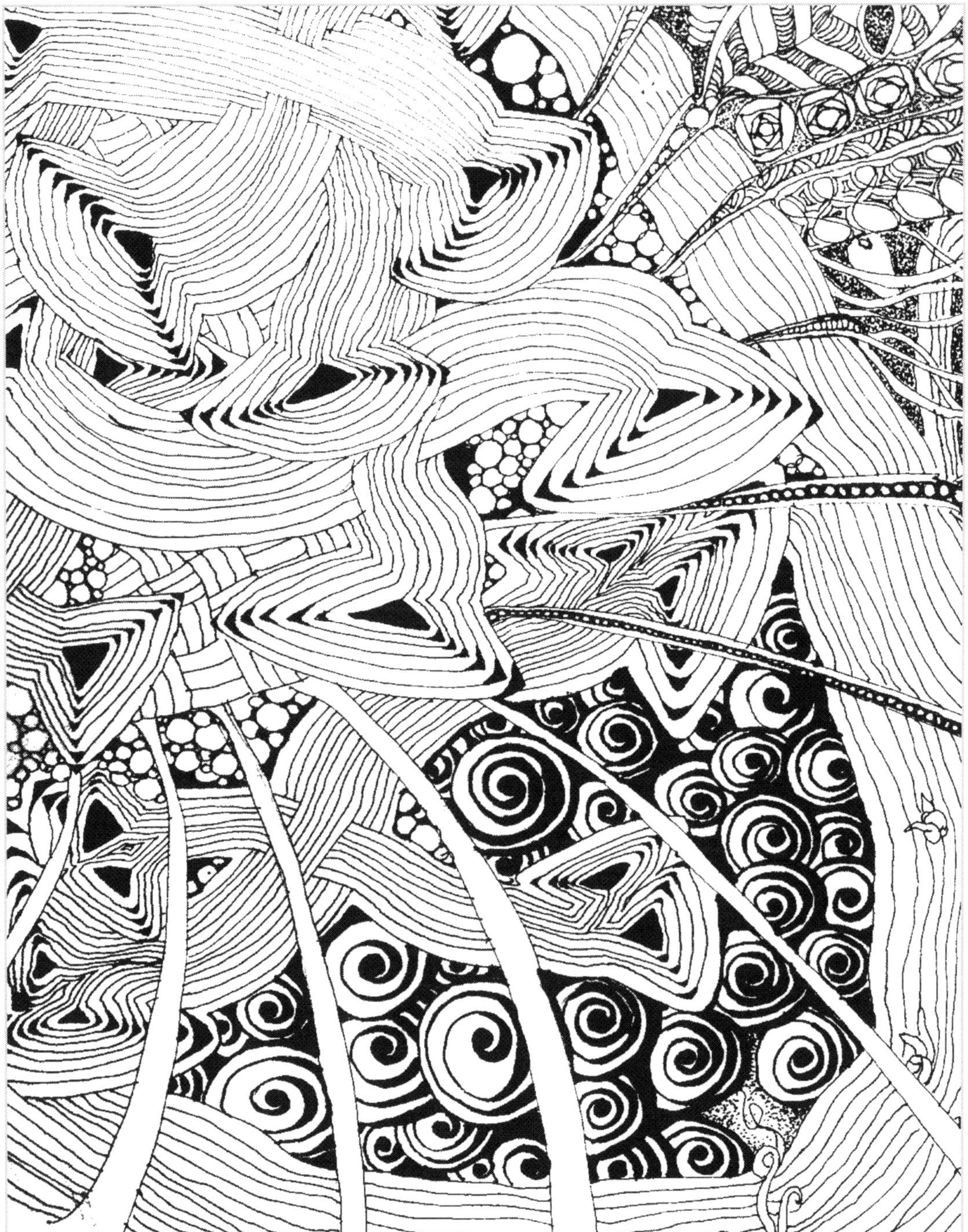

You've seen beau tiful artwork by Brinn McFetridge throughout this book. Here is your chance to shade a piece of her art. Will you use it to try your stippling?

GLOSSARY

A

abstract: not imitating external reality or objects in nature.

ATC: artist trading card.

B

blender: another name for the blending tool.

blending: rubbing the shading lines with a blending tool so smooth the texture.

blending tool: anything used to evenly distribute graphite over the paper to improve smoothness.

C

cast shadow: a dark area cast by an object onto another surface.

Certified Zentangle Teacher: one who has taken training from Rick and Maria, the founders of Zentangle.

composition: the arrangement of objects in a drawing.

contour hatching: shading using curved hatching that follows the contour or form of an object to emphasize its shape or add dimension.

contrast: calling attention to the difference between values that are next to one another.

cross hatching: shading by using tiny criss-cross lines.

CZT: acronym for Certified Zentangle Teacher.

E

Ensemble: Two or more tiles that share a common string and fit together like a puzzle.

F

focal point: the part of a piece of art that draws your eye first.

form: a 3-dimensional geometric figure, like a sphere, cone, or cube.

form shadow: the part of an object that is darker than the rest because it is not in direct light.

G

gradation: in art, the gradual blending of one tint or value to another.

grading: a system of rating the hardness or softness of a pencil.

graphite: a stable form of carbon, named from the Greek grapho: to write.

H

hard light: light casting shadows that have crisp edges.

hatching: a shading technique in which very fine parallel lines are drawn to create the illusion of shade or texture.

highlight: the lightest part of an object, where light bounces off the surface.

K

kneaded eraser: a soft, pliable eraser that can be molded to a point or wedge to erase fine lines or small sections.

L

loose: not overly controlled. Loose art is representative instead of photographic.

M

mandala: from Sanskrit word for circle. A geometric pattern that represents the Cosmos and is used for meditation.

mask: to use materials to protect areas of art from change.

movement: the path our eyes follow when we look at a work of art.

O

organic: composed of free-flowing and curvy shapes like those in nature, not rigid and geometric man-made shapes.

S

shading: adding shades of gray to artwork to enhance or define it.

shape: a flat (plane) shape, like a circle or square.

soft light: light that casts diffuse shadows with soft edges.

sparkle: A deliberate break made when drawing a tangle to suggest a highlight or sparkle.

string: A line that divides a tile into sections.

T

tangle (n): a named pattern that can be broken down into simple, repeated strokes.

tangle (v): to draw tangles.

tangleation: a variation of a tangle pattern.

tile, Zentangle: a 3.5 inch square of beautiful print making paper used as the surface for tangling in the Zentangle method.

tooth: the surface texture of paper. Paper with more tooth will feel bumpier than smooth paper with less tooth.

V

value: how light or dark a color is.

value scale: a range of different values from light to dark or vice versa.

Z

zendala: a ZIA drawn in a circular pattern similar to a mandala

Zentangle: a trademarked method of creating beautiful images by drawing structured patterns that is easy-to-learn, fun, and relaxing.

ZIA: an acronym for Zentangle-Inspired Art. Any art consisting of tangles that is non-traditional, either larger, containing color, or representational.

RESOURCES

Books

- **The Book of Zentangle** by Rick Roberts and Maria Thomas

This book is an amazing collection of wisdom and information in words and pictures, direct from the creators of Zentangle. If you can't get to a CZT for a class, this is the next best thing.

- **The Joy of Zentangle**, Drawing Your Way to Increased Creativity, Focus, and Well-Being by Design Originals.

Inspiration, instruction, and over 100 tangle patterns to get you started tangling and keep you going for a long time.

- **Totally Tangled** by Sandy Steen Bartholomew

This is the book that got me hooked on Zentangle and one I still refer to most often for a shot of inspiration.

Websites

Zentangle.com and blog.zentangle.com - Learn about Zentangle, buy products, locate a teacher, and keep up to date on what is happening at Zentangle, Inc. This is also where you will find a list of CZTs and links to their blogs.

Tanglepatterns.com - the name says it all.

Tools and Materials

Zentangle tiles, pens, and pencils are available from Zentangle.com or your local CZT.

Artist pencils, kneaded erasers, blending stumps, and tortillions are available at any local art and craft store or Amazon.com.

Index

S

T

V

W

Z